I AM NOBODY

I AM NOBODY

NOBODY

CONFRONTING THE
SEXUALLY ABUSIVE COACH
WHO STOLE MY LIFE

GREG GILHOOLY

GREYSTONE BOOKS

Vancouver/Berkeley

Greystone Books Ltd.
www.greystonebooks.com

Cataloguing data available from Library and Archives Canada
ISBN 978-1-77164-245-3 print
ISBN 978-1-77164-246-0 epub

Editing by Nancy Flight
Copy editing by Lesley Cameron
Jacket design by Will Brown
Text design by Nayeli Jimenez
Typesetting by Shed Simas/Onça Design
Proofreading by Alison Strobel
Jacket photograph by iStockphoto.com
Printed and bound in Canada on ancient-forest-friendly paper by Friesens

We gratefully acknowledge the support of the Canada Council for the Arts, the British Columbia Arts Council, the Province of British Columbia through the Book Publishing Tax Credit, and the Government of Canada for our publishing activities.

Canadä

To all who have suffered:
    You are not alone, you will be heard,
    and you will be understood.

Grief fills the room up of my absent child,
Lies in his bed, walks up and down with me,
Puts on his pretty looks, repeats his words,
Remembers me of all his gracious parts,
Stuffs out his vacant garments with his form;
Then, have I reason to be fond of grief?
Fare you well: had you such a loss as I,
I could give better comfort than you do.
I will not keep this form upon my head,
When there is such disorder in my wit.

—*King John* (Act III, Scene IV), William Shakespeare

CONTENTS

A CALL TO ACTION

‖ F YOU HAVE been sexually abused, fight on, no matter how
dark things may seem, no matter how difficult your situation
may be, because you can come through and survive your battle
and live a good, meaningful life. Reach out to others and let their
goodness shine upon you and help carry you along your journey to
inner peace, wherever that may lead you.

If you haven't been abused, please give freely of your love and
support to those who have been abused, for we need you and your
help more than you can ever know.

But if you have sexually abused another, pay your debt to society and get all the help you need to ensure that it will never, ever
happen again—for it can never, ever happen again. Accept responsibility for what you have done, no matter how unfair it may seem
to you, and accept all of the consequences you may have to endure
because of your actions, all of the restrictions you will face in your
future. Respect your victims. Do not make excuses. Do not in any
way minimize the impact -of what you have done to your victims.
Do not try to pretend that there was any good you may have done
along the way that could in any way offset even part of the bad that
you have done. Failing that, go to hell.

I AM NOBODY

'M STANDING IN the parking lot of a local community hockey arena. The rink—plain, rectangular, designed like an industrial warehouse—could be anywhere. It's a cool, still, gray day in the middle of a Canadian winter, snow gently falling, the type of day where every kid should be outside skating and playing, living life to its fullest. It makes me think back to all the hours we spent playing hockey outside, how good it felt to skate with the wind at our backs, how brutally awful it was to have to turn around and skate back into it. In an instant I am again feeling that cold air biting through my equipment, I am remembering how it felt to freeze into my own sweat. For a moment it's real, and I want to fall back into it, I want to give myself completely over to the memory of the sound of our skates squeaking as we stood and rocked back and forth in the intense cold, listening while our coaches set out the next drill. I want to be that kid again, getting ready for the next drill while sniffling back a runny nose in the thick fog of our heavy breathing, all of us needing to start moving again to generate some body heat. I can even smell the hot chocolate that was always served to us when we were very young and came inside after our battle with the elements, the true victors being those who could get their skates off quickest and be the first to grab the hot water bottles to warm their frozen feet.

But I'm not a kid anymore, and the game left me with other memories, too.

I enter the arena. I see people milling about, kids dragging equipment bags bigger than the bags I took with me when I went away to university. The scene is chaotic. The arena, like most others, is crowded, not designed for the crush of people. There are children and adults everywhere. And then it starts, something that always happens to me whenever I am at a rink (or in any public space, for that matter). I start scanning the room looking at every adult male trying to figure out why each one is there in the midst of the kids. That one in the corner—is he a parent? Have I seen him before? What is that guy doing over there? Are those kids by the door being watched by their parents? That coach kidding around with the kids on his team—is that normal, or is he getting a little too personal with some of them?

Ten steps later and it has passed. I've made it into the dressing room of the team that I coach and all is well. Just the hockey team enters, the boys and the other coaches. Here we can all have fun and the kids can revel in the pure joy of playing hockey. That world out there, the big scary one we all encounter daily, that world doesn't exist in the energetic lead-up to going out on the ice and playing. On the ice, the kids do things with such speed and grace that you sometimes have to remind yourself just how young they are. Here, one thing and only one thing matters to them: hockey. When they are at the rink hockey becomes their entire world. There is no school, no homework, just a safe place where they can push themselves athletically and at the same time play.

At least, it's supposed to be safe.

I loved hockey. I still do. Hockey was where I was most comfortable. On the ice I felt completely in control of everything around me. I excelled at hockey and was confident in a way I never was anyplace else. I saw the game and understood its patterns. I was a part of teams and understood the internal dynamics of how teams operated. I could see who was struggling, who needed to work harder, who needed to be pushed, who needed to be supported. It all just came naturally to me. I was at peace in my hockey equipment—the world made sense, I had an identity, and I was proud.

But then, in 1979, when I was fourteen years old, I met Graham James, the once-prominent, celebrated hockey coach. Graham groomed me and then sexually assaulted me over a period of several years into the early 1980s. That changed the way I would see hockey, the way I would see life, forever.

Books like this are usually written by people who are "somebodies"—celebrities, athletes, prominent business people, politicians, or other persons of note. They have a built-in audience, and their views are accorded greater weight and importance than those of a nobody. That makes sense, because as much as the media (and those who sell books) love a good story, those stories need an audience.

But I am nobody, just a victim (or *survivor*, if you prefer that word, and I understand why many do). I'm not a former professional hockey player, nor was I ever that close to being one. I'm not a "woulda, coulda, shoulda" type who can't get over the fact that but for this or that I might have been a star. All one can ever know is who I once was, who I became during and after the abuse, and who I am now. I'm just me, once a young boy with promise who had the misfortune of crossing paths with, and then drawing the attention of, a serial sexual predator. Now I am a man who is, decades later, finally putting his life into place.

Because I'm a nobody, you have no connection to me. You don't know me, so you don't bring with you any preconceived notions of who I once was, who I am now, and what my struggle did to me. You have no particular reason to care one way or another about me.

You haven't compartmentalized me in any way as somebody you see in the media, in the headlines, on the screens. I'm completely removed from your world while still being a part of it. There is distance between us.

But I could be somebody right next door. I could be the kid from around the corner, the one you used to see playing on your street but who you never really knew. I could be anybody you see when you look out your window. What happened to me could have happened to anybody around you. Maybe it happened to you. And that's what makes this a horror story, because child sexual abuse happens far more than most people realize. It happens in places where most would never believe it possible, and it is committed by people you would never believe capable of committing such a heinous act.

Most people around me know nothing of the real me, the one I have hidden for far too long. I promised myself when I set out to write this book that I would not gloss over how bad things got or the living hell that sexual assault inflicts on its victims. I promised myself that I wouldn't make myself out to be stronger than I was and that I would explain that survival and recovery are not always easy or even possible. I promised myself that I would show just how awful abuse can be as I try to come to grips with it and its impact, accepting the past for what it is, and moving forward with recovery. Anything less, any sanitized version of things, would disrespect anybody else who has suffered sexual abuse. Anything less could lead those who are dealing with the same things I am to conclude that there must be something wrong with them, to ask, "Why isn't he having the same trouble I am having? Why isn't he facing the difficulties that I am? What about these things that I have to do to try to protect myself that seem to be nowhere on his radar?" I hope that by being completely honest about my struggles I can show others who may be dealing with the same things that they are not alone in their efforts to survive, to find meaning in life, and to flourish while showing the full horror of sexual abuse and its long-term impact.

Still, even after all of these years, after years and years of therapy, I don't really get it. None of it ever really makes sense.

We all live with our inner voice, the one that is always with us. It is the voice from which we cannot run, the constant in our life that brings us back to our reality, no matter how good we may try to make things look to others in our social media postings, in our daily lives with our smiles and our banter, in our routine comings and goings. Our inner voice does not express an objective truth but rather the way we see ourselves in our world. My inner voice has tormented me:

Why did this happen?
How did it happen?
Who were you?
Who are you?

I can try to explain it, but deep down I just don't know. I can say all the words, but they are empty, meaningless attempts at ascribing reason to something so outside the realm of what could even be contemplated as a remotely reasonable experience. And that's what makes all of this so difficult to live with. That's what makes his abusing me so horrific to me. I don't understand how it happened to me. I may never be able to understand and accept to my core what happened, why it happened, and how it happened. I understand at an intellectual level how a victim can become powerless and succumb to a predator, but I still do not fully accept that it could have happened to me, that it did happen to me.

Writing this book has been tough for me. I had to revisit how Graham got to me, controlled me, made me do things I didn't want to do. I have to admit and accept that he was able to get at me, defeat me, tear me apart physically and mentally, rip the life out of me. Everything in my recovery has been about taking back my life, asserting my power and control over who I am and what I will be. Stepping back into my past to write this book was to relive my destruction. Yet in doing so I somehow found my voice, I managed to better understand and accept what had happened, and am better and stronger for having done so.

I am nobody important, nobody of note. I'm just a nobody who was sexually abused by that once-prominent hockey coach, a nobody who because of the abuse actually became nobody at all and believed that I deserved everything that had happened to me, that I deserved to fail at everything in life, that I deserved to be shunned, that I deserved to die.

Except I am still here.

This is my story.

ONE

JUST A BOY

I AM A CHILD of the Canadian prairies, born in Winnipeg in 1964 in the middle of a very cold winter while my dad, choosing his first love over the waiting room, circled the hospital in his car, listening to the radio for hockey scores from the Innsbruck Winter Olympics.

"Winnipeg" comes from the Cree word *win-nipi* which, roughly translated, means "muddy water," an apt metaphor for a story about sexual abuse. And with a population of about 750,000, it's more of a big small city than a small big one. When I was growing up, it was Canada's fourth-largest city, but having gone through some very tough times it has now slipped to eighth. It is solidly working class, it can sometimes seem a little unsophisticated to outsiders, and its charms can remain somewhat hidden. But if you look just a little deeper, you will quickly see that it is also a magical place with so much to offer, a place of character, one you would never leave if you could just take the time to get to know it a bit better.

Winnipeg is the quintessential Canadian city, a place known and loved by people who have lived there but misunderstood and underappreciated by those who haven't. Winnipeg is, geographically speaking, where east meets west in Canada. It's the kind of place that in winter it isn't just cold but cold-cold. If you've moved away and then come back home to visit, you'll think you remember how cold it can get but then realize as you take your first step out of the airport, and your lungs immediately freeze on taking your first breath, that you have forgotten how cold it really gets. Every day in the winter the newscasts give the number of seconds in which exposed flesh will freeze. Movies and stories about climbing Everest present the windy, freezing "death zone" near the top as a serious problem, but this is what Winnipeggers deal with for weeks on end every year. We Winnipeggers are tough. We walk in the freezing cold because we have what it takes to survive in Winnipeg, we prepare and we wear the proper clothing. We embrace the cold because that's the type of people we are.

Not everybody is strong enough to handle Winnipeg. Its only hill is artificial, a park created on top of an old garbage dump that is a great place to toboggan in the winter. Winnipeg has amazing summers, but they last for only a few very short months. The freeze-thaw cycle is so intense that the roads are continually destroyed by potholes that form when the ground warms again in spring. Winnipeg's mosquitos are so bad that even in these enlightened times most people are in favor of aggressive chemical fogging, if only to allow us to kid ourselves into believing that the problem isn't as bad as it really is. And as for things to do in The Peg, a prominent professional football player once said that the city was a nice place to live but that he needed to be traded away because he could only take his kids to the zoo so many times after he'd run out of things to do with them.

But Winnipeg was a fantastic place to be a kid. With its long winters and outdoor natural ice to play on, it was an especially amazing place to be a young hockey player. Like all who grew up there, I am a proud Winnipegger, and we share a secret world with knowing references to the special ties that 7-11s, Slurpees,

The Guess Who, BTO, socials, Neil Young, "going to the lake," Sals, orbit, K-tel, the BDI, bumper shining, garbage mitts, and Sylvia Kuzyk all have to our city. A fatwa on any non-Pegger who may ever speak ill of my hometown.

I see a lot of myself in Winnipeg. It's the place where I grew up, where I first went to school, where I learned who I was, where I became a young boy with big dreams, where I learned to laugh and play. It's the place I have in my mind when I look back on my life, the place where, as Garrison Keillor says, everybody was good-looking and above-average. And I have so many good memories of Winnipeg, of my house, my school, my friends, my little corner of the world where nothing went wrong, where all of us kids rode our bikes to the park around the corner, where we went down by Sturgeon Creek back before it was dammed and played in the mud, where we played in the snow, where we set up our pick-up baseball games and the older kids taught us younger ones how to properly taunt the batter. It is that place we all have in our memories when life was perfect and we were kings, that we know we were a part of yet never really existed.

I grew up in Winnipeg and I love it so much, but I don't live there anymore. I love it from afar now because what happened there makes it very difficult for me to return. I want to go home. I make plans time and again to go back. But I can't just click my heels together and make it all better because the storm, well, when it blew, it blew hard, and Dorothy sure wasn't in Kansas anymore.

———————

MY PARENTS BOTH grew up in Saskatchewan. My mom, Patricia, came from a farm family that eventually acquired some property outside of the town of Pense. My dad, Michael, was from a family of athletes who, after leaving Ireland and landing in Montreal, made their way west to Regina, leaving behind a good portion of the clan in the jails of what is now known as Thunder Bay. After marrying in Regina, my parents set out for the relatively bright lights and big city of Winnipeg just in time to have me.

Eventually we became a normal suburban family of five. I was the eldest of three children; my sister, Dawn, was born a year after me; and my brother, Doug, was born a year after that. We lived in a modest bungalow built the year I was born in a modest baby-boomer subdivision where the streets all had alliterative names: Amarynth, Alcott, Antoine, Alguire. It was decidedly upper-lower-middle class, but back then nobody really knew how the rich lived because, unlike today, we had only a small television window into their world, and we didn't know anybody rich, so we never thought we were doing without. My parents were entirely average, and there was absolutely nothing that would have caused anybody to give them a second look. That was just fine by them and fine by us kids as well.

My dad dropped out of high school after Grade Eight and then immediately took a job loading and unloading trucks with the Regina branch of Northern Electric Distributing. Eventually he moved up the ranks and became a salesman of electrical supplies to contractors. He stayed with Northern Electric and its distribution subsidiary Nedco until he retired. Think about that. He dropped out of school, never went to high school, took a menial job, and stayed with the company virtually forever. The thing is, I'm pretty sure that he hated every minute of his job from the day he started until just before the end, when he was finally given the chance to manage other people. He excelled at that. All his working life he had been a square peg in a round hole until it was almost too late. He was a large man with a soft smile. People liked him. He was gentle and kind-hearted, and yet he understood how to get things done and was firm when necessary. Turns out he had a great touch with people and was an amazing manager, a leader, somebody people wanted to perform for, somebody who was both liked and respected and who people didn't want to let down.

Despite having only a Grade Eight education, he was far smarter than many people I went to school with or later worked with. And that is something I have always carried with me. It's always a fifty-fifty chance whether the people leading the meeting are any smarter than the people who will come in hours later to clean up the offices after them. I've seen this firsthand over and over again during my career. But I went to school and worked with many who seemed to view themselves as better than others. No one should ever presume they are smarter or know more than anybody else. No one.

My mom was a high school graduate and thus the educated one in the family. She went on to work as a lab technician, earning a certificate but never completing a university degree. She was naturally bright and had been very attractive in her day, though the title of Miss Pense, Saskatchewan, which she earned one year at the town's summer fair, may not have been the most hotly contested pageant. Her sense of humor showed itself every once in a while, but for the most part she carried with her a darkness that suggested she had seen a bit too much of the world to ever be truly happy. She never seemed to be present in the moment but instead always had her eye on something that could or was about to go wrong. Picnics were always on the verge of being infested by bugs, candy was just about to be choked on, rain was just about ready to fall.

Our family struggled financially. Mom and Dad hid it very well, but I would sometimes take phone messages from collection agencies and would see bills that were long overdue. We were by no means destitute and always had the basics, but I know that it must have been tough for my parents. I remember having to get up from the old beaten-up piano I loved so much so that it could be taken away and sold for money we needed to get me a new pair of skates. And, when I finally became a lawyer and applied for a credit card, I was initially refused because Amex thought I was my father, who had numerous unpaid debts.

Sports had been a way of life for the Gilhooly family for several generations. My grandfather and great-uncles played professional football and hockey. My father grew up playing hockey in the Regina Pats organization, right beside future NHL stars like Bill Hicke and Red Berenson. One of my dad's favorite possessions was a team picture from when he was an assistant captain. He has blood all down the front of his jersey and is smiling, just behind a young Berenson, whom he protected. In short, my dad followed in the Gilhooly tradition and loved my mom, hockey, and the Saskatchewan Roughriders, although not necessarily in that order.

So it was not surprising that I started skating just before my fourth birthday and was participating in local organized hockey by the time I was five. I started my hockey life as a very large forward. I was so big for my age that I stuck out in the crowd. At the local park I was once mistaken for being a somewhat slow pre-teen when in fact I was only five or six. I was a very good skater, given my early start, and that combination of size and ability was a recipe for a disaster in the early 1970s, when kids of all ages, shapes, and sizes were still body-checking each other. And that's where the story really begins, when I became a goalie not by choice but as a result of an incident at an outdoor rink that showed both the good and the bad in my father.

We played most of our hockey at outdoor rinks. My local community club was Heritage-Victoria, and that's where I was first signed up to play. It's in the west end of Winnipeg, in the center of a group of very modest suburban homes built near the end of the baby boom. Outdoor hockey in the winter meant kids played while parents huddled on snowbanks, shifting their weight from one foot to the other to keep their feet from freezing. Even back then the parents were at least as engaged as the kids playing, if not more so. The problem is that when they're young, kids can be of wildly different sizes and abilities, and that can impact a parent's state of mind, especially if your kid isn't as big as or as good as somebody else's and you're the type who wishes otherwise.

At one of the games I inadvertently checked a boy on the other team. At least, I'm pretty sure my bodycheck wasn't intentional, but since I was only six or seven years old I can't in all honesty be sure. Afterward, his mother spat on me as I came off the ice.

When my dad saw it happen, he froze. He later told me that the others who saw it all froze too, as if what had just happened was beyond comprehension. There I was, a little kid all bundled up to play hockey outside in the freezing cold, coming off the ice to walk through the snow and into the clubhouse to warm up and take my skates off and get my boots on and go home, with half-frozen spit all down the front of my hockey sweater.

In the aftermath, my dad showed both the best and worst in him. The best was that he immediately de-escalated the situation. The worst was that he didn't stand up for me but instead more passively worked toward a less confrontational resolution that was not in my best interests. He immediately grabbed my arm and walked me into the dressing room, where he took off my skates, warmed my feet, and kept telling me how well I had played. Then he took me straight to the car and we went home. I didn't know what to think of what the woman had done to me, but I remember that my dad made me feel good. By the time we were home it felt as if nothing had happened. He did an amazing job. But at the same time he kind of didn't.

Today there would be lawsuits, calls for suspensions, and media coverage. Back then there was nothing. And my dad's next step prevented the situation from ever happening to me again. Maybe, he suggested, I would like to try being a goalie? Maybe I could try it out next time?

And with that suggestion—though I had no concept of this at the time—the worst in him came through, his passivity in the face of another's wrong. Why did he think that I needed to make a change? Why wasn't I free to play hockey without having to change positions? Did I deserve to have an adult spit on me? Had I somehow done something wrong? Are adults allowed to do things like that to kids?

But at the time, the proposition of changing positions seemed like an opportunity. As a kid, there was nothing more exciting than putting on all of that cool goalie equipment, so I didn't exactly feel as if I was missing out on anything, and I probably thought this might actually be even more fun. The fact that I could skate well gave me an advantage in the position, and kids like to do things they are good at. So just like that, I was a goalie. And looking back on it, I guess it would have been difficult for my dad to be among the other parents while his ginormous kid on the ice was with the other kids, knocking them around, skating circles around them. Now that I know more about my dad, I believe that pulling me—and himself—out of that spotlight and not being the center of that ongoing conflict would have suited him just fine.

And he couldn't have predicted what would happen next, when things really started to happen. Because I could skate and was large for my age at a time when the worst skater usually became goalie, I had that incredible advantage in the position. Nobody figured out until years later that given the importance of the position, the better athletes should be made goalies. I moved up a year to play with older boys and then was advanced even further to our area hockey team. As far as I was concerned, it was as if the spitting had never happened, and I couldn't have been happier with my new place in hockey. It's only when I look back on it that I wish my dad had stood up for me and my right to play the game in whichever position I wanted.

HOCKEY'S PLACE IN Canadian society has been well documented. My first real brush with that *zeitgeist* was while playing for Heritage-Victoria at age nine in a league that featured several boys who went on to become professional players. Playing in the area league championship gave us two chances to defeat our bitter rivals, Kirkfield-Westwood. I know how funny that sounds, having a bitter rival at age nine, but at the time we were living the dream and hockey was everything to us. Spring was coming and there was that certain smell in the humid air, a smell that means two things in Canada: summer is coming and playoff hockey is upon us. This was back when most hockey was still played outside, so because the ice was starting to melt during the day, our games were scheduled long after the sun had gone down at times that seemed ridiculously late in the evening given our ages. If we won the first game, it was over—we were champions. If we lost, we still had a chance the next night to win in a winner-take-all game.

All I can remember is the last part of the first game, a game we lost. Do I remember anything at all about the second game, the game we won to advance to the Winnipeg finals, the celebration, the awards, the party afterwards? No. The only thing I remember is that we lost the first game on a very controversial late goal. And the only reason I remember that is because of what the adults did.

There was a play around my net. The referee blew his whistle and then pandemonium erupted—screaming, yelling, allegations that the referee was blind, a complete idiot. The game was stopped, but then everything quieted down after the referee went to the benches and explained to the coaches what had happened. The goal was finally counted and put on the scoresheet, a face-off took place at center ice, and shortly after that the whistle was blown to end the game. We had lost and had to play another game. To everybody watching outside that cool spring night, it looked like we had been ripped off. Except there were two people who knew for sure that our bitter rivals had scored on us—me and the referee. Because I told him.

The shot had come in hard and off the ice. It looked like I had made a great save, blocking it with my glove and then smothering it. Except that when I went down to smother it in the crush of players crashing in around the net (maybe crashing the net is bit of an overstatement, since we were just little kids, but it remains epic in my mind), I nudged the puck over the line as I covered it. Even the other team didn't know they had scored. But the referee, standing in perfect position, thought he had seen what I knew had happened. He skated over to me to get the puck and said he couldn't see for sure and asked me if the puck had gone in. I told him it had. And with that, he signaled a goal and a face-off at center ice. And in doing so, it was if he had started a war.

Now, understand what was at stake here. We're talking the highest level of competitive hockey for nine- and ten-year-olds, so of course that meant hockey scholarships, agents, pro hockey careers, entire futures, right? You would have thought so given how the adults acted. In the midst of the outrage, the referee skated over and told both coaches that the goalie had told him it was a goal. All the other players on the benches heard this, and all the players on the ice who had followed the referee looking for an explanation heard this. I only found this out after the game. I was not a popular person. And on the way home in the car, my dad and I had a conversation that I didn't understand.

"Nice game. Are you tired?"

"No. Why is everybody mad at me? Why don't they like me anymore?"

"Well, you're at an age now and you're playing at a level where it wasn't up to you to do the referee's job for him. You don't have to tell him that the puck went in if he asks you."

I was confused by everything I had seen that night, by how the adults had carried on at the rink, by what my dad had told me on our way home. And that's all that I would have taken with me from that year of hockey, that would be all I would have remembered from the glorious Heritage-Victoria Olympic Nines of 1972–73, except that something else happened later that night. After I had gone to bed, and while I was lying there alone in the almost dark, looking at the shadows of my hockey posters and thinking about the game, trying but failing to fall asleep, I heard my dad's footsteps come down the stairs toward my room. He knocked at the door, opened it a bit, and stuck his head in.

"Greg, are you still up?" he whispered.

"Yes."

"You did the right thing tonight telling the ref. I'm proud ofyou."

"Thanks."

"You OK?"

"Yeah."

"OK. Goodnight. Good game. Goodnight."

He closed my bedroom door and went back upstairs. That's the last thing I remember about that night, and the only thing I remember about that entire year of hockey.

I CONTINUED TO progress quickly in hockey. By 1975, when I was eleven, I began playing for the St. James Canadians at what today would be considered the AAA level. I eventually became one of a small group of players in the city who played at that level in every year of eligibility without ever being cut. I was usually at or near the top of our league statistically in "goals against average" while playing on a team that often finished only in the middle of the standings. As I moved through the ranks of age-group hockey, I was becoming known outside of my local area and was being scouted and recruited for both junior and college hockey teams.

But I wasn't close to being the best athlete in my family. My brother, Doug, was blessed with a remarkable physical make-up and coordination, the kind of guy who later in life could pick up a set of golf clubs after not having played in a year or two and score in the mid-70s. And my sister, Dawn, blew us both away by becoming a nationally ranked swimmer, a national age group record holder, and later a champion triathlete.

Yet, while all three of us seemingly had a common bond through sports, something that would connect us and bring out all of the emotional support that a functioning family needs to provide its members, that wasn't the case. I was always on my own as the eldest, while Dawn and Doug were more of a team. They were simply naturally more comfortable with each other, they were more fun to be around, and they were cooler kids at school. Unlike me, they had many friends. Me, when I was young I was always a little different, off by myself, intellectually a bit older than my peers and with different interests.

All three of us were always straight-A students, but I wasn't just a straight-A student, I was a straight-A-virtually-perfect student. I could tell that I was ahead of the rest when my kindergarten teacher let me lead the flashcard vocabulary program. She had figured out on the first day that I could read all of the words, pronounce them correctly, and give their proper meanings.

Not only that, but I completely kicked ass at nap time.

The next year I was dragged out of my class to perform a reading test for another teacher who had heard about me. I became a bit of a circus act, and I was increasingly asked to solve puzzles or answer questions on command for others to show just how smart I was. But I also had a most amazing teacher, Ms. Belding, who always made time for me. She took me aside and set me up with my own academic program. That elementary school of mine—Arthur Oliver—is long gone, but I hope she isn't.

Ms. Belding was the perfect teacher for me because she kept challenging me while encouraging me. She started giving me my own schoolwork during class. I loved it. I was getting from her what I wasn't getting at home: somebody who understood me and my need for more. And while schools now rarely advance young children ahead of their natural grade because they better understand the social and psychological risks this presents to students not old enough to interact appropriately with older classmates, she and the rest of the staff at my school only ever did what everyone thought at that time was best for me.

It wasn't long before external educators were showing up at school and I was being pulled out of class to be tested by strangers.

"Greg, today we have something special set up. Don't worry. It will be fun. Here, come with me, we're going down to the office to meet somebody."

And with that, I got up and went with Ms. Belding, the class snickering behind us as she held my hand, oblivious to my immense crush on her.

I was introduced to a woman who was pleasant yet who also seemed overly serious about what we were about to do. I was tested on a set of materials, with blocks, math puzzles, timed tasks to perform, language puzzles, things like that. At one point she broke into a wide smile and thereafter was more akin to a best friend. She told me that I was the first person she had tested who had managed to solve one particular puzzle.

About a week later, the same scene played out. I asked why I had to do it all over again and was told that they wanted to make sure that my score really was what it was. All I know is that the next week I was moved up a grade. A week later, I was at the top of that grade too.

I was "academically gifted," as they say, and if I in any way make this out to be a potential weakness I also understand how that will come across. I did well at school and was moved up a grade and probably could have been moved up a few more. I was a parent's dream. I was, to anybody looking at me from the outside, a massive success. How could any of this in any way ever prove to be a problem?

Today, children are rarely accelerated through the school system ahead of their age group as it is better understood now that school is as much about life as it is about education. School is about learning the basics, learning how to learn, learning how to socialize, and gaining the ability and confidence to facilitate your own development. If you aren't developing emotionally as well as academically, you're in a very dangerous place. And with all that was going on, I was in that dangerous place, an isolating place.

When I moved ahead in hockey, at least I had my school friends. When everyone figured out I needed more in school, they reasoned I could deal with it because I was already playing sports with older kids. Except, by moving me up a year in school, they took me away from the very group of kids who were keeping me socially integrated at my emotional level. As large as I was physically when I was young, I was not an emotionally strong child. I was not ready to live in a world where my hockey and school peers were all older and more emotionally mature.

Because of my size, I wasn't exactly a normal-looking kid. I was the one in the center of the back row in all the school pictures, the kid with his head sticking up while his neck sits next to the smiling faces on either side of him. Everywhere I went I felt as if I didn't belong, and that was imprinted on me at a very early age. Emotionally, I was a gentle soul, very much like my dad in that regard, though fortunately I had also acquired my mom's aggression, which gave me a drive he never had. Emotionally and socially I was a late bloomer. Although physically large, I was very late to reach puberty. And because I was already finding it difficult to fit in, the last thing I wanted was to look different, to actually be different. Yet I was different. I kept growing and growing, I started stumbling over my limbs, I started to gain weight as my body anticipated a puberty that just never seemed to kick in. It was a very difficult time for me. I was a giant with the voice of a choir boy and an athlete who was now bumbling and having to work hard just to keep up at the back of the pack while running laps or doing other training drills that I had once led.

After having started out as very athletic and extremely coordinated, I went through several years of being very tall but also chubby and somewhat uncoordinated. I struggled to keep pace with my height and lingering fat, and had a body composition I thought would never change. Yet, while I was tripping over my own legs, I was still able to fight through the extra weight and keep succeeding at hockey at the highest levels as patient coaches could see in me both my natural talent and my willingness to work at least as hard as the hardest worker on the team.

By age fourteen I was again truly becoming an athlete. I was active in football and other sports besides hockey and had no difficulty excelling at school while keeping up an extensive list of extracurricular activities.

But a disconnect between the reality of who I *was* and who I *thought I was* had been cemented. The negative image I had of myself from those difficult times stayed with me longer than it should have. Further, that image, formed by others too, probably stayed with them longer than it should have.

I had just turned fourteen and was away at a hockey tournament in Thunder Bay, Ontario. One afternoon, we had nothing to do between games and were hanging around in one of our hotel rooms. Somebody came up with the idea of having a push-up contest. There had been a time, when I was ten or eleven, when doing even just a handful of push-ups would have been difficult, if not impossible. I tried my best to get out of it, to hide, but when you're my size (I was by then well over six feet tall) there is nowhere to hide. Eventually, near the end, I was called forward and forced to do my push-ups. To this day, I remember how shocked we all were when I finished second to Scotty Allan, a physical specimen of perfection.

I shouldn't have been surprised, though, as I'd been quietly working very hard downstairs at home by myself to get my body into shape.

Less than a year later, our team was in Bloomington, Minnesota, for a tournament, and one of the billets we were staying with had a weight room set up in his basement. A couple of guys on our team who were there couldn't believe it when I went over to the weight bench and effortlessly pressed the entire set. And the thing is, they were shocked that I even went over to the bench, let alone pushed the weights with ease.

Barry Melville, one of our hockey coaches when I was eleven and twelve, later saw me at one of my football games and didn't realize it was me. Once he found out, all he could comment on was my changed shape. He had been so patient with me, so encouraging, so dedicated to helping me improve, and I felt proud to make him smile at the athlete I had become.

I was also lucky to have had a remarkable gym teacher, Mr. Warkentin, in Grades Seven through Nine at Ness Junior High School. He was always so kind, patient, and supportive of me as I grew into my body. There was nobody happier than he was as I went from being a kid who couldn't hold myself up to the chinning bar to one who excelled at the flexed arm hang, a rite of passage for all Canadian kids of a certain vintage who had to complete the Canada Fitness Test.

When I look at pictures of me from back then, the change in my physical makeup through those early years was dramatic, more dramatic than I realized. But the image of that eleven- and twelve-year-old heavy, uncoordinated boy persisted with all of us, myself included, despite my new body. We saw only what we had once seen, not what was really there.

I SEEMED TO have it all. I was a star student, an athlete, and a nice, friendly kid. Athletic success came easily. When I played baseball, I was a pitcher, and I threw harder than the other kids the very first time I tried without knowing a thing about baseball. When I played football, I was voted one of the captains. I didn't know it, but I was in the process of becoming me. Yet, I was different from my athletic peers because school was even more important to me than sports. I liked sports but I loved school, always in that order. Kids like what they are best at, and no matter how good I was at sports, I was always even better at school. I was, in effect, a teenager cast as a jock among the geeks and a geek among the jocks. But underneath it all, I was a jock who hadn't always been physically solid, who was in many ways anything but.

And if you dug just a bit deeper into my family situation, you would also have seen something that was different from what it likely seemed to be. Families are like that, and mine was no different.

My mom, as much as she appeared to be loving and caring, and as much as she was loved by others outside our home, was incredibly cold and demanding. She was a closet alcoholic, one only we could see. She most definitely was not a happy drunk. She scowled at us, snapped insults, always had a demeaning comment about how we could be doing more or doing better than we were. I grew up thinking that white Bacardi rum was a cleaning supply because I always found bottles of it under our sink—and that's what my mom told me it was when I was little and asked her what was in the bottle and, well, she was my mom, so I believed her.

Somewhere along the way, somebody or something had taken away her sense of life and fun. The joyful mother she appears to have been in a journal she kept after my birth quickly gave way to an overwhelmed mother of three who struggled to cope. Drunk and belligerent at dinner, or passed out on the couch after drinking to try to escape, life was just too much for her.

That made her incredibly difficult to live with. The sad thing is that every once in a while, maybe twice, three times a year, she would become the person we didn't usually see, happy, carefree, laughing, and just really cool to be around. I remember her helping me build a crystal ball radio, just the two us, and it was as if she was a different person as we bantered back and forth until we sorted everything out. She joked that if we could figure this out then we could probably build a television and maybe we should just get rid of ours so that we would have to get right onto that next project. It was such a simple moment, yet because such moments rarely happened with her, that conversation is etched in my memory. And those few moments of joy with my mom kind of made it worse, because after seeing her so full of life, it hurt even more to see her the way she usually was around us.

At her funeral, I heard all about the person she had been before life got the better of her. It was like listening to stories about a complete stranger. I wished that the woman who others had seen had been my mom—someone warm, kind, open with her emotions, helpful, encouraging.

And I know this is awful to say, but I never believed she really loved me. I mean, of course a mother loves her child, and of course I must have memories of loving moments stored somewhere, right? But even as I write this I struggle to find memories of any loving moments. The truth is, I have none. She wasn't wired that way. Maybe she was a product of her generation, maybe a product of her stern farm upbringing, maybe a product of her alcoholism, but whatever it was, she could not show love.

Of course, if anybody outside the family had said, or were ever to say, a bad thing about my mom, I would be livid. That's the way it works. You keep it within the family. I did, until now. But I loved her, and I tried so hard to be as loving as I could.

Now my dad, he was a good guy. I have no idea how he survived as long as he did with my mom. They clearly loved each other at some level, and they were each other's best friend, but after my mom started drinking, she became stubborn and cold and ruthless, and it wasn't easy being in the house with her. My mom would be in a conversation about something, anything, and would always find a way to lash out at my dad.

"Michael, if you're so smart, how come you have your crappy job and your crappy car and your crappy clothes? See, you're not smart. You're not smart. You're crappy." It wasn't exactly Shakespearean iambic pentameter and it most definitely wasn't nice. Mom did have standards though. She would not swear in front of us, so "crappy" was the go-to word.

She would withdraw into herself, cut short or dismiss any interaction by reflexively turning her back to us to hide her drinking, I guess thinking that if she couldn't see us, we couldn't see her. She would go silent to try to hide her slurring. And on the nights when she lost the ability to hide herself, she would just go on and on at my dad about the same thing, whatever the complaint may have been, until everybody sought refuge somewhere in our tiny bungalow, though we were never able to completely avoid what was going on. We never talked about it with each other. We just tried to pretend it wasn't happening. Yet, my dad never fought back or argued with her, he just accepted her for who she was. I always admired him for acting like a gentleman with her in the face of some of the worst things imaginable. He loved her to the end, for better or worse.

But the thing is, my dad had to take his frustrations out on somebody, and that somebody was me. I'm not talking about physical abuse or beatings or anything like that. First, that just wasn't in my dad's make-up. Second, he simply wouldn't have been able to take advantage of me physically after I got to be a certain age given my size and strength—he was a big man for his generation 6′2″ and strong, but nothing compared to me in my teens. The abuse was verbal, and something our entire family had to witness.

His mantra with me was "book smart, worldly stupid." It started when I was about nine or ten years old, when it became apparent that I was more than just academically gifted. I'd give my view on politics or current affairs. "You always have been and you always will be book smart and worldly stupid." I'd fetch him a Robertson screwdriver when he'd asked for a Phillips. "Book smart, worldly stupid." I'd finish mowing the lawn and not coil the electric cord properly. "Book smart, worldly stupid." In a certain sense I guess it was sort of a cute, almost endearing way to approach me, because he was actually acknowledging that I was smart. Except it wasn't cute, because it came with much more.

No matter how big or small the issue, my father had to go after me verbally. He couldn't ever just leave me alone. He was always on me. Sunday dinners were the worst. My sister, Dawn, later told me that she feared them, dreaded them, for she knew that whatever I said about anything, my dad would challenge me, and not in a productive way to encourage critical thinking, but in a way that belittled me, that tried to tear me down, that was designed to make me feel inferior to him. "You're nothing. You're not as smart as you think you are. Oh, come on, that's stupid, you're stupid. You're a loser. What, you think you're better than me? You think you deserve more than I have? You'll never make it! You'll never succeed! You're nothing!"

My sister would cry. My brother would be thankful it wasn't him.

It hurt. It hurt so much, until eventually it didn't anymore. And then it became a game with me to provoke him, to get him whipped up into a frenzy, for me to sit there and be belittled. I just didn't care anymore. And my inner voice would kick in:

Go ahead. Yell at me all you want. I don't care. I don't care about you. I don't care about anything anymore. You've told me I'm stupid, I'm a loser, I'm never going to succeed. What more could you possibly tell me?

But you think I'm a loser? I'll show you.

Looking back on things, that all makes sense. He had never been able to achieve all that he wanted in life. He saw me, his eldest child, achieving everything that at one time had been his to obtain. He had dropped out of school after Grade Eight, but knew in his heart that he was better than that, that he was smarter than that, but that he was trapped in a situation he couldn't escape. He was stuck having to do whatever he could to raise a family, and here I was about to get all of the benefits of his miserable hard work. But at the time I didn't have any perspective. All I could see was his anger toward me.

I fought back. I said things I never should have said.

"I'm a loser? You're a loser! Look at you! How could I ever be proud of you?"

At some level I knew what he was going through, what he was dealing with, but as much as I tried to focus on the good and love him, it didn't make any difference. The tragedy of life is that you can't see then what you can see now. I know now that he was envious of me, but I couldn't see that back then. All I could see was the anger and his inability to show me any approval for what I was doing, not resentment, jealousy, or a fear that maybe his first born son, a son he loved and admired so much, saw him as looking small and inadequate.

And yet, unlike my reaction to my mom, a part of me always knew that he was indeed proud of me. I would, every once in a while, hear from others the things that he was saying about me to them. But he was too stubborn to ever say these things directly to me and I was too stubborn to ever force the issue with him. So, while he played the tough guy with me, I think I knew that deep down he was proud of me, even in the face of his relentless verbal assaults. Sure, there was his demeaning mantra of "book smart, worldly stupid," his outright dismissal of anything I ever said or wanted to try to achieve, and his saying I wasn't nearly good enough for those types of things. Still, I think he was proud of me.

In the midst of this trainwreck at home, I was now moving on to high school alone because the guys I played hockey with, as well as my best friend, Carl Torbiak, all remained in junior high in the proper grade for their age. I became increasingly isolated, a geek living in a jock's world and a jock living in a geek's world, now without my best friend.

Please don't get me wrong. My life at home and at school was not even close to the worst imaginable, and I did deal with things in my own way. I had friends, just no close friends. I know that many have much worse family situations than I did. I wasn't some lost soul nobody loved or appreciated. But I was a boy with vulnerabilities.

Being an outward success at external things didn't fulfill my emotional needs. Already isolated within my family, seemingly unloved and unappreciated by my parents, and now displaced at school, I wanted more of a connection with the world around me. And the thing is, when you want something so badly and aren't getting it, it makes you vulnerable to somebody who comes along and offers you understanding and an acceptance of who you are and what you want out of life.

I may have pretended otherwise, but when I was a young, awkward, giant misfit of a kid I had never wanted to be special or different. Being successful didn't make up for being different and alone. I craved the acceptance that I wasn't getting at home, the normalcy that I wasn't getting at school, and the understanding that I wasn't getting from friends outside of hockey.

Still, no matter how tough things may have been for me on the inside, I always had hockey, my safe place, the place I belonged.

That is who I was when I met Graham James.

TWO

THE PREDATOR

N THE 1970S, everyone in the Winnipeg hockey community knew Graham James. He was an innovative minor hockey coach focusing on talent and speed, not size and brute force. He produced winning age-group (under sixteen) hockey teams while serving as a successful scout for major junior hockey teams in the Western Hockey League, one rung below the NHL. And he was based in St. James, the western part of Winnipeg, where I grew up.

Graham seemed to live and breathe hockey.

You might find it odd that I refer to the man who abused me as "Graham." Yet that is how I see him, how I think of him to this day. He is, was, and always will be "Graham." I have tried to pretend otherwise, and I have been encouraged to try to distance myself from him by referring to him as "Mr. James," "the accused," or "the defendant." But to me, he is and always will be "Graham," and so "Graham" he is.

I had only seen Graham from afar, but I, like the rest of the hockey community, saw him as somebody of importance. He was a winning coach, a scout, an innovator, a hockey intellectual working among less-educated and less worldly coaches. His demeanor at the rinks was somewhat aloof, and he always seemed to be deep in thought, analyzing and processing everything going on around him. He had an aura about him, and he was somebody you wanted to impress. And then suddenly you would see him laughing with a group of coaches or players, and in an instant he went from unapproachable Hockey God to regular guy. Everybody either knew or knew of Graham, and it seemed as if everybody wanted to impress him.

Impress is an interesting word to use, because Graham himself was anything but impressive. He was short and pudgy, with a boyish round face and unkempt curly hair. He had a sad face and was poorly groomed, and his presentation could best be described as "disheveled." Yet because he was someone of importance in the hockey community, none of this seemed to register. He was somebody to impress.

It was Graham's job to know about every hockey player who might be of potential interest to a junior hockey team. It was Graham's job to get to know young boys. He was coaching the St. James Midget (sixteen-year-olds) AAA Canadians, a team from my area composed of boys two years older than those on the Bantam team I was playing for. We were both involved in hockey at the highest level in Winnipeg, and Graham most definitely knew who I was.

I finally got to meet Graham in January 1979, when my St. James Bantam Canadians traveled to Minneapolis for the North American Midwest Regional AAA Silver Stick Championships. Although Graham was coaching the St. James Midget Canadians, something that itself would have involved a massive time commitment, he somehow found time that weekend to help a friend of his, Mike Tishler, the coach of our arch rivals, the St. Boniface–St. Vital Saints.

In January 1979, people saw only good in Graham. They looked fondly upon him for giving even more of his time to the game of hockey by helping coach another team at that Silver Stick tournament in Minnesota, a team he was not directly involved with. The tournament was an opportunity for him to scout the best players in our age group. And there may even be people who to this day believe that Graham's motive was solely to help coach that team and give his time freely to the game he loved.

As a scout, Graham was interested in identifying the best upcoming players, and the tournament featured the region's best teams from both Canada and the United States. Our rivals, the team he was helping out, featured several outstanding players who were already attracting significant attention in the hockey world. Looking back, it is almost ridiculous to think about the talent that was playing hockey in Winnipeg in our age group. The St. Boniface–St. Vital Saints featured Darren Boyko, who would eventually play in the NHL and later set records in the Finnish Elite League; Dale Derkatch, who would set records in junior hockey while starring for the Regina Pats; and Mark MacKay, who would end up playing professional hockey in Germany and eventually captaining the German national team. The Winnipeg South Monarchs had among their players Brett Hull, Bobby's son and himself now also in the Hockey Hall of Fame; and Richard Kromm, a highly sought-after prospect who eventually played for the New York Islanders.

There were other extremely talented players in our league in our age group. We played a very high level of hockey, and there were opportunities for an adult to latch on to a boy's success. There was money to be made and coaching and management opportunities to be had by showing an eye for developing successful hockey players.

Graham was neither a parent nor a relative of any of the players. Still, it would never have occurred to anyone that he might have an ulterior motive. It would have been beyond contemplation in 1979 that Graham was using his position to develop relationships with young men, to access potential prey. Nobody considered for a moment that he might be putting himself amidst young, athletic, and even, some would say, good-looking boys for his own satisfaction.

Everybody on our team knew that Graham was there. As hockey players, we desperately wanted to impress him. But at the same time, we saw his helping a team from a different district, our rivals no less, as an act of treason against both the St. James team he coached and our team representing that same district. We used this seeming treason as motivation throughout the tournament. Hockey is about many things, with loyalty and respect for the jersey very high on the list. How dare he disrespect our jersey, his own team's jersey, and help another team against us? Oh, the silly things that motivate young boys.

And of course, things being what they are, our two Winnipeg teams had traveled all the way to Minneapolis only to end up facing each other in the Mid-Western Regional AAA Final, a game that could have been scheduled just a short drive from everybody's house back home.

I don't remember much about that game except that I did not play particularly well and we lost to the team Graham was helping. For some reason, I'd been very calm on the bus taking us from the hotel to the rink for the game and couldn't understand why I wasn't more energized for the final. So I mentally "worked myself up," that being the mantra for successful athletes back then. But I had completely misunderstood what was going on. My perfectly calm state had actually been something I'd never experienced before—perfect preparation for a big moment. As the game wound down I realized that in working myself up, all I'd done was get in the way of my ability to play naturally to the best of my ability. I was so disappointed, so mad at myself.

Me being me, I blamed myself for the loss and was both angry and somewhat despondent as our team left the ice with our second-place trophies or medals or whatever they gave us—it was just a loss to me, and second-place awards meant nothing to me that night. And just then, as we were walking down the pathway from the ice surface to our dressing room, there, almost incredibly, was Graham standing just off to the side, alone, watching us but looking as if he didn't want us to see him. I looked over and saw him and couldn't help myself: "Hey! Graham! Nice job helping them. Traitor! You have to leave St. James to be a winner?"

Back then, I would have been the last, and I mean last, person to say anything rude to an adult. I immediately felt sick about what I had done and resolved to do whatever I could to try to take it back.

Except you can't ever really take words back.

After getting out of my equipment and eventually leaving the dressing room, I searched for Graham to apologize to him. I was nervous and ashamed. I expected the worst. Instead, I was met by a very calm, very reassuring, almost nurturing man who said that he understood that things are said in the heat of the battle and that I shouldn't worry at all about what I'd said. He said that if he'd been in the same position, he likely would have done the same thing. I was relieved.

"Hey, Greg, this is just one game," he said. "Focus on what you've accomplished. Focus on your skills, on what you can do. That's the real you. You know you're better than today. Today, tonight, was an exception."

"It's Gil. The guys call me Gil."

But it got even better. Graham went on to compliment me on my play. He told me to put this one game aside and learn from it. He let me know that he was aware of my ability and successes and that he thought that I had a future in the game if I kept progressing in the right direction. He said that he was prepared to help me, that he had some thoughts on things that could help me, but he definitely did not want to interfere with my current coaches (who, he thought, weren't that good but must be respected) so we would have to keep this between us to avoid causing offense. Same with my dad—don't tell him, as my coaches would eventually find out. Keep this to myself, at least for the next little while, and we'll see what we can do. He said he would get in touch when we were back in Winnipeg. And with that, we agreed to speak when back in Winnipeg.

I remember getting on our team bus to head back to Winnipeg not caring one bit about the fact that we had lost the regional finals. Instead, all I could think about was that one of the leading figures in our hockey world thought I had a future in the game and was prepared to work with me.

That was the random event that caused our paths to cross. Those were the random words uttered by me in frustration that changed my life. Some might assume that I would wish I had never apologized to him. But I see it differently: it was my fault and I wish I had never been rude to him. In the end, nothing mattered. I was nobody to him, just an opportunity, a potential victim.

Not too long after we were back in Winnipeg, Graham started following my team around and showing up at games. Seeing him there, knowing he was watching me, I felt flattered. In those days before email, texting, cell phones, even voice mail or home recording machines, he could have just called my house and asked for me. But he never made direct contact with me anywhere other than at a hockey rink. He was always surrounded by other coaches or kids in hockey jackets, near the canteens at the rinks that everybody passes on the way in and out of arenas. It provided him with a perfect opportunity to grab a quick minute of conversation with me while my dad was waiting for me in the car. If he ever needed to get in touch with me, he could always easily find me.

Eventually, Graham suggested that we get together at a local restaurant. I was so excited that somebody of his stature in our hockey community wanted to meet with me, and I could hardly wait until the day came.

THE DAY FINALLY came. I had just turned fifteen and didn't yet drive, so I had to walk there, about a fifteen- or twenty-minute walk. I was so excited. I wanted to make a good impression, and I most definitely didn't want to be late, so I arrived very early. Because I had very little money with me, I sat drinking several glasses of water while I waited for him. The waitress asked if I was going to order something or just sit there. I was quiet and nervous. Eventually Graham showed up.

"Greg, sorry, Gil, sorry I'm late."

He wasn't late. Graham can be very charming. He was just less early than I was and wanted to put me at ease for being a dork who showed up way too early for our meeting. He immediately made me feel like the most important, successful young person he had ever come across. He gushed with praise about my hockey talents as well as my success at school.

"So, I hear you're a bit of a genius. What's your favorite subject?"

"Yeah, right. I don't know. Math, English, stuff like that."

I was clearly a brilliant conversationalist.

It was apparent that he had done his research, as he seemed to know more than I thought he would about who I was and what I had already done. He said that he had seen me play a game at a tournament the year before and was amazed at my talent. He complimented me on how others spoke of me, both as a player and as a person off the ice, saying I was well known as an intelligent, well-mannered, respectful, and very hard-working young man.

Besides flattering me, Graham started digging for more about me.

"You know, I think that a strong family upbringing can be helpful in developing character. Most of the guys on my team have great parents. But it's also possible that coming from a tough family background can make you into an even stronger person. What's your family like?"

I gave him a bit of information, but not the whole story. "We're OK, I guess."

He told me about his team, shared some hockey secrets, asked about my school, and touched on current affairs. Our discussion was very exciting for me, and I felt as if I were being brought into the inner workings of the local hockey community. Knowing about my success at school and my interest in academics, he played up his position as a teacher and let on that he was highly educated. And he immediately homed in on the potential issues that might be at play.

"I know what it's like to be very smart and good at school while also playing sports. The other guys can sometimes make it hard on you. It can be a lonely place. I understand."

By engaging me, adult to youth, as somebody who mattered, by listening intently to my every word without dismissing me or yelling at me, Graham instantly became somebody I thought I could talk to, somebody I wanted to talk to, somebody I respected and admired for the simple reason that he made me feel that I finally had a meaningful voice outside of the classroom. It was the first time my intellectual side had been respected and encouraged outside of school, in the real world. I didn't have that at home. And all it took was this one conversation to make me feel good about myself.

I don't remember things like what he was wearing or what we ate, the kind of things you think would be etched in my memory. I do remember looking down as he went on and on about me, breaking eye contact with him out of embarrassment, and seeing a stain on my hockey team jacket next to the team crest and worrying that he would see that stain and think I was a slob for having spilled milk on it earlier and not cleaning it properly.

Mostly, I remember getting up from the table and feeling almost dizzy, slightly removed from the situation while thinking that this couldn't be happening. How lucky was I? How cool was this? It was amazing.

And of course, I had a long time to think about it because I walked home. It wouldn't be right, he said, for us to be seen together. And he told me to keep our contact secret—something he would reiterate at each of our meetings.

I thought it had been one of the best days of my life.

WE CONTINUED TO meet at the same restaurant every few weeks or so for a few months.

Over time I became increasingly at ease discussing things with him. From answering with a simple "OK" when he asked about my relationship with my parents at our first meeting, I increasingly opened up when he later circled back to the issue. I slowly, gradually let him in on the isolation I was experiencing at home and divulged how difficult it was no longer having my best friend around all the time.

He would tell me that I was better than the rest of my teammates and that I deserved better coaching, coaching that respected both my physical skills and my brain. He would go on and on about hockey strategy, stressing that a goalie should know more than anybody else on the team about how the patterns of the game work because goalies have to participate actively in a team's own defense while at the same time responding to the other team's offense.

"You know, traditionally, goaltenders in minor hockey have been ignored when it comes to teaching hockey theory. Do your coaches teach systems of offense and defense?"

"Well, they run drills for us with the guys having to be in different places in different situations."

"But do they give it an overall structure, something cohesive where everybody has certain fundamental responsibilities?"

"Not really."

"You need to know what the other team is trying to do in your zone. And you need to know what your team is trying to do to defend that. There's a reason for all of that positioning."

"I think our guys are just trying to remember where the coaches want them to be."

"Look, I appreciate the role of the goalie in a way others can't. Because you're smart, once you understand the patterns, the systems, you can use your head in connection with your talent to move far beyond others playing your position. I'm sure your coaches already recognize that. Maybe your guys just aren't ready for systems, or surely they'd be teaching you how to play, wouldn't they?"

He asked about my parents and my relationship with them. What were they like? Where did they come from? What were their interests? What had they done in their pasts? What were they doing now? Surely, given their backgrounds, they would understand that I needed to be challenged, and they were already encouraging my intellectual pursuits and supporting me in my athletic and academic efforts, weren't they?

The seeds of doubt were sown. Who was there to teach me? Who understood me? Who was there to champion me? My parents? My coaches?

Graham asked me what I wanted to do with my life. Did I want to pursue hockey, or did I want to do something with my education? If it was hockey, he said, there would be no stopping me—provided I received the right coaching and training, and he could help me with that. If it was something else, he, a teacher, could also provide guidance as I worked toward university. But if it was a combination of the two, he, as both a leading figure in the hockey world and a teacher, was ideally situated to be my mentor.

I wanted to do both. I had always wanted to do both. I told Graham that my dad had only gone to Grade Eight and that I would be the first in our family to go to university. He would have heard the way I said it, the determination in my voice. He would have understood that I wanted to be different from my dad, better than my dad.

"My dad focused on hockey and look where that got him."

And with that statement, without realizing it, I had crossed a line. I was now speaking disrespectfully about my own father to somebody outside the family, somebody who until very recently had been a complete stranger. The one thing Graham would most easily have learned about me and my relationships with my own family was that I wasn't going to be like my dad. Graham instantly saw that as a way to connect to me, to bond with me.

Those seeds of doubt. Who was there to teach me? Who understood me? Who was there to champion me? After our meetings I would think long and hard about what he had said. He didn't tell me that my parents were bad or that my coaches were bad. He left me to come to my own conclusions. He prompted me to ask myself what I wanted and how I might best achieve that. But before prompting me to ask myself those questions, he had already positioned himself as the answer to my dreams.

We increasingly discussed how I could best develop as both a player and a person. He now knew that I wanted to play varsity hockey at university, and there was no way I was ever going to change my mind about that, notwithstanding his position as a junior hockey scout. There were rumors of a new rule that would make those playing major junior hockey, the level of the teams for which Graham scouted, ineligible for NCAA university hockey in the United States (this rule was, in fact, adopted the next year), so he never pushed me to the Saskatoon Blades or the New Westminster Bruins or whoever else he may have been helping. Graham took great pride in steering players into what is now the Canadian Hockey League, but that was never on my radar.

"I understand you. You want to do what I wanted to do, exactly what I wanted to do. I wanted to get a scholarship and play hockey in the States too, but my asthma got in the way. It's smart. You get the best of both worlds. You'll have your hockey and an education to fall back on. That education will always be there."

"Graham, I'm not ever going to play in the NHL."

"You have no idea just how good you are and how much potential you have, do you?"

"No."

"Well, I understand you. Only somebody like me can understand you. People like us, we need to stick together and help each other."

He would never let too much time go by between our meetings, but he was also never so in my face that it became off-putting. He walked a delicate line between keeping me on a string and appearing to allow me to move on with other aspects of my life with other people. He was able to maintain an emotional hold on me, and I would increasingly ask for less and less time to pass until we could get together again to talk. Yes, in a way, getting together became my idea. His time was now something he was doling out in limited amounts while I craved more. Not only did have me on a string, he had me swimming toward him.

Graham started revealing himself to me. He told me that he believed that he was misunderstood, that he was a good guy but that many people seemed to be insecure around him, almost in awe of his education and coaching talent. What he hated most, he said, was having to dumb himself down in certain circles to be accepted. He was frustrated that he was in many ways a loner dedicated to making the game of hockey better. He never understood how sportswriters, especially Jack Matheson of the *Winnipeg Tribune*, could keep their jobs after supporting goon hockey. He thought it was unfair that sportswriters, who, he said, generally knew nothing about hockey, had the right to comment about anything to do with the game. He believed they were hurting the game, and once told me that the definition of a sportswriter was somebody who had failed English but could remember the winner of the last twenty Stanley Cups.

That was Graham. He would say anything to make a point that served his immediate interests and made him look better than everybody else. He was trying to get me to see that he was smarter and funnier than everyone else while appealing to my intellect and my sense of humor.

It worked. More and more I wanted to be like him.

Graham sympathized with me, saying that people like my father, who had dropped out of school before high school, could never understand people like us, people who lived a different life inside our heads. One night at dinner, my dad was talking about somebody's son who was in engineering at university. He couldn't understand why somebody would go to university to learn how to work on a train. I just nodded and looked away. But I laughed with Graham about it, thinking that he understood me and cared about me. I laughed with my eventual abuser about a perceived short-coming in my dad. I can't ever take that back.

Graham told me he could help me develop to the point where he could get me a scholarship to an Ivy League school. *He* could develop me. *He* could get me something. It was now all about what he could do for me and how I needed him to get what I wanted. Except, there's no such thing as an athletic scholarship to an Ivy League school, not that I knew anything about that at the time (there is need-based financial aid, which often amounts to virtually total funding when a student-athlete comes from a family with a low income like mine). A simple sentence, but one with so much embedded in it, designed to position him between me and my dreams. Yet, all I could see at the time was that he was encouraging me to chase my goals.

Near the end of one of our meals at the restaurant he was very clear: "Look me in the eyes. Look hard. I believe in you. You can do this. It doesn't just have to be a dream. But it will require commitment. You're going to need a lot of help. Nobody makes it without a lot of help. But I believe in you. You have every right to succeed, no matter who doesn't believe you can do this, no matter who believes this is beyond what somebody like you can achieve. I believe in you. We can do this."

No matter who doesn't believe in me?
No matter who believes this is beyond me?
Somebody like me?

I felt panic. My body tightened and my ears started to ring. What didn't I know about myself that he knew? Who was he speaking with who had told him I wasn't good enough? Maybe my dad had been right all along.

But at the same time, I could see in his eyes that he believed in me, that my goals were attainable, that he accepted me, that he understood me. I was starting to believe that maybe I had found my place, that here was someplace I belonged, that I had finally found my true home.

I didn't see the dead eyes of a shark hunting its prey. Instead, I saw the compassionate eyes of somebody who knew what was going on inside my head because, in his telling of his story, he too had been a brilliant student and a top athlete, and nobody but people like us could understand just how difficult it is to be a jock in a geek's world and a geek in a jock's world.

"People like us"—those words haunt me still.

Maybe the problem was that I wasn't enough of a jock to truly be a jock? Maybe I wasn't enough of a geek to truly be a geek? Maybe I was nowhere, lost, and without his help and guidance I would always be lost, alone, one of a kind? Maybe I was just nothing special? He understood me, he knew what it was like to be caught between two worlds, he would help me with both worlds.

I was one of a kind, but he was too, so the two of us would be one of a kind. "People like us have to stick together to help each other," he said.

"People like us..."

After a short while, everything he said made perfect sense to me. He was increasingly becoming the major voice and guiding light in my life, and I was slowly becoming isolated from the people closest to me. My coaches couldn't know, my family couldn't know, the others on my team couldn't know about our relationship, and that was pretty much it for me at that time. If any of them ever found out, it would be all over.

And Graham was dangling a pretty big carrot in front of me for immediate gratification. The older team in our area that Graham coached, the Midget (sixteen- and seventeen-year-olds) St. James Canadians, was in contention to represent Manitoba in the Air Canada Cup (now Telus Cup), the national Midget hockey championship. Graham told me that if his team qualified, it would have an expanded roster for the tournament. He thought I should be added, given the potential need for a third goalie for the tournament and his belief in my abilities. I was shocked, as that would mean he'd be lifting me two levels, bypassing the two AAA goalies in the age group ahead of where I was playing, two goalies who were also highly regarded.

Graham's team did qualify for the Air Canada Cup. It was held in, of all places, Winnipeg that spring of 1979. I'll never know whether he was telling me the truth, but he told me he tried to get permission to add me to the roster and was denied because he wasn't allowed to bypass the boys who were older than me. Graham told me he protested. The three players (none of whom were goalies) he called up from the team a year older than mine were James Patrick, a defenseman who went on to star in the NHL; Dave Farnfield, who ended up playing at Yale; and Rob Scheuer, who ended up captaining the Princeton hockey team.

While the first of those names is what hockey people will focus on, it is the second and third names that were relevant to me, as they were recruited by and eventually accepted at Ivy League schools. To me that indicated that Graham was able to deliver on his promises. The reality, of course, is that Graham had nothing to do with their being recruited by Ivy League schools. But I didn't know that back then.

GRAHAM HAD GOTTEN to know me very well. He understood what I wanted to achieve and had positioned himself as ideally suited to help me achieve my dreams. He saw that I was particularly vulnerable because I was a bit of a loner caught between two worlds. I looked to Graham and not to my dad—a man who, I am sure, loved me but just couldn't show it—for guidance. I opened up to Graham. I let him in.

A goaltender has an interesting perspective on the game of hockey. In many ways the game unfolds in front of the goalie, its patterns revealing themselves sometimes quickly, sometimes slowly, but usually in recognizable ways. An adept goalie adapts and reacts to the moving parts, most often without even consciously thinking about what is happening. The goalie is said to be "in the zone," and the pucks are stopped, controlled, and redirected with ease.

I thought I was on my game. I was in the zone, a dominant player on my team, in my league, and I was now being tutored and mentored by a leading figure in the game. I thought I could see everything in front of me, that everything was finally coming my way. It all looked so promising, so attainable, so very real.

But in reality, I couldn't see anything.

THREE

ATTACKED

THERE WAS NEVER a clear start to what he was doing, never a moment to look back on where I could say to myself, "There, it's so obvious what he was doing, I should have never let it happen." But then again, when I look back on all of this, all I can see now is that every single interaction with him was just such a moment, when "Of course, it's all so clear what he was doing. How could I have been so weak, so stupid, to let this all happen?" is the only possible response.

In a sense, our relationship just evolved from our initial meetings. I devoured Graham's progressive theories about hockey systems and his love of fast-skating defensemen and speedy forwards who went deep into their own end to win back possession of the puck. I craved the attention he gave me in our meetings, being treated as a peer, as an adult, as somebody more than I was at home. I felt fortunate that he was willing to help me progress with my hockey and my academics, that he was willing to mentor me and bring out the best in me. So, when he suggested that we meet not at a restaurant but at a school field for a training session, I was ecstatic.

Graham started setting up training sessions where he would show me various stretching exercises and body-positioning techniques to incorporate into my own off-ice workouts. This was in addition to the reading material he brought to our meetings which confirmed my belief that Graham was indeed a most different type of hockey coach. I was already completely captivated by his detailed analysis of the shortcomings of North American hockey and the benefits of learning Swedish and Soviet systems. Those systems were known for their focus on off-ice learning, so it was only natural for him to move on to dryland (off-ice) training, something they focused on and which at the time was still seen as somewhat revolutionary.

I was the perfect willing subject. Beyond wanting to excel at hockey and take advantage of what Graham had to offer me, I was still, deep inside, the insecure, overweight young boy who in my own mind needed to work extra hard on my physical conditioning. No matter how tall, strong, and athletic I had become by age fourteen, in my mind I was still the uncoordinated, pudgy boy who hadn't yet grown into his body.

Graham had picked up on that, and he was very good at taking the stories of my past and using them to home in on my insecurities to convince me that I needed his training methods.

"You know, a guy like you with big legs has to work hard to keep up with the play."

"You know, a guy like you has to fight for everything you'll ever get, because nobody's ever going to help you like I will."

"You know, coaches hate smart players, because they fear they can't control them, they can't teach them."

"You know, just because you're smart and you know what to do doesn't mean your body is going to do it all on its own."

I was hearing the echoes of "book smart, worldly stupid." I was once again seeing myself as an uncoordinated, overweight young man. Neither could have been further from the truth, yet both were the reality I inhabited.

Graham would never participate in any of the physical exercises or drills, blaming his asthma (or a hernia or an arm in a sling or some other excuse). I have no idea why it never dawned on me back then that these ailments would in no way have prevented him from, say, at least doing some of the stretching with me. I guess I was just so caught up in the moment and what I was doing that I never even noticed that he preferred to just lean back and stare at me. I would stretch, I would do squats, I would do push-ups and sit-ups, all under his watchful eye. I would mimic a goaltender's stance and shuffle side to side and lunge laterally back and forth and back and forth until my thighs ached. I was always a model student for him. I viewed this as my opportunity to learn from an expert and impress a leading figure in the hockey community, one who could give me everything I had ever dreamed of.

It must have been a very difficult time for him. Having identified me, having taken steps to bring me under his wing and groom me to be receptive to his thoughts and desires, and having isolated me from my family, coaches, and friends, and having made himself the most important force in my life, he now had to test my boundaries and assess whether the time was right for him to make his move on me. Would I be compliant? When could he safely take tentative steps to find out? How could he move forward without fear of getting it wrong and potentially opening himself up to being found out?

Because he did not have constant exclusive contact with me, he would have to be very careful in making his next move, for while he had won my trust, there was no natural setting for him in which he could physically take advantage of me since I was still living at home with my parents. He only had our meetings and these workouts.

But Graham was brilliant in his own way, the Rhodes Scholar of sexual predators.

One night during a training session, he pushed me until I was exhausted. I had worked my legs so hard that I could already feel them stiffening as I sat down, leaned back, and gulped for air. I was sweating hard, my shirt was soaked, and stopping felt so good. The intense exertion gave way to the usual post-workout euphoria that I craved so much and that felt so good, so intoxicating. I loved to give my all to the task at hand and work to the point of utter exhaustion. That had always been my reputation in everything I did. I was the guy who worked the hardest in all the drills, the one who never stopped short in the skating drills but went all the way to the end of the rink and slammed the boards with my stick, who always stopped on the line, never before it. That's just who I am. Or rather, who I was before him.

Graham started going on about the physiology of a hockey player. He noted that a hockey player was required to perform everything on skates, two small edges of steel.

"A hockey player looks with the eyes, which starts everything. Power to move where needed comes from the core and torso, and this power must be transferred to the hips and down to the legs. From there, all of that power has to be carried by the feet in the skates, which each sit on top of the ice on thin edges of steel, which transfer all of that power to the ice. A hockey player requires very strong feet, very special type of feet that can withstand the enormous forces. Can I take a look at your feet?"

Not a demand. Not a command. A request. A simple request that at the time made enormous sense to me.

"Sure."

I reached down and took off my socks. I leaned back and put my feet in the air for inspection. He took one foot and cradled it, stroked it. He squeezed it, twisted it slightly, ran his palm from heel to toes. He pressed into the arch. He released the first foot and grabbed the other. Same thing, an inspection, a slow, deep analysis of my foot. He stared at each foot for what seemed like a long time. It all seemed so scientific, so analytical.

"You've got good feet. Big, strong feet. They're perfect. Perfect."

The physical barrier was broken.

From then on, post-workout foot massages became part of the routine. It didn't seem strange to me but instead made perfect sense after what he'd told me about the physical mechanics of hockey. My feet felt so good after his massages, and I'd thank him for making me feel better and helping me recover from the pain of the drills.

Said another way, I thanked him for touching me.

The pattern was repeated. He made it the new reality as my training continued, despite any injury he might at the time have—a bandaged hand, an arm in a sling, whatever might have otherwise stopped a less persistent and less needy connoisseur of feet. So now, in addition to being my mentor and my friend, he was my massage therapist. He had already broken me down intellectually and emotionally. Now, finally, he had made his first physical move.

This new pattern of foot massages continued for several months. Some foot massages lasted longer than others, some involved wedging a foot against his chest when he could use only one arm because of injury, some seemed a little different from the rest, but nothing, absolutely nothing, seemed to me to be at all inappropriate or anything other than a foot massage.

But of course, Graham wanted more, and eventually "more" happened.

"MORE" STARTED OUT as a training session just like the rest. Only this time he wanted to show me a book about hockey theory,

Tarasov's Hockey Technique. We talked a bit about it, nothing out of the ordinary.

"How do you feel? Tired? Sore?"

"Of course."

"Here, why don't you lie down and I'll work the pain out of your feet."

A foot massage, but this time, it wasn't like the others. I sensed something was different even as he started normally, with my feet. He seemed different, a bit aloof, not completely present. He had shown me the book, but we hadn't spent much time looking at it, and I sensed it had been a pretense for something else. Maybe these thoughts are something that I've created to make myself seem smarter about what eventually happened, or maybe I always knew that this was going to happen. I don't know.

He started to move beyond my feet and slowly work his way up my legs. I froze. I did nothing but lie there, my eyes closed, wondering what was going on. I was afraid. I was confused. I opened my eyes, trying to get my bearings and understand what was happening. But all I caught was a glimpse of him, his face, his eyes.

It's his eyes that I remember the most. His dark, dead eyes, the kind of eyes that show absolutely no emotion at all, that seem to look right through you as if you aren't there—the eyes a shark has, cold, searching eyes that see without engaging, eyes that are always on the hunt for prey. I will never forget those eyes. I can never forget those eyes.

He moved slowly up my legs, never saying a word. I kept my own eyes shut as much as I could after seeing those eyes. They scared me. But it was too late. I had seen his eyes, the dead eyes, and they would be with me for the rest of my life.

I had no idea what was happening. I mean, I knew exactly what was happening, but I had no idea what was happening.

Where is this coming from? Why am I not pushing him away? What should I do? What could I do? Why is my body responding? I must want this. I must like this. This must be who I am. I have to get out of here. But what will he do? What will he say? What will I do? Who will believe me? How do I explain why I was with him? How do I explain all of the meetings I've had with him for months? Who can I speak to who will understand? How do I make this go away? Why am I responding? Why is my body responding? Why can't I stop responding? Why can't I say anything? Why can't I stop him? WHAT THE FUCK IS GOING ON?

It all happened in utter silence. There was a radio on, no doubt to muffle sounds, but I could no longer hear a thing. All I could hear was the blood pumping through my temples, pounding in my ears, the sensation of being removed from the world around me and locked in my own space. At least, that's how I remember it. Or maybe that memory came from the hundreds, if not thousands, of nightmares I've had ever since. What I know with absolute certainty is that I couldn't hear a thing.

He rubbed my legs. He fondled me. He masturbated me. He exposed himself. He rubbed himself on my face and inserted his penis in my mouth. He returned his focus to my feet. He masturbated and ejaculated over my feet and shins.

I did nothing. Well, I guess that's not completely true, as I did respond in a small way, with a kick, but it was, at most, a half-hearted one, more a straightening of a leg than anything else, something you do when you're pretending to wake up with a jolt rather than hit somebody deliberately. Whatever you'd call what I did, it certainly did not prevent him from accomplishing whatever goals he had set out to achieve.

He groaned. He turned away, turned his back to me, and walked away, leaving me by myself for several minutes. And when it was over, once he had finished with my body—well, how could I make sense of what had just happened? How could I explain that I didn't attack him, that I didn't lash out and stand up to him and stop him right then and there? And today, how can I reconcile what I wish I had done back then to avoid this, to stop it, with what I didn't do then?

I covered myself back up as quickly as I could. But I didn't run. I didn't know what to do. I sat there until he came back in. And then we talked. Rather, he talked, I listened. He talked for a long time. He calmed me. He comforted me.

"You're progressing so well. You have so much talent, your legs are so strong, you have limitless potential. You know, people like us have to support each other. We're not like others. They would never understand who we are. They don't see things the way we do. I know you're a bit lost right now, but I understand you. I see who you are and what you can be. People like us have to look out for each other. We have to support each other. But people like us, working together, can make anything happen."

That expression again: "people like us."

Graham had just shown me he was different. Now, with those words, he was telling me. Maybe he had been telling me all along and I just hadn't understood. I thought "people like us" had referred to the talented jock as geek, geek as jock. Now, with what had just happened, I was pretty sure he was telling me that I was gay.

And then he confirmed it: "If our secret ever gets out, everyone will think you're gay. Nobody will want you on their team or in their program. It would be the end of everything for you because nobody wants to deal with people like us."

I don't know if he meant it as a threat. I mean, of course he did. But back then I saw it as something he feared would happen to me if "the secret" ever got out, something he didn't want to happen to me because it would cause me pain and suffering and he was there to look out for me.

The things a goalie doesn't see when he's screened.

I should have run away from him forever. I didn't. I could have stopped him right there. I didn't. If I had stopped him, nothing would ever have happened to Sheldon, to Todd, to Theo, to all of his other victims who came after me. Except that I didn't. I didn't stop him from anything, and that is my shame. I'm not ashamed of what happened to me. My shame is that I didn't stop him and that others after me had to suffer as a result. Their suffering is all my fault. I could have prevented it all.

Instead of running, I felt sorry for him. Oh, I was full of rage and fear, but at the same time he had somehow made himself come across as a victim in all of this, presenting his homosexuality as something that caused him pain. He showed a vulnerability and needed support. I felt sorry for him. I actually felt sorry for him.

I walked home, a zombie detached from the world around me. I cried like I'd never cried before in my life. It was a long walk, a route I usually jogged at a leisurely pace, but I couldn't breathe properly. It was very cool outside, that I remember, but that's about all. I couldn't feel anything. I was off in my own world, far removed from this one. Lights were blurry, and once again I couldn't really hear anything. Was I in shock? Probably. I cried in solitude during my walk home. There is so much that I don't remember, that I don't want to remember, that I have actively tried to forget over all of these years. But there is also so much I will never, ever be able to forget.

When I got home it must have been late, but there were several lights still on.

"Where were you?"

"Out."

It was the normal reply of a normal teenager. I, the supposed golden child, had never had a curfew. I had my own room in the basement all by myself, and I could pretty much come and go as I pleased, often without anybody even noticing that I was away.

With that one word I went down the stairs, taking the twelve quick steps down to the low-ceilinged basement I had to duck to enter, and stumbled into my dark bedroom with the one small window up at ground level, the room that flooded whenever it rained.

Alone in my own home, I had no one to turn to, and I certainly wasn't about to start talking to anybody about what had just happened anyway. I was supposed to be perfect, and what had just happened was not perfect. I had no perspective that night, no ability to take a step back and process what had happened, what was happening. I was caught up in the middle of something I did not understand, something so horrible that it was beyond anything I could remotely consider. Who do you turn to when the only person you have to turn to is the person who has just done something horrific to you?

His words haunted me: "People like us have to stick together." I thought I knew him, that I had understood him. I hadn't. Who was he?

More importantly, who was I?

That's a question we all ponder at some point in an attempt to find the meaning of life. But that night it was just something that kept echoing in my head as I lay in bed unable to sleep, quietly crying through the night until the darkness was broken by the early morning light straining to make its way through our back windows and downstairs into my room, the only place where I would ever again feel safe.

Even though Graham's homosexuality was something I couldn't really understand, it didn't scare me. The way he had constructed things, positioning himself as a lonely and misunderstood victim, made me sympathetic toward him. In fact, it made me think he was even better than the rest. He, a lonely man, an outcast in society (remember, this was nearly four decades ago), was still engaged in the most manly of Canadian sports and at a level where he was seen as more progressive, more intelligent, simply superior to others. I liked his story and its appeal of an underdog triumphing against all odds over the know-nothing Neanderthals. His story got to me at both an emotional and an intellectual level.

The reality, of course, was that he was no underdog. He was just a sociopath, a serial sexual offender. He was the powerful one. I was his victim and the true underdog. But I couldn't see that, for he had groomed me to see the world his way.

Graham had been very clever. After physically assaulting me, he didn't come out and tell me he was gay. He simply referred to "people like us," leaving it to me to connect the dots (a disgusting metaphor given what he had just done to, or rather on, me). He left me to process what had happened and reach my own conclusions. He hadn't presented me with something I could reject out of hand. Rather, he positioned his own desire for a sexual relationship as an inevitable conclusion for me to reach myself, for me to conclude that I wanted what he wanted.

His implications that I too was gay, that people like us needed to stick together and support one another, that we needed to keep our secret, and that I needed to come back to him for his support all fit into the narrative that he had constructed from the information I had given him over the past months. Graham had slowly made his world my world, and my world was now being further defined by him as he wanted me to see it. In this construct, his physical actions toward me made perfect sense. He was bringing me out of my shell and showing me my true self. He was liberating me.

To me, Graham's interest and support were the actions of someone who cared about me. They were actions that respected who I was and what I needed to do to become the best me that I could be. The furthest thing from my mind was that I was being groomed by a sexual predator so that he could abuse me. No, to me he was the one delivering to me all that I needed, all that I wanted, all that I deserved. The physical actions were just a new dynamic in my development of who I was and what I would become. In this light, he was helping me be me. I believed that he and only he knew anything about me and who I really was. I believed that he cared about me.

At least, that's what I kept telling myself when I was crying the hardest.

Maybe he was right. Maybe I was gay. I had thought I knew who I was. I mean, I had an ability to understand who I was through outside feedback about school and hockey, but my sexuality had never been on my radar except in respect to the normal issues all teenagers deal with. Graham was now introducing something dramatically unexpected.

I had previously always thought, never doubted, that I was heterosexual, and had never for a moment thought otherwise. I had never fantasized about anything other than girls and women and, while I was quite shy, I was very interested in girls. So it was confusing for me to find my body responding to him physically. I try to make it easier on myself now by noting that the average teenage male can have an erection simply because a breath of wind hits the right place. This protects me from facing a difficult reality that I continue to grapple with to this day, notwithstanding all of the therapy and the greater insight I now have into how the body operates. Whatever he was doing to me, I was responding to it physically.

Although I had always thought that I was heterosexual, evidence to the contrary was piling up. The result was a great deal of confusion and a huge impact on my personal development and self-image.

The easiest part of assessing the impact of sexual abuse is considering the actual physical actions themselves. Still, words like *massaging, touching, fondling, groping, masturbating, oral sex,* and *ejaculating* don't come close to describing the horror of what was going on. And all victims, whatever they have experienced, live with that horror of the physical actions. There is no erasing the memories, and until they invent a pill that allows you to control your own dreams and nightmares, I will never know from night to night whether I will or won't revisit those horrors in my sleep.

It is harder to deal with the lingering uncertainty and confusion created by the disconnect between who you once thought you were and who you now see yourself being. A single incident of abuse by Graham left me with deep questions about myself, questions I answered in ways that left me less than whole.

Who am I? I must not be who I thought I was.
Why did my body respond to his advances and actions? I must have liked it.
Why didn't I stop it? I must have wanted it and I deserve what I'm feeling now.

But there would be more than just a single incident. Much more.

I was, on the outside, still succeeding at everything. But sexually confused, isolated from my parents, and without close friends at school or a support network within my own hockey team, on the inside I was now alone with a secret, which, if revealed, he had told me, would shatter all of my dreams.

But was I gay? I didn't have any girlfriends during high school. Oh, I had crushes on girls and I had dates with girls, but I had little free time outside of my extracurricular activities for dating. As much as I thought that I was heterosexual, I couldn't honestly and unequivocally confirm to myself that I wasn't gay, especially now that I had had this physical response to a man. There was no Internet to consult about sexual abuse. There was nobody I could speak with, nobody to counsel me. My physical responses to him were all I had to form a judgment against myself.

And I still had him, his interest and his support. In poker parlance, he was now all in with me. All in.

Me? Who was I? I had no idea. I thought I did, but not anymore.

Me, that teenaged kid, lost, all by himself?

I, as I had known myself, had ceased to exist.

I was now nobody at all.

FOUR

TRAPPED

⸻

I WENT BACK TO him—and hated myself for it. Part of me knew I should run away from him, but the rest of me knew I needed to go back and stay with him because my dreams depended on him. I couldn't run away, because I was locked inside a reality established and controlled by him. I had no ability to step back and rationally assess the situation.

Why couldn't I run? Why couldn't I just end it? The one truly at risk if our secret ever came out wasn't me but Graham. He was the adult, he was the teacher, he was the hockey coach, he had everything to lose. It should have been easy for me to tell somebody what had happened, right? It should have been a no-brainer to go to my parents, to a teacher, to my coaches, to anybody, and let somebody know what Graham had done, right?

Wrong. Wrong not because it is wrong, but wrong because I couldn't even conceive of a world where Graham was at risk for anything, where reality was never anything but what he was telling me it was. I just couldn't. I saw him as having the power and me as having none, because that's the way it was.

I was alone, I was stuck, and I could see no way out. And so several weeks later, after he contacted me again, I went back to him.

I walked to meet him in a trance, numb, constantly asking myself whether or not I should keep going. I walked with my head down, looking only at my white athletic shoes with red striping (the brand of shoes is lost in the ether of memories long gone, though for some reason the red against aged white remains clear). I didn't want to see anything or be seen by anybody. I fell into myself, a hulking young man slowly, inevitably retreating as much as possible into nothingness. I barely noticed where I was or what I was doing. I was almost run over by a car, unaware that it was barreling toward me until its horn briefly startled me out of my self-interrogation. I kept asking myself the same questions, over and over again:

Whose feet are these?
Why can't I control where I go and what I do?

I promised myself that I would ask him to explain what was going on and what he had meant by everything he had said the last time. I convinced myself that I had to see him again so we could talk things through together so he could see that he was doing something that he liked but that I didn't. I told myself that he would see things from my perspective, that he would understand that if he wanted me to succeed, it could never happen again.

By the time I met him, the easily won debating points I had secured when facing only myself in my own head fell away in his presence. So did any resolve I had been able to arm myself with. But it didn't seem to matter. He acted as if nothing had happened, and for a few brief moments I was able to make myself believe that maybe what had happened before was an aberration, something that would never happen again.

But I was wrong.

He started by breaking me down mentally. I was too afraid to stand up to him. He said that I needed his help to succeed and that I would risk losing everything if anybody found out what he was doing for me. Just like that I was back to being a puppy dog, an athletic giant, but ultimately nothing more than a toy he was playing with.

This time he was less tentative, more confident, and more aggressive. This time I was less surprised but more terrified of him because of what he was doing, more terrified of myself for simply being there in the first place. Fool me once, shame on you. Fool me twice, shame on me. I felt total and complete shame for being there, for letting it happen to me.

You stupid, stupid boy. You're pathetic. You knew this was going to happen. You knew it all along. Big talker, all the things you were going to say to him. What, he's got some magical control over your mouth? You can't even speak now? You must like this, you must want this. How awful are you that you would go through this just because he wants this? How weak are you? This is you. This is who you are. He knows it. Now you know it too. He's the only one who understands you. He knows you better than everybody else. He knows the truth. Stop pretending you're anything else.

Afterward he was, as before, calming, seemingly understanding, even nurturing in positioning himself not just as a hockey mentor but also as a life mentor who understood who I really was. I hadn't done anything I had planned to do. I hadn't stood up to him. I hadn't asked him to explain. I hadn't tried to get him to see that this wasn't what I wanted. No, in his presence I believed everything that he said about me. I couldn't wait to leave, yet as I was leaving, I also knew I would come back. I knew that he had me. I knew that there was no way I was going to be able to get away from him, even though getting away was as simple as walking through the door and never coming back. I just knew.

I have zero memory of taking the bus and walking home that night. I have zero memory of anything that followed other than that I cried so hard into the afghan blanket that covered my water-bed in my basement bedroom that I didn't notice until the next morning that I had heaved so heavily that part of it was covered in vomit. Fortunately, Renaissance Man that I was, I was able to do my own laundry as the washer and dryer were in the basement next to my bedroom, and nobody in the house was any the wiser.

An attack followed up with complete capitulation. In these two meetings the template for our "relationship"—for lack of a better word—had been defined. My "mentor" had me in his grasp, he was never going to let go, and I knew it.

BY NO MEANS was it an everyday thing—in fact, far from it.

Although he said he tried, Graham never managed to arrange things so that he was my hockey coach and thus was denied the opportunity to control me every day. Since there was no reason for the two of us to ever be seen together, Graham had to pull on different strings to abuse me. Sure, we had the cover of train-ing sessions and general mentoring, but that was still somewhat unusual and would be better kept secret. It would always be easier to hide what was going on if nobody ever saw us together any-where except at the hockey rink. Secrecy was the key, and he hammered that home to me time and time again.

Oddly, this made it easier for him to control me. I was a teen-ager questioning who I was, I was sexually confused, and he had become the most important person in my life, my mentor, the only person I could talk to about the things that were important to me. At the same time, I feared that our secret would be discov-ered, meaning that I had to comply with his every wish. The daily distance between us made things worse for a very simple reason: the easiest way for him to control me was to withhold from me the thing that I now needed most—him.

I was trapped. I wanted to run away from him and never see him again. Yet, at the same time, he was the one thing in life that I needed the most in the face of personal crisis—his support, his mentoring, his interest, his understanding. In the bizarre world of abuse, I couldn't get away from my abuser because he had positioned himself as my one and only savior. I wanted to run away from him so badly, but the only place I wanted to run to was right back to him. So all I ended up doing was running in place.

Get away from him. Run away, now! This isn't you, this isn't who you are. You're a boy, a young man, with so much ahead of you. You don't need him. This will all just go away. Just stop this, stop it now. You can do this.

Except he knows who I really am. He knows I need this. He knows the real me. He is just like me and can see right through me. He isn't making me do anything, I am. He can help you. He's making me a better me, a stronger me. He's showing me who I really am. Stop hating him, he's helping you.

It was so hard, so mentally and physically exhausting, so futile. It yielded nothing but more pain and weakness as over time both my body and my mind became worn down from the struggle between the need to escape and the need to be with him. All that all you can do is stop, breathless, in exactly the same place you started.

I found myself desperate for his ongoing understanding and approval, all the time not knowing what was going on at his end. I frantically asked myself: *What is he doing? Is he helping anybody else? Is he still helping me? Am I still his chosen one?* Those were the days before cell phones, email, texts, even answering machines in homes, so absent direct contact, there was no contact. The isolation from him in the midst of my isolation from everything else while living in his reality was unbearable.

Because we met infrequently (usually after several weeks, a month maybe, sometimes more frequently, sometimes less so, as when he went away in the summer), there was a certain level of anticipation and excitement about reconnecting, discussing current events, hearing about what he'd been doing for me and what new insights he might have into positional goaltending. He knew exactly how to play me. At the same time, while always hoping that the next time would be different, I also knew deep down what was expected of me.

I rationalized everything by choosing to see Graham as he wanted me to see him: a lonely man looking out for my interests who just happened to be gay, a man who needed me as much as I needed him. I convinced myself that Graham must have been torn up inside and that he would never do anything to hurt me, that any pain I was in was just because I was selfish, that he needed support, that he needed love, that I needed to give love back to him.

"You're a very special young man. You mean so much to me. I see so much of me in you."

All the while, I had to carry on in the outside world as if nothing was happening. I sat in an English class covering the major themes in Dostoyevsky's *Crime and Punishment* while my teacher, Harry Pauls, compared Raskolnikov to the *Übermensch* in Nietzsche's *Thus Spoke Zarathustra*. He joked to our class that a Nietzschean society of supermen "would look like a group of perfect Gilhoolys." I smiled and looked down, knowing, unlike the rest of them, the opposite to be true and that Socrates' statement at his own trial, that "the unexamined life is not worth living," could be turned on its head to mean far more to me than it ever could to Raskolnikov.

The longer the abuse went on, the more difficult it became, because I knew that if our secret ever got out I would have nowhere to go, nobody to turn to. My inner dialogue became oppressive as I would constantly debate with myself, negotiate with myself, justify myself.

A one-off experience with him might be understandable to others as something he forced on me, but then again who would believe me? A longer-term series of meetings where it happened again and again and again? First, nobody would ever believe that a longer-term series of meetings hadn't been consensual. Second, do I even know whether or not it's consensual? Who am I?

Beyond that, it was a different time, a less enlightened time, a time before "not that there's anything wrong with that" was in the cultural lexicon and understood by the masses. I was, to my deep personal regret, afraid of the stigma of being gay that I would have faced had I been "outed" for my relationship with him. I feared being caught, being labeled as something I didn't think I was— but didn't know for sure. I feared being seen as something that at the time was seen by many uninformed people (including me) as bad or wrong. I was afraid my dreams would evaporate if my secret got out, that anybody who knew me would shun me, that I would be isolated even by those who were, though not close, still very much a part of my life.

Of course I should end it with him, right? But where would that leave me? Where would telling somebody about Graham leave me? More alone than ever before, that's where. More dependent on him than ever before.

The only viable alternatives that I could see to consenting to what Graham wanted were ones that further isolated me and that would take me back not to where I had been before I met him, but to a place far behind that, a place with no future, no dreams, no support, a place where I would be all alone, misunderstood, and lost. I wanted out, but at the same time I needed him more than ever. Graham's genius was identifying me as somebody who could be trapped. He knew that I would comply with his wishes because he had left me with no options, and he knew his secret would be safe with me because he understood how isolated I was and how dependent on him I had become.

But a victim doesn't just comply and leave things at that. A victim still knows there is something wrong going on. So, if I couldn't confront my abuser, there was only one other logical target to go after—the person I thought was truly responsible for everything that was happening. I went after myself.

CLINICALLY STATED, I "acted out," "exhibited anti-social behavior," "self-harmed." These words and phrases, which we read so often, all try to set out in a neat and tidy fashion what it is we victims do. But they don't begin to describe what actually goes on and what we do to confirm our pain, our guilt, our lack of any sense of self-worth.

Graham controlled me and my body. So I fought back in a bizarre battle of me against me, a battle that in winning I lost and in losing I lost even more.

> *He loves my feet. So I'm going to rip out my toenails. That'll show him. He abuses me, but what he does to my body makes me react physically. I hate that I feel pleasure, so I'm going to punish myself for feeling good. I'm not good. I deserve to fail. I will fail. I'll fail at school, at sports, at relationships, at everything. Nothing matters.*
>
> *He controls me. I'm going to inflict intense pain on myself, pain that shows I'm in control of what I feel.*
>
> *He's attracted to me. I'll gorge myself and get so fat so he won't want to touch me again, nobody will want to touch me. Nobody will want me. Nobody will hurt me again. I'll be safe.*

And so on.

The world looks a bit different in the midst of abuse. Things that used to seem important to me didn't seem so important anymore. And as I increasingly realized what was going on in our "relationship," I figured out that I was able to attack myself out of self-hatred while at the same time attacking him indirectly by diminishing what he had come to love.

Well, to say that "I figured out" anything is to overstate how it happened. It just happened, a natural reaction to an unnatural set of circumstances.

I LAY IN bed one night, unable to sleep, tossing and turning, thinking about "it," what was going on, what I could possibly do next, wondering whether or not I was gay. I told myself that I wasn't, that my constant crush on Diane Mohr ever since I'd met her in Grade Four pretty much confirmed that. Still, I really didn't have all the answers.

Maybe I am? Of course I'm not. How do you tell? He says I am. What if I am? What would I do? If he thinks I am, other people must think so too. Do other people think that? Do they know something I don't? If I am, what will people say? But I'm not. So why I am doing this? Why do I respond to him? Why does my body like this? But I don't like this. Maybe I do? How do I know? How can… Stop!

Except you can't turn off your brain.

But you can focus it on something else.

I reached down and started rubbing my feet. Just like he did, except I was grabbing at them hard, with my fingernails scratching, pulling the skin back tight against the toes, then against the heels. I grabbed at the skin on the top of my feet, drawing my fingertips as close together as possible, making a fist, stretching the skin as tight as possible. Pain. Over and over again I dug my fingernails deeper and deeper into the skin. More pain. I grabbed my big toes, right hand on right foot, left hand on left foot, and scraped the tops of them with my thumbnails, my fingers grabbing the thickened pads. I worked my thumbs into the nails of my toes, into the nail beds. I ripped away as much of the nails as I could, deep into the skin. Still more pain. But compared with the thoughts that just minutes earlier had been racing through my mind, this was pure bliss. Those thoughts were now gone, nowhere to be found. All I could think of, all I could focus on, was the intense pain, my fingernails digging into my own skin, my own blood flowing onto my bedsheets.

I closed my eyes and fell into the pain. I was free. I could sleep.

THAT MAKES PERFECT sense when you're living in a world of abuse. And when I lived in a world where something like that makes sense, how could I ever believe I was worth anything?

I thought I was crazy for hurting myself. It scared me to know that I could do that. But at the same time, I knew, I absolutely knew, that all of this made sense at some level, that I was doing whatever I could to make something mine, to take my life back as much as possible in the midst of the carnage, in the midst of him controlling me and my body.

MY WEIGHT BENCH, dumbbells, and barbell were set up in the basement just outside my bedroom. Down there, I was alone in my own world. I was no longer a pudgy young kid, but a strong athlete playing a number of sports. That transition had taken place in large part because of those weights my parents had bought for us and that I knew they couldn't really afford. That transition to strong athlete had been hard fought, something nobody had seen as I worked all alone in my own little world. That transition was so very short-lived that it was over almost as soon as it had taken place, before many people had even noticed.

At first, I kept working out in my basement. It was a safe place, a place I could retreat to. Initially I thought of making myself huge, a force nobody could ever overcome. But at the same time, I wondered, what was the point? All getting in shape had ever done for me was get me into this mess. I was already big enough, strong enough, that he posed no physical threat to me. I could already easily overcome him, yet I was still with him. This wasn't about strength. All I was doing was making myself into something more attractive to him, to others. I didn't want him to find me attractive, and I wanted the rest of the world to see me for the fraud I was. I didn't deserve to have anybody respect anything about me.

Why was I doing this? Why was I working so hard? It made no sense to me. One day, I was lying on my back on my weight bench, sweating, in the middle of a set of chest flies, arms extended out to the side, a dumbbell in each hand. Why? I put the left dumbbell down on the ground. I set the right dumbbell on my chest. I put both hands on the single dumbbell and extended my arms directly toward the ceiling. Then I let go, dropping the dumbbell onto my chest, ribs, and upper abs.

Pain. Intense pain. Nothing but pain. Nothing.

I deserved this pain for what I was doing. I loved the pain for releasing me from my thoughts. All I could think of was pain.

It was perfect.

SELF-HARM. SELF-ABUSE. A lack of self-worth. A belief that I was a fraud, that I didn't deserve success. Sometimes the thoughts just didn't go away. Some nights I couldn't sleep because I knew I deserved to die but was too chicken to kill myself. I was ready for those nights. I kept a bottle of something stashed in a secret place, above the basement ceiling tile next to the light. One sip tastes awful, two not so bad, and by three or four I was already losing focus about what it was I was worrying about. I liked not worrying about things. Soon the only thing to worry about was remembering to hide the bottle before I passed out.

Still, when that wasn't possible because there was nothing around to drink, or if I just feared the headache that came whenever I drank, I would dig. It was always much more satisfying to dig into myself. Because he liked my feet, they were my preferred place to go to, and the blood that came out pulsed with my heartbeat. I had very good circulation.

Digging is the entry drug to cutting. I eventually got there too.

THE ALARM GOES off in the morning.

It's the start of a day like any other day, just some random weekday for a seemingly normal high school kid who came home from school the day before with some homework to finish and then a hockey practice to attend. Today is a new day. *Carpe diem.*

Maybe I was lucky and had a fitful sleep. Or maybe instead the nightmares about him were too much and I couldn't fall back asleep after waking in the middle of the night drenched in sweat, heart pounding, images of him on me, laughing at me, inviting others from our hockey world to follow him on me. Maybe my head is pounding with an intense headache from the constant crying ever since I awoke, crying that I muffled in my pillows, in my bedsheets. Maybe my head is buzzing from the rum or rye whisky or whatever else I could raid from my parents' supply and hide above the tile of my basement ceiling and then guzzle in the middle of the night without anybody knowing. Or maybe my body is sore because, without realizing it, I have been mindlessly picking my skin open and ripping little bits of flesh from myself as I try to find anything to take me away from the horrible feelings arising from my nightmares.

Whatever kind of night it has been, all I can hear now is that alarm going off, and with that the inner dialogue begins. I know that it's curtain call, time to start acting, to carry on as if none of this is happening. I know that I have to get up and take my place in the world. I can't let anybody see that I am weak, that I am a loser, that I am a complete failure, an utter fraud.

But deep down, the only thing I can think of is that it's all just a complete waste. All of that work to get into shape and excel physically? All of that academic achievement? That kind, gentle, polite personality? All of that just made me attractive to him. All that did was make me unsafe. All that did was put me front and center and right into his sights. I will never make that mistake again. I know there is safety in being anonymous, in being unattractive, in being undesirable.

In fact, what's the point in getting out of bed? I'm safe here, nobody can hurt me here, nobody can get at me. Besides, it's a world where people like him not only exist but also flourish, where people like him hold important positions, where they are respected in the community and have people supporting them while I am crying myself to sleep alone in my basement bedroom. What kind of world is that? Why would I want to live in that world? What kind of life is that to live among him and people like him?

But I'm lucky. I somehow realize that not every day is going to be one of those dark days when everything looks bleak. I remind myself that I still have good days when I believe that anything is achievable, when I absolutely know in my heart that life does have meaning, that there is more to life than him, that I am still me no matter what else might be going on. I make myself remember who I really am and remind myself of my drive for life, for hard work, for success, for kindness, and for laughter.

All of this fight, the daily battle with myself inside my head, just to get out of bed. It's a lot for a high school kid to deal with.

Sometimes I wish that the alarm had never gone off, that I could just go back to sleep, nightmares be damned, because going through all of that effort just to get out of bed doesn't seem possible or even worth it. So I choose revisiting the demons in the dark over fighting just to take my first step into the unknown day ahead. But that's not even close to the worst. No, when it's really bad, I wish that I had never awakened in the first place, that I could have just fallen into a deep and never-ending sleep so I would never have to face another minute of hell on earth.

But today I hear the alarm. *Suck it up, buttercup, and get moving.*

Carpe diem indeed.

I HAD ENOUGH self-awareness that I came to understand that my secret meant my life was going to be a battle between wanting to run and needing to stay. But I didn't understand what that would do to me. And because what was going on was a secret, my secret, our secret, no one knew what was behind my self-destructive behavior and odd actions. Why wasn't I the engaged student I had once been? Why was I regressing as an athlete, no longer putting in the extra work that had once transformed me? Why was I always tired and moody? Why was I always wearing long sleeves and not showering with the team after practices and games? Why was I increasingly funny, loud, and disruptive at school? Yet because teens are not known for their stability of character, it was easy for me to get lost in the crowd of the angst-ridden.

My natural abilities gave me cover. No matter what Graham was doing to me, he couldn't take away my natural abilities. I still had enough natural talent to survive and move on to the next challenge. I still played and excelled at what is now AAA hockey, and I still excelled at school. But I had changed. From the outside it probably appeared that I was going through a phase, a natural teenage rebellion, and because I had built up so much goodwill, people respected me. They didn't ever think to dig any deeper than asking me if anything was bothering me, if maybe something was wrong at home. Nobody ever asked a follow-up question after I brushed them off, for, in spite of it all, I was still outwardly very, very successful.

But had they looked more closely, people would have seen that I had lost interest in sports and academics. I was still succeeding in hockey and attracting interest from junior and college hockey teams, but I was no longer running or working out at home. I was letting my athletic body go soft almost as quickly as I had moved past being heavy. I was still succeeding at school and winning awards, but I was no longer completing all of my assignments. In Grade Eleven I had won the silver medal at the University of Manitoba Open Debating Championships, but now I no longer participated in debating tournaments or math championships or anything academic, other than maybe attending classes whenever I felt like it.

But these changes could be passed off as merely a little bit of rebellion. People had no idea what was really going on, that these were passive-aggressive, desperate cries for help.

In the meantime, Graham continued dangling carrots in front of me. He was always telling me what he was doing to help ensure that I'd be scouted for college hockey teams. He told me that he was behind my getting called up by the St. James Canadians, our local junior hockey team, to travel with them, even though I was underage. It was because of him that, as a sixteen-year-old, I progressed through training camp and stayed with the junior team into their season. He kept telling me about the recommendations he was supposedly making to scouts. Sure he was. But I believed everything he said to me about all of that.

A girl at school liked me, a tall, beautiful girl whose father just happened to be the assistant general manager of the New York Rangers. She tried hard to get me to go out with her. She came to my hockey games, she sat near me in class, and she got her father, who already knew much about me as a player, to invite me to the Winnipeg Arena to meet the Rangers coaching staff, team management, and goalie John Davidson when the team came to Winnipeg to play the Jets. No young hockey player in his right mind wouldn't have succumbed to her advances, as on top of everything else she was a very nice person. But I didn't want to bring her into my world, for I believed that she deserved far better than that.

It's hard to be an athlete when you no longer want to be one. I had loved hockey from the very first moment I put skates on as a very young boy. Now I hated it. I stopped training outside of actual practice and games. I went from being an underage member of the St. James Junior Canadians early in the 1980–81 season to a soft, out-of-shape regular-aged Midget AAA goalie by the end of the year, no longer a dominant player in our league.

Make yourself safe. Do whatever you can to protect yourself. Make yourself unworthy of attention and affection. After all, you are unworthy of attention and affection. He controls you, he controls your body. Take back control, show him who controls your body.

The easiest way to hide from sight is to become somebody nobody wants to look at. So, make yourself into somebody nobody wants to look at. Nobody abused me when I wasn't in shape, but Graham noticed me when I was.

I control what I put into my own body. I can make myself safe by making myself repulsive by gorging, by ceasing to be an athlete. I can control me and show him that I control me.

I can show myself that I am still in control by purging, by releasing the food from inside and taking back my body, by showing myself that deep down I still believe that I deserve to be somebody, that I deserve to be an athlete, that it's me ruining myself and it's me who can save myself.

Back and forth. But because of my less than perfect ability to purge all that I had binged, I continued to put on weight. I became a physical mess. I did whatever I could to take attention away from myself. I didn't want anybody to look at me, I wanted to hide. I didn't believe I deserved to live. But if I couldn't kill myself because I was too afraid to try to take my own life, I could kill myself by ceasing to be the person I was. On the outside I still looked almost the same, kind of fit, but soft and not athletic. On the inside, well, nobody could see anything. There are lots of ways to kill yourself without having to die.

School became a game. I questioned the point of even reading the textbook and went into exams cold and wrote essays without reading source material, figuring anything important would be mentioned in class. I excelled at that. Then I went the other way and decided I was I probably smart enough to skip entire units of classes and teach myself and still receive a perfect score on the tests if I just read the textbook once. In an open challenge to authority, I did that in my physics class. Mr. Narayansingh caught wind of what was going on after noticing that I was repeatedly absent and thought he would teach me a lesson by setting a very difficult test. I aced it.

I ended up, not for the first time, in front of the vice-principal. The principal, who the year before had congratulated me in a long school-wide announcement over the loudspeaker for an academic-athletic award I had received, was too angry to deal with me.

"Greg, last year you were... we don't understand why you're now... this attitude of yours has got to... if you don't... Greg, are you even listening to me?"

And I'm sitting there, off in a completely different world, one where the issues he's bringing up just weren't my biggest concern right then, lost in my own thoughts about what was going on, lost in a world more horrific than anybody could possibly understand, filled with a violent rage nobody could see:

Fuck Graham. I want him dead. I want that fat fuck dead, I want him to go to the Civic Centre and get out on the ice and stand naked in front of one of the nets, and I want everyone I know to shoot pucks at him as hard as they can, and I want them to do it over and over again until he can't stand up anymore. And then I want them to shoot at him some more. Fuck him. Fuck him and his fucking hockey and his fucking hair and his fucking dirty khakis and his fucking Swedish hockey theories and his fucking foot massages. And then, as he's crying in agony, begging for somebody to help him, I want him to look up, I want him to look me in the eye, and I want him to apologize. And then I want somebody to shove one of my skates down his throat and kill him. But not me. I never want to touch that motherfucker again. Never.

What could anybody ever say about what was going on inside my head other than "Say three Hail Marys and the Lord's Prayer and come back next Sunday."

I could have told the people at school about everything, but I couldn't tell them about anything. I was silent. I nodded my head, I said I was sorry, that I would be better and more respectful going forward, and I left the office and went back to class. Of course, I then promptly skipped the next class and went to the library to read.

The darkness that I carried with me every day was real:

Why did he pick me? He must have seen I was weak. People must see me as weak. I must be some sort of joke.

Why didn't I stop it? I must have wanted it. I deserve what I'm feeling now. I deserve to feel like his leftover garbage.

How could somebody like him control somebody like me? I'm worthless and weak. I'm not the strong, tall, intelligent, athlete people see on the outside. I'm a fraud.

I'm weak. I can't stop it. But I can cut, I can binge and purge. I can get fat and make myself so gross he'll stay away from me. Everyone will stay away from me.

What you see isn't real. I'm a failure, a worthless and weak fraud, and I deserve failure, not success.

Who am I? I'm a fraud, his garbage, his enabler. I'm somebody who doesn't deserve to live.

But I am also one of the lucky ones. No matter how hard I tried to destroy myself after internalizing the abuse, I never could keep myself down. I still graduated from high school with honors while playing AAA hockey. I still retained my dream of playing college hockey. And my natural talents made that dream a possibility, despite my best efforts to make those talents disappear. I still wanted to achieve my dreams, even as I self-sabotaged by not training and not staying in shape. I was meeting with college coaches who came through Winnipeg, and I could see a possible escape in my future. But I couldn't connect the dots in a way that allowed me to leave Graham while he still had the power to take that escape route away from me by disclosing my secret, a secret that he told me would scare away the college coaches.

Never in this perverse reality did it ever occur to me that I could simply apply to a university myself on my own merits and get in. I believed that I needed him for anything I wanted to do. He told me that he was still helping me achieve my dreams and was working with all of those coaches to get them to recruit me to their programs. He reminded me that we had to be careful, as they wouldn't be interested if they knew the truth about us.

I now know that it was all a lie, that he was just telling me whatever he could to keep me compliant. I've since been told that he had nothing, absolutely nothing, to do with my hockey success or any scouting that was done, that he had nothing to do with getting college hockey programs to approach me. But back then my reality was the reality he had created.

Still, I was not without self-awareness. I could see that I was destroying myself, but I was powerless to stop it. I also knew that I had to fight this battle on my own, that nobody else could ever know there was even a battle going on. Deep down, I knew that this was a battle I couldn't win. Knowing that you are alone and that the real you is broken and defeated, that the successful young man the world sees is a fraud, is very difficult and lonely knowledge to live with. Although I kept trying to succeed, I also kept trying to destroy myself—day after day.

And Graham had his tricks. He would talk about others he was interested in to try to make me jealous, to make me think that maybe his attention was moving elsewhere. That's right. At the same time as I wanted to kill myself for being involved in this mess, I craved his attention and support. He had me hating myself for being with him while at the same time working hard to please him, to keep his attention. I wanted to die because I was with him, yet he made me jealous of others who might take my place.

Jealous. I was jealous of others who might cause his attention to shift elsewhere. I was being abused, yet the more I unraveled, the more I feared that he was losing interest in me.

The self-doubt, the lack of any sense of self-worth, the self-sabotage, it all got worse and worse. I continually questioned who I was. More than wanting to hurt myself, I wanted to kill myself, but couldn't get up the courage to actually do anything about it, so I was a failure at that too. But if I was not strong enough to kill myself, then this was the only reality in which I could operate— his reality. In my mind there were now only two options: death, or more of the same, with more of the same being a victory of sorts, an extended lease on life, however meaningless that life might have been.

It was a vicious cycle. The longer it went on, the more I hated myself for it. The more I hated myself, the easier it was for me to give up on myself and just give myself over to the abuse. Oh, I would find ways to fight back, but it was never a fight against him—it was a fight against myself. I dug into my own skin. I ripped out those toenails on those feet that he loved so much. In class, I would find myself digging my pen into my hand, blood suddenly on my books. But it had to remain a secret. I never, ever took my shirt off or showered after hockey or other sporting activities in the midst of one of my self-abuse cycles for fear of showing my self-inflicted wounds.

But I also kept picking myself up and finding a way to fight on, to try to rescue myself from myself. In my last year of high school, my grades were nothing like the top marks I had received in Grade Eleven. But they were still very good. And back then the Scholastic Achievement Test was still seen by admissions departments in U.S. universities as important in assessing academic competency and qualification. I knew that I would have to take these exams at some point, but I didn't give them much thought and took them without doing any preparation. Weeks later, when I received the results, I discovered I had done well. Very well.

From Graham's perspective, it must have been a very scary time. He didn't have direct control over my daily life, only control over my dreams. He could see that my dreams would eventually take me away, away from him, and with that came the risk of exposure. His best chance of preserving our secret was to earn my goodwill by making me believe that he had delivered my dream to me, that he had given me exactly what he said he would. If only I had known what a fraud he was.

Nobody's life is ever as good as it seems, and nobody's is ever as bad as it seems. I went through hell with Graham, but I was also lucky to have been given some natural gifts that allowed me to make it thorough to the next stage of life in spite of everything.

We take our victories in life where we can. I'm very proud that I was named the first star in my last game with the St. James Canadians of the Manitoba Junior Hockey League, which was a 3–1 victory over the Selkirk Steelers. It's a small achievement, but to me it was a sign that there was still somebody lurking within the nobody I had become.

I had been approached by many universities and seriously recruited by several, but in the end I formally applied to only one university. After all, I "knew" I would get in because he was helping me, right? Some of the universities that had shown interest in me had renowned hockey programs, programs that were much better than the one at the university I eventually applied to. But my focus had never been on hockey alone, so I didn't apply to those schools. I applied to just one university, the one Graham said he had targeted for me from the start. And so, one Sunday afternoon in March 1982, I received a phone call after the admissions meetings had been held, followed a few days later by the fat envelope in the mail that confirmed you had been accepted. It was set. I would be going to Princeton.

IT WAS THE first moment since I had first spoken to Graham— in 1979—that I had felt any freedom from him. It wasn't total freedom, for he could still interfere with my dreams of playing hockey if he revealed our secret. Still, I knew that I could have a future and that the end of our "relationship" was in sight. Graham had to prepare for a separation. In fact, he likely had already begun preparing.

Graham faced a huge risk when the relationship ended. He knew that the secret may at some time come out once I had time, space, and an opportunity to reclaim my own reality. And it was the knowledge of that risk that informed how he needed to act during the relationship and that was the reason he did certain things during the relationship. He had every incentive during the relationship to plant the seeds of doubt in others' minds about what was happening, what had happened. He needed to prepare stories for the future, should I ever come forward. He needed cover for his actions, things to point to that would show that I was lying, was making things up. An abuser will change his habits, do different things, involve others in somewhat similar situations where nothing happened so there are others who will say that they were there and he never did anything with them.

And yet no matter how hard an abuser like Graham may try to do all of this, an abuser knows he cannot underestimate that massive risk of being caught, of being found out, because that risk can never go away. All that Graham could ever do was manage the relationship as best as he believed possible in the hope that I would never come forward.

Graham managed me through to the end, positioning himself as the man who had delivered me my dream, pushing me to acknowledge what he had done to make my life better than it would have been without him in it, making me feel in his debt for what I had achieved. There was no tearful goodbye. There was only a parting, a moving on, an end brought about by my physical move away to Princeton University, which, at the time, I thought he had delivered to me. The last time I saw him was nothing special, and just as it had all begun so innocently and without drama, it ended abruptly without any discussion or even mutual acknowledgment that it had happened.

I think Graham knew that he had dodged a bullet with me. Although I was in so many ways perfect prey for him, I was not nearly as captive as the others who followed given that he never directly coached me and I never lived with him as did some of the others who followed. It turned out that the distance between us actually worked to his advantage, as it made me crave his attention and presence in my life, but it could have gone the other way. He hadn't coached me and he had a different, less tangibly direct hold over me. And that again shows his genius in being able to identify me as a victim who would respond in a certain way to a certain set of circumstances.

But now I was about to be free. I didn't understand, however, that my life as I had known it had already been destroyed. Yes, I was able to hold it together amidst the self-harm, the self-destruction, and move on to the next stage of my life. I assumed that once I was away from him everything would be fine. But physically leaving Graham turned out to be the easy part. Living with the carnage of the abuse would prove far more difficult.

I had once had an unstoppable drive to be the best at everything I ever did. Now, after my experience with Graham, I still wanted to succeed, but I also wanted to fail and show the world the true me, the fraud that I knew I truly was. I was escaping my abuser, but I was about to find out that he had left me with something worse.

I was now my own abuser, dedicated to bringing myself down.

FIVE

ESCAPE TO PRINCETON

PRINCETON UNIVERSITY IS a glorious combination of physical beauty and limitless opportunity for learning and self-growth. Set in the midst of lush, gently rolling New Jersey countryside halfway between New York and Philadelphia, it is more Hogwarts than Hogwarts itself. One of the world's great learning institutions and often ranked as the United States' best undergraduate university, it is Ivy League in every sense. Its Collegiate Gothic buildings are blanketed with dark green ivy, though to be fair, the campus also features buildings of innovative modernist design along with others that can only be described as brutalist in spirit, if not technically a member of that school of architectural design. Yet even the most seemingly out of place structures are all somewhat softened by the ivy that permeates the campus in an almost calming, spiritual way.

Princeton is somewhat isolated. The university is located in its namesake, a small town that grew up outside its campus gates. The town's hub, Nassau Street, with its old brick-and-awning shops and restaurants, fronts onto the university's Nassau Hall, which served as the base for the U.S. capital in 1783. Nassau Street is the dividing line between town to the north and gown to the south, while the campus itself rolls gently down a hill to the south, unbounded, dissolving into vast open fields, treed countryside, and Carnegie Lake.

Though Princeton had been a dream of mine, I had actually known very little about it until late in high school. My parents hadn't gone to university and I had just assumed that it would be something like the only university I had ever seen, the University of Manitoba. My only real knowledge about Princeton growing up had come from the "Flintstone of Prinstone" episode of *The Flintstones*.

The student body is far smaller than many might think. When I attended, there were approximately 4,400 undergraduate students (about 1,100) in each class, meaning that it accepts only a tiny fraction of the countless thousands of applications it receives every year. Virtually all students live on a campus where cars are essentially absent except for campus police and service vehicles. The few students who bring cars to school park them far away from the dormitories and other buildings, and use them only for infrequent off-campus excursions. That was also true in my time there.

It is a magical place, an intellectual nirvana where you can walk, stroll, play, and fully immerse yourself in a world unlike the one you came from, or at least in my case, a world unlike the one I came from. It is, as former student F. Scott Fitzgerald described in *This Side of Paradise*, a collection of spires and gargoyles, a paradise indeed where time seems to slip away among the quadrangles and arches and fields, marked only by the ringing of the bell atop Nassau Hall. But make no mistake about it, as Fitzgerald's contemporary and nemesis would have said, that bell, well, it tolls for thee.

My mom was pretty sure I was never going to make it there. Not that I wouldn't be accepted, but that I wouldn't physically make it there. I had packed and was ready to go, my life now consisting only of whatever I could fit into a single duffle bag, a suitcase, and my hockey bag. But my mom firmly believed that at some point along my journey (a flight from Winnipeg to Toronto, a transfer through customs with my student visa, a second flight to New York's La Guardia airport, a connecting transfer via van to the Newark International Airport, and a wait of several hours in the airport until being picked up there by the hockey coach for the drive down to campus) I would be abducted by the Moonies. Seriously. She thought that there was more than a good chance that I would be taken in by the followers of the Reverend Sun Myung Moon, who were, like the Hare Krishna, known to seek donations and recruit lost souls at airports (I use "known" somewhat loosely). She worried I would be lost forever, never to be heard from again. She warned me again and again, and again one final time as I said goodbye at the airport, to be careful and not get swept up by some cult.

I understand the angst that a mother must feel when her child goes away to university. My parents had little money, and they couldn't afford to take me to Princeton and set me up on campus. In fact, my parents never came out to see me until I graduated. While it's easy to look back and laugh at my mom's fears, she was actually on to something but didn't know it. I already was a lost soul, taken in not by the Moonies but by a far more dangerous monster.

Like most people, my mom feared the monsters she saw in the news, the faraway threats and bogeymen thrust upon us by those exploiting our weaknesses and greatest fears. But also like most people, she couldn't see the monster that had been lurking among the children in her own community, the one who had ensnared her own child.

I MADE IT to Princeton, somehow miraculously avoiding the Moonies, though sweating profusely because of the amount of clothing I was wearing given the limited baggage I could travel with without incurring extra fees.

Once at Princeton, I knew immediately that I was home. It was perfect. It was everything I had dreamed it would be. It was the ideal place for me because of who I still was deep down. I still get very emotional whenever I think of this moment, because I only wish I had been able to experience my time there as the true me, not the me of the aftermath of him.

Holder Hall, which was to be my home for the next two years, is one of the classic dorms at Princeton—a three-story, gray stone Collegiate Gothic quadrangle, with arches on each of three sides to allow access to the inner quad and the doors into the dorms. There's a tower in one corner with spires reaching to the sky, and a dining hall and library along the fourth side. At that time there weren't hallways in the dorms but entryways, with about four-teen doors, each opening up into the quad. The entryways were like vertical hallways—open a door, take a few steps up to a land-ing—and there were doors into rooms on each side, one room to a side. Up the stairway was the next level and landing and two more doors to two more rooms. On the third level there was a landing and one door for a double wide room sitting on top of the rooms below on either side of the stairs. A group of sopho-mores lived on the third floor in the ultimate luxury of a spacious room. My group was lucky, and in our second year we too lived in such comfort.

Although this was a dorm, these were not utilitarian stair-ways, landings, or rooms. The wood was dark and stained, with wainscoting everywhere. Each room had a main living area with a fireplace—nonworking but providing ambience—and two bed-rooms. In the past, one bedroom had been for the student and the other one for his servant (I use "his" on purpose, as Princeton did not admit women until the late '60s, and it was still only 35 percent women and 65 percent men when I attended). The rooms were now configured as quads, each bedroom outfitted with bunk beds and desks.

I'll never forget the somehow exotically musty smell of the dorm on that hot and humid September afternoon in 1982, a smell that persists to this day. It was a magnificent smell, and the room itself was more than I could ever have hoped for. I was a student who went away to university, lived on campus, and actually saw my standard of living rise.

My roommates had all arrived earlier that day: one from Detroit, one from just outside of New York City, and one from the Washington, DC, area. I met their parents. I met their siblings. I met their other relatives. Coming from Canada and being the first in my family to go to university, I had no appreciation for how far I had come and how big a deal going away to a university like this was. To me, I was going away to an excellent university. To the American kids, it was as if they had won the lottery, and they couldn't believe their good fortune at having been accepted.

Our closets and storage areas were small, but I had no problem fitting in all of my stuff with room to spare. My roommates, on the other hand, had more difficulty, though they were very creative and made it work. By the time I arrived, everyone else in our room had already been there for a few hours. It was almost a fight to see who could help me the most to unload, and they couldn't have been more welcoming and supportive. Unlike them, I had no car or station wagon or van to unload. Everything I had was in my arms.

We sorted out rooms, beds, and desks, and just like that we were in the next phase of our lives. I saw their painful goodbyes with their families, I saw the love present everywhere as similar scenes played out elsewhere in the quad, and for a fleeting moment it made me feel very calm, knowing that even though

I was all alone, even though I was seeing what I wished I myself could have been a part of, I could live vicariously through the others and imagine a similar love and support. And sure enough, to this day, my freshman-year roommates—Ken Cook, James Fischer, and Brian Crane—remain three of the best people I have ever been lucky enough to know.

There is a picture of the four of us, taken on our first day at Princeton. My roommates all look so excited, but I have a distant look, the eyes of somebody who at a young age has already seen too much, who already knows how this next chapter of his life is going to play out.

THAT FIRST NIGHT it started to set in just how far away from home I was. Fortunately, the school set up small parties to help get us to know each other. We mingled, we were introduced to upperclassmen, and there were games to further integrate us. One of the tasks we were assigned was to interview a fellow freshman at the party and report back to the group. My roommates prodded, actually pushed, me toward a tall, beautiful woman named Melissa Marks to interview her. I was already so taken aback, almost in shock at everything new around me, that apparently I had just stood in place, trying to figure out who to talk to until my roommates intervened. Melissa was the most beautiful woman I had ever seen. She was also a professional model who had already been on the covers of major fashion magazines. She would go on to marry a friend of mine and become Melissa Marks Sparrow, now a leading doctor at Johns Hopkins. But that night, the only thing that mattered was that, though she was far more worldly than I was at the time, she was the nicest person imaginable and she made me feel at home, broke me out of my trance, and in the process let me know that I was among good people. She won't remember a thing about our interview that night but it kept me from going home. I will remember it always.

As a recipient of substantial financial aid, I was required to take a job on campus to support myself during the school year. It was my good fortune to get a job working in the dining hall for my residential college. I could work the breakfast, lunch, or dinner shift, or all three if I wanted to. This job came with an added benefit: it was a fantastic way to meet other students who like me needed to make money. While the reputation of the school may suggest otherwise, the reality is that there are a great number of students at Princeton who come from very little money.

That's the interesting thing about Princeton. Notionally a bastion of conservatism and elitism within American society, like many elite U.S. universities, it's actually in many ways one of the more socialistic and progressive institutions you may ever come across. Don't get me wrong, it is a very expensive place to go to university when you actually have to pay. If, however, you come from a family with little or no money, you don't have to pay. Admissions to the university are made on a need-blind basis and financial aid is allocated once the students have already been admitted. I was also the recipient of the Canadian Alumni Association of Princeton scholarship, which paid for a portion of my tuition, room, and board. Princeton, a school without athletic scholarships, was still virtually free for me.

As it turned out, Graham had no contacts at Princeton, and my scholarship from the Canadian Alumni Association of Princeton was something I had earned on my own and with no help from him—something I learned only later.

DESPITE BEING FAR removed geographically from Graham, despite making new friends, having new roommates, and meeting the guys on the hockey team, I still could not get Graham out of my mind. He was with me every step of the way. Never, ever did I believe that I belonged at Princeton. Worse, I believed that the only reason I was there was because of what Graham had done for me. Although I was on the cusp of living out my dream, in my head that dream was still, even in his absence, controlled by Graham. Everything I had in front of me was to me something I had because of him. My new roommates were because of him. My ability to study at Princeton was because of him. My place in the hockey program was because of him. And that belief that everything good in my life, that everything there in front of me, was because of him, made me not want to be there at all.

Princeton was supposed to be a new beginning. Yet I was in shock, stressed beyond belief by the jolt of simply going to the airport, getting on a plane, and instantly starting my new life, the one I was always supposed to be living, a life more in touch with who I really was, one removed from Graham and the abuse. I was free of him. Except I wasn't. The change was so sudden, the confusion so unsettling, the stress so intense.

Who am I? I'm a fraud. If they only knew who I really was, how weak I am, how pathetic, how I actually got in here through his help, they'd know I don't belong, they'd laugh at me. What am I doing here?

My body started to shut down. The very day I arrived my left thigh went completely numb and I didn't regain feeling in it for about a week. It scared me. I scared me. He still scared me. And I couldn't tell anybody about it, and I couldn't go to the infirmary and seek treatment, physical or otherwise.

How can you tell anybody? What are you going to say? "I'm here to report that my left leg is going numb. Nothing happened, I just, um, well, see, it just started after I kind of freaked out a bit after realizing that even though I had made it here, nothing was ever going to change the way I think about myself even after I've left my sexual abuser behind"? That's how to make friends and influence people. They'll commit you.

I went back and forth between absolutely loving Princeton and all that it had to offer and detesting everything about it because I associated it all with Graham. Princeton, my magical place, was at the same time a living hell because to me it represented the very worst in me, the truth about who I really was. I had sold my soul to him to get there. What should have been a shining achievement I saw as further evidence of the fraud I was. I had not earned my place at Princeton. It had been delivered to me by my abuser. I was only here because I had let myself be with him.

I had the bottom bunk in our bedroom. At night I would roll into bed and pretend to fall asleep quickly, attempting to avoid small talk about who I was, where I came from, what the details of my life were.

It's not important, you don't need to know about me, you wouldn't want to know about me.

I would stare up at the bottom of the mattress above me and trace its soft blue stripes pushing through in diamond shapes formed by the intertwined metal mesh that ran from end to end of the upper bunk holding up its mattress. I would do this from each bottom bunk bed I slept in over the next four years. So many hours of staring mindlessly while not being able to sleep, not being able to think of anything but him, not being able to do anything but wonder why. My diamonds in the sky, made by the weight of another pressing down upon me from above.

Don't think about him. Don't think about it. He's not here. He can't hurt you anymore.

Except he was still with me and he was still hurting me.

I threw myself into everything in front of me in an attempt to hide from my reality. I took as many shifts at the dining hall as I could get. My days usually began around 6:30, when I would get up to work the morning shift. Classes would follow, then it would be off to dryland training in anticipation of the hockey season, then dinner, and then off to the library. I did my best to ensure that there was little or no time that wasn't filled with scheduled obligations in an attempt to force myself to keep my mind as far away from Graham as I could. I tracked my money, logging every expenditure, and I recorded our team workouts, anything to divert my mind. I was disciplined. I was very hard-working. I was successful. But I wasn't sleeping well, and still he was always with me.

ONCE I'D REALIZED I was actually going to go away to Princeton, there had been only a few months to prepare. I wanted to take control of my body in hopes of a new start and becoming the athlete I really was. Having gorged myself to make myself as unattractive to him as possible, I now desperately needed to get in shape.

During that summer before university, I started to eat better, I ran, and I worked out again. I started losing weight. Yet I still saw myself as fat and unworthy, so I lost more weight. But the more weight I lost, the more I thought I was still hideous, fat, ugly. I couldn't look at myself in the mirror without thinking that I was deformed, that he had ruined me, that I had ruined myself with him. I kept thinking that I had to change who I was, that I had to cut him out of me. So I kept running, stopped lifting, and pretty much stopped eating.

I showed up for university lean and mobile, but I had little muscle and no real strength, my body running on fumes. I could no longer see what was real. I had completely lost any connection with my body. I could no longer properly build my body because I could no longer properly see it and thus could no longer truly be an athlete.

Still, when you're working hard to make your dreams come true, good things can happen. My midterm grades in my first semester were all A's, with an A-plus in a physics lab course. Being the complete geek-fest that it was, I won a wall chart of the periodic table for the highest score in a multidisciplinary assignment, and I loved it. That was me at Princeton—all A's and an A-plus. As always, school was easy.

I was slowly making friends and having fun both in class and while working. I was popular at work and in my classes. I was fun. I was hard-working. I was everything I was supposed to be. That job I had at Commons, our college cafeteria? I worked countless mornings as a short-order cook and was awarded "Best Trash" at the end-of-the-year party for the ease with which I emptied garbage cans into dumpsters and threw around heavy bags of waste. That turned out to be the highlight of my college career—"Best Trash."

But I could only work so hard for so long before Graham crept back into my life. He never contacted me again, I assume because he too was escaping me and any further involvement that would risk my coming forward. No, the things creeping back into my life were all in my head, all part of the carnage that abuse leaves behind.

Because I wanted to run from Graham, I also wanted to run from the Princeton hockey program, believing that I had only been accepted into it through Graham's assistance. At the same time, I wanted to succeed in the hockey program because it was everything I had ever dreamed of achieving. That had always been my nature: a drive to be the very best, a need to work as hard as possible to succeed at whatever challenge I was presented with. But that drive to succeed created a very difficult, almost impossible dynamic given my need to fail as a result of the abuse. It was the very essence of self-sabotage. Wanting to succeed, I couldn't just walk away, I wanted to participate and succeed. Needing to fail, to show the world the true me that nobody but I could see, I could never sustain those best efforts. But because I was still trying, I had to keep working to succeed. Yet at the same time, needing to fail, I couldn't not get in my own way.

Back and forth, over and over again.

I wanted to be free of Graham. I thought that if I could get away from him, go away to Princeton, succeed on my own, make the hockey team, and get a varsity letter, I would have shown that I could defeat him, that I could win back my life. But all of those questions were still inside me:

Why did he pick me? He must have seen I was weak. People must see me as weak. I must be some sort of joke.

Why didn't I stop it? I must have wanted it. I deserve what I'm feeling now. I deserve to feel like his leftover garbage.

How could somebody like him control somebody like me? I'm worthless and weak. I'm not the strong, tall, intelligent, athlete people see on the outside. I'm a fraud.

What you see isn't real. I'm a failure, a worthless and weak fraud, and I deserve failure, not success.

Can't you see that I'm a fraud? I'm a failure, not worthy of this success. I'll show you I'm a failure, worthless and weak.

Who am I? I'm a fraud, his garbage, his enabler. I'm somebody who doesn't deserve to live.

BAKER RINK IS located at the southern end of campus, at the bottom of a gentle hill that rises up through the campus toward Nassau Street. Baker is an old stone structure, one of the oldest indoor hockey rinks in the United States. Just across from it is Poe Field, a vast expanse used for virtually anything athletic or recreational. One late September weekday afternoon after classes had concluded, our hockey team met at Poe for one of our usual dryland training sessions. The leaves on the trees were just starting to turn color, there was no wind of any kind, and the clichéd smell of fall was in the air. The skies were darkening as if a storm were coming, but the rain never fell. We were stretching and doing other exercises, push-ups, sit-ups, all the types of things that Graham used to have me do. And just then members of the rowing team came running by in a pack, all in their gray shorts and gray tops with Princeton emblazoned on them in our orange and black colors. On the other side of us, another team was going through its paces. In the midst of it all a group of students carrying books was walking across the way.

It was the most beautiful scene I had ever been a part of. It was everything I had ever wanted to be a part of, an athletic scene set in the midst of this idyllic academic institution. It was everything I had ever imagined Princeton would look like. It was perfect. And all I could think of was that my dad, the Grade Eight dropout hockey player, would have loved to have been there with me, would have loved to have gone to Princeton.

And then I thought exactly the same thing about Graham.

RIGHT FROM THE start, I took aggressive steps to threaten my place in the hockey program. Bruce Delventhal, the assistant varsity hockey coach who was responsible for recruiting, had been my prime contact at Princeton. Because Graham had told me that he was doing extensive work behind the scenes to ensure that I was recruited by Princeton, I assumed that Graham had been working with Bruce.

I came to see Bruce as somebody like Graham, somebody who knew everything about me. Bruce had a moustache, but other than that was very similar to Graham in both physical makeup and demeanor. Beyond that, Graham's story about helping me get into Princeton didn't really make sense unless Graham was very close to Bruce. Since Graham had told me that I needed his help to get into Princeton, how could I have been recruited unless Graham had called in a favor with Bruce, the gatekeeper at Princeton? But why would Bruce owe Graham a favor?

I was starting to see ghosts, to see everything as some con-spiracy leading back to Graham. To me it made perfect sense that Bruce and Graham would have a special relationship of some sort and that they both knew everything about me, my innermost secrets. I was captive to that alternative reality, one that Graham had initially fostered, one that he nurtured in me, one that now made me fear Bruce, one that made me come to detest Bruce. I couldn't process reality itself.

I had to fight them, I had to win. And the only tangible way I could win would be by earning a varsity letter from the hockey program. That varsity letter increasingly took on a deeper mean-ing. Yes, Graham had gotten me there. Yes, Bruce had colluded with him to make it happen. But Graham wasn't here now and I could do this on my own. A Princeton varsity letter would be my success. Mine. Not his. Then I would be alive. Then I would be truly free of him.

Some chase a huge white whale, others tilt at windmills. Me, I had an orange "P" to strive for. To me, it embodied everything.

SELF-SABOTAGE. WHEN THE hockey equipment was passed out, the trainer mistakenly confused me with another tall freshman, a defenseman, and issued me a pair of regular hockey pants with minimal protection instead of much larger and more heavily padded goaltender pants. If you don't know hockey this will mean nothing to you, but if you do, you'll understand that to play in net with inadequate equipment is simply insane. I said nothing to correct the situation. Who doesn't get proper equipment to play with? Who doesn't put his hand up or even simply tell the equipment manager that there's been a mistake and that he should go back and get me another pair of pants? Somebody who isn't really there, somebody with no sense of self-worth, somebody who is nobody. When you don't think you're worth anything, you act as if you're not really there.

I had brought my own equipment, no longer good enough for me to use, with me so that I'd have something to put on when I first got there. My upper-body protection was virtually nonexistent—thin felt from the 1970s and meant for younger players. At my size—at that time perhaps the tallest ever to have played the position in any meaningful way—even equipment made for professional players would have been too small, yet my old equipment was beyond insufficient and left my outer ribs, forearms, shoulders, inner legs, and lower thighs all exposed. I said nothing.

I came to see using this equipment as a type of penance for my sins with Graham, and I never got through a single practice or game without a significant bruise of one sort or another. I deserved to feel pain. Yet, as before, there was a certain peace to be found deep within my pain, for when I felt nothing but pain, I wasn't thinking about him.

Cap Raeder, a former professional goaltender, came to work with our team for a week during that first training camp. As we were doing drills, it became apparent to him that I was doing whatever I could to avoid blocking the puck with my body, instead letting my hands do the work. That is about the worst thing a goaltender can do, but that was my innate sense of self-preservation kicking in to avoid injury during practices, using my gloves as much as possible to catch or block the puck rather than letting my unprotected body absorb the puck. Whenever games came around I was fearless, getting caught up in the excitement and feeling no pain while playing properly. But at practices, well, I owed my ongoing existence to my avoidance of the puck.

I had played this little charade in practice for years and gotten away with it because of my performances during games. But Cap saw what I was doing, something only a real goaltender could pick up on, my reliance on my gloves while shifting my body out of position to remain safe. I only realized late in the week that he had picked up on what I was doing. I immediately went into game mode and started squaring to the puck and using my body to cover as much of the net as possible, but it was too late to show him I truly played the position. Having never seen me in a game, he had seen all he had needed to, and it was too late for me to change his mind. I had never before encountered anybody who could see what I was doing and was totally unprepared for this. The jig was up.

There are moments in life, small but significant moments, that can make all the difference. As I skated up to him and looked him in the eye, I immediately knew that he knew. I knew that I had to explain myself to him, that I had to show him the equipment that I was wearing, that I had to tell him why I was wearing it, that I had to tell him everything about why I suffered the way that I did while playing the game that I was supposed to love, that I had to tell him everything about Graham and why I was even at Princeton in the first place, and that I had no intention of wasting his time while he was there to help us, that I knew what I was supposed to be doing, and that I did it properly when I played in games. I knew that I had to take off my jersey right then and there and show him that my ribs were exposed, that my shoulders were only partially covered, that my clavicle was not completely covered. I knew that I had to take my shirt off and show him my bruises, show him that I was paying a price for all of this insanity. I knew that I had to tell him that I wanted all of this to end, that I wanted to move on and play and enjoy the game that I loved so much.

But in that moment I did nothing. Because I couldn't admit to the stupidity of it all. Because it didn't make any sense. Because it sounds absolutely crazy even now.

I DIDN'T MAKE the varsity team coming out of training camp in my freshman year. I played junior varsity (coached by Bruce) and earned a JV letter. I played very well. I practiced all year with the varsity team, and many of the varsity players came up to me from time to time and expressed surprise that I wasn't on the team. But I knew why. I knew what Cap had seen and what Cap had told our coaches, who couldn't see for themselves, coaches who, because they had been told something by an expert, now it was all they could see.

Coach Higgins placed another freshman, Tony Manory, on the varsity roster ahead of me, though we both played alongside each other in junior varsity games and he too earned only a JV letter that year. Tony was a very good guy. I liked him immensely, and he was a good goalie.

Coach Higgins revisited his decision after I dramatically out-played Tony. My call-up, however, was short-lived. I saw him look away in disgust as I waved at some pucks in a practice warm-up shooting drill, confirming what I assume had been Cap's assessment.

Still, he had me practice all year with the varsity team in the hope or expectation of things to come. I had some moments where I would stand out, and our star player, Ed Lee, once shook my hand in front of the team at the end of a drill after I had stopped everything he threw at me, much to his frustration.

Coach Higgins would skate up to me during practices and ask how I was doing, ask me how I felt about things, about my game. He apologized several times for not having room for me in the varsity locker room (I had the JV locker room to myself all year for varsity workouts), and he was very supportive and encouraging. He thought he was being helpful in apologizing to me. He didn't know that he was only making me focus on darker thoughts.

My own dressing room? Bruce knows, and he's told everybody. They all know. They have to isolate me from the rest. It's just like Graham said, if our secret ever got out nobody would want me around, nobody would want me on their team, nobody would stand to be associated with me. They know. They have to keep me by myself. I'm not a part of this team. I never can be, so I never will be.

Hockey practices often became futile attempts to remain focused.

What am I doing here? They know, they're laughing at me. Come on, shoot, shoot harder. Maybe I'll get out of the way. Or maybe I'll stop it, maybe I'll let you hit me, hurt me. I deserve the pain. You don't know anything about me, about who I really am. The real me, I deserve to be here, the true me is good enough, real hockey programs wanted me. But I'm here, and I get it, you know everything about me. You know who I am. I'm a fraud. I don't deserve to be here. Shoot harder. Come on, this is a joke. What am I doing here? How did I ever let this happen to me? Why can't I just stop it, stop all of this, and just have fun and play hockey. Why won't this go away? Why can't I just be normal?

That's not exactly being in the zone and reacting naturally to the flow of the game, or practice, in front of you.

I kept fighting through the madness enough to hang around. I wanted to run away, but I couldn't, and I kept showing up, never missing a practice, three hours a day, sometimes more, day after day. A part of me still wanted to win. And at the end of the year, Coach Higgins called me in with the rest of the varsity players to go through equipment catalogs to select new gear for the next season, pick stick brands and patterns, and discuss training plans for the summer.

IN HINDSIGHT, THAT first year of Princeton hockey was still a wonderful experience for me. A hockey trip to West Point to play the cadets, with dinner with them afterward in their immense dining hall—the one where General MacArthur addressed the cadets and said, "Old soldiers never die"—watching the plebes serve dinner to the upperclassmen. Away hockey at Yale, games at prep schools, against senior men's clubs on the east coast. And so many laughs along the way.

Coach Higgins presented us with no shortage of humor. He was such a good man and he tried so hard to do his best for all of us. But he was a hockey man, and for the most part, we were never the hockey men he was. "The Bagger," as he was known, was not one to suffer fools, and in terms of what the hockey world had to offer, we, unfortunately, were fools. His frustration with us was intense.

Coach Higgins was a balding man. That was unfortunate, not because there is anything wrong with being bald, but because his scalp served as a type of barometer for his level of frustration with us. He could set up the most elaborate of drills only to see them fall to pieces within seconds of us actually trying to implement them. His scalp would increasingly redden, and then further brighten, to the point where his head almost matched the orange of his Princeton jacket. And the thing is, once his scalp reached that certain color it was a very short step until he would blow the whistle, throw his stick, throw his gloves, remove the whistle from his neck and throw it too. It was at this point that we thought we knew how "The Bagger" got his name—namely, by putting his teams through "bag skates," the name denoting a workout where you skate until you throw up into a bag. As much sense as that made, it was only later that we found out that his wife had given him the name when he was working as a checkout boy to earn money to go to school.

Some of the Coach Higgins stories were experienced directly. Others were passed down as if from the hockey gods. From "A goes to B, B goes to C, and C goes to One," to "Blue jerseys down there, red jerseys down there, yellow jerseys down there, and gold jerseys down there"—yellow and gold, of course, being the same color and certain players literally doing pirouettes trying to figure out where to go—the stories are told with affection. But the classic Coach Higgins story involves his assessment of the modern economy. One early evening at a practice, the team not performing well and the Coach Higgins scalp-o-meter rising to increasingly dangerous levels, he chose a different approach. Blowing his whistle, he called the team over to the boards and in his deep Boston accent implored the team to work harder. "Men, you gotta work hahhd. You gotta work hahhdah. You can't just loaf around. You gotta work. You gotta focus. You guys, look around. You got everything. This place, you got everything. But you loaf! But you're not working hahhd enough! You gotta work hahhd!!! You're not... you're not... you gotta... you gotta... IT'S WHY THERE'S SO MUCH UNEMPLOYMENT IN THIS COUNTRY!!!!!"

I HAD HOPED that things would be better in my second year, that maybe, just maybe, after spending the summer in Winnipeg and consciously avoiding the places that would bring back bad memories, I could say that I had made peace with my past and move forward. Maybe things would be different and offer a new start.

Instead, on arriving back on campus, I felt a crushing realization that things would be exactly the same no matter how hard I tried. In fact, because there was less distraction arriving as a sophomore, because things were less new and patterns had already been established, it was actually worse. The published college hockey scouting report pinned to our locker bulletin board, the one touting me as the new Princeton goalie who had big skates to fill with the graduation of our senior goalie, Ron Dennis, did nothing to take away my certainty as to what was about to happen.

The hockey equipment that Coach Higgins and I picked out in his office? I never asked for it when we started up the next year, and it sat, unused, while I continued to wear my old, undersized, flimsy stuff. Insanity.

During my medical I sat down for my eye test.

"Greg, what's this letter? OK, what are these? Now these?"

"I can't make those out."

"You'll need to get glasses or contact lenses."

"OK."

Except I did nothing. Breakaways? Easy. Shots from longer range? Much more difficult. Insanity.

A goalie who can't see? A goalie purposely refusing proper gear so that he can suffer pain? Insanity.

Yet it all made sense to me at the time.

I was halfhearted on the ice, letting down everyone in the hockey program. I wanted so badly to succeed, to find myself and my place among my peers. But the moment I was back with the hockey team, all of my past with Graham came rushing back.

I didn't care, and it showed. But of course I did care, and it crushed me on the inside.

On the outside, however, I wasn't going to let anyone know that I hurt one bit, because I had already run from the scholar-athlete who had shown up first year. A part of me hadn't really wanted to go back to Princeton, and in a passive-aggressive manner I participated but really didn't.

———————————

IT WAS LATE afternoon in our dorm room, one of those double wide units on the third floor of Holder with angled ceilings, dormers, leaded windows that opened to slate tiles on the roofs and offered views far across campus, dark wood on the lower walls. I was there by myself. The phone rang. And it rang. And it kept ringing. I didn't move to pick it up.

I knew who it was. Already cut from the varsity roster, I was supposed to be at Baker Rink to get on the bus and leave for a JV game. But I wasn't in the mood to play hockey, for I was having a dark, a very dark day lost in my thoughts about it, about him.

The phone kept ringing. I didn't move.

The phone rang some more. I still didn't move.

Ring after ring after ring after ring. It kept ringing. I didn't move. This was war.

Finally, I'd had enough. I was ready to give in. I got up and answered it.

"It's me."

There was no response. A few seconds later, the phone clicked dead on the hang up at the other end.

My hockey "career" at Princeton had just been terminated. No amount of begging the next day in the inevitable attempt to try to succeed after having ensured failure could change anything. I had just killed the scholar-athlete within me.

But I do have some good Princeton hockey memories. In spite of what I was dealing with, not every day was all doom and gloom. The waves of pain and self-loathing came and went. In between, there were great moments, fun moments, normal moments, times when I could just be who I really was. And there was laughter—always laughter, whether manufactured to hide the pain or real, genuine laughter.

Coach Higgins gave me an opportunity. I was unable to deliver. I'm sorry I let him down. He was a good man with a good heart. His job depended on us delivering for him, on me delivering for him. I failed him.

And, of course, I failed me. I never played a varsity hockey game, I never earned that orange "P," and it haunts me still. He won.

———————————

THE WILSON SCHOOL of International Affairs at Princeton offered a departmental program to which sophomores could apply and, if selected by an admissions committee, enter and make International Affairs their major. All other departments at Princeton (and now the Wilson School itself) were open. You could major in whatever you wanted to provided you had taken the required preliminary courses for entrance.

Because the Wilson School was selective, it attracted huge interest. Because it was a program I was interested in, and because its main prerequisites were an interest in the field of study and very high grades from first year and midterm second year, it seemed only natural to me and everybody who knew me that I would apply. After all, in second year I had taken an extra calculus class on a pass-fail basis (we could take several extra courses this way, where the actual grade we received wouldn't show up on our transcripts other than to note whether we had passed or failed, allowing us to give less than full attention to an extra class at no risk to grade point averages) and scored 100 percent on the midterm. A dean told me I was one of the few to ever move a course from pass-fail to graded, which I did after that midterm.

But beyond interest and transcripts, you also had to submit letters of recommendation, including one from a professor. I immediately knew who I'd get to do that.

My transcript was fine. My professor's recommendation? Well, I never asked for one. I just slipped a note with the required form under his office door the night before applications were due asking him to see what he might be able to do for me in the circumstances.

Self-sabotage.

When the admissions were announced, I told everybody that I had been wait-listed, but that wasn't true. I wasn't remotely prepared to tell anybody that I hadn't really applied in the first place, because that self-sabotage was tied to this story, and this story was something I wasn't sharing with anybody.

ONCE HOCKEY WAS gone, things became dramatically worse. If I aced one exam, I would make sure to not do my best on the next. I'd trash a string of easily attained A's by not doing all of the required course work in another course. Princeton's atmosphere of success brought out my worst feelings of being lost, excluded, misunderstood, and undeserving. I would eventually self-implode time and again, unable to come to grips with how somebody as pitiful as I was could even have the right to live, let alone thrive. I was on automatic pilot, recklessly sabotaging myself both academically and physically.

Because of my athletic failure, my early academic success meant nothing to me. I had never been just a scholar or just an athlete—I had always been a scholar-athlete. In my mind, it was easy to excel only at school or only at athletics—anybody could do that. The important thing was to excel at both at the same time. Once hockey was gone, any good grades I had already achieved were meaningless, I was a failure. And that was good, because that was how the world was supposed to see me.

During those dark periods, when I questioned the meaning of everything, I would skip lectures, miss seminars (where class participation was of paramount importance), and fail to hand in assignments. In our upper years, we were assigned faculty members to supervise independent research, which was an opportunity to work closely with some of the greatest minds in our fields of study. Thinking I wasn't worthy of being there in the first place, I figured I'd just be wasting their time, so I skipped appointments. My grades suffered.

And yet I loved being at Princeton. I had so many magical experiences. I was in so many ways succeeding in the face of so many obstacles.

Years of black-tie dinners, sometimes with dates from other colleges who came to visit. Traveling to watch the football team at Harvard (I so loved "Repel them, repel them, make them relinquish the ball!"). Seminars that I could drop in on any night of the week to hear somebody speak on a topic I'd never thought would interest me. Dinners at the homes of my professors. Studying until late in the night and then walking back to the dorm with my roommates and sharing a laugh about the day. Working as a short-order cook at the cafeteria and serving eggs to Brooke Shields. Making friends for life with my roommates. Going my own way when things got just a little too tough. Long runs along Carnegie Lake with the girl who had a crush on me. Back rubs, the safe sex of the time.

Christmas at Princeton was special for many reasons. First, a beautiful campus became even more beautiful when it was covered with snow. Second, the academic schedule was set up so that first-term exams were held after Christmas, meaning that while we had classes in December, we weren't in exam frenzy. Instead, we had winter parties, winter formals, arch sings with a cappella singing groups performing under the Gothic arches of the various halls, the sound resonating under the stone canopies. And there was nothing more romantic for a Christmas date than getting the keys to Baker Rink from the manager of the varsity team and taking your crush for a late-night skate around an unlit Baker Rink, a magical place on its own, after your dinner. Marc Daniel, manager of the varsity team and keeper of the key, remains a good, lifelong friend. I can never thank him enough for lending me the key to the rink on several occasions. Still, nothing could match the magic of that first freshman year Christmas skate, if only because when we all showed up the next day to get ready to go to Yale, nobody but Marc could figure out why the otherwise pristine ice was marked up close to the boards all the way around the ice surface.

Whenever things got too difficult for me I would go for a walk by myself. I would lose myself in the beauty of Princeton. I would stare at the spires and gargoyles on the buildings and listen to the ghosts. I would search for meaning in my life, for something or somebody to help.

But I couldn't tell anybody. I couldn't admit to anyone else that I had been weak, that I had been defeated by my abuser, that I was not the person they saw from the outside. I had made new friends at university, but those friendships were with the person people thought they were seeing, not the real me, and I couldn't tell them who I really was for fear of losing their friendship. And then, when things were very dark, I just assumed that everyone knew anyway and that they were all laughing at me behind my back.

In spite of all of this, I learned a great deal. I still had the drive that had kept me alive, and I still got excellent grades in the courses where I hadn't purposely sabotaged myself. I immersed myself in campus life, attending lectures after hours, exploring intellectual pursuits in areas outside my field of study, engaging in long conversations with professors and classmates. I enjoyed the ability to pursue learning in a wide variety of subjects, from economics to history to literature to math and physics. I loved learning, studying, reading, discussing. I loved everything that Princeton had to offer. If only I could have stayed out of my own way and escaped the feeling that I was a fraud and that I had sold myself to get there.

Every once in a while I would have moments of clarity, brutally terrifying moments, almost out-of-body experiences, when I would vividly see what I was doing to myself and understand without any doubt that I was actively trashing my own dreams. Those moments of clarity were my insight into the depths of my own inner hell, they made me see that I could not escape myself and my own reign of terror. When they happened, I would have to work very hard to try to remind myself that I still belonged at Princeton in spite of whatever stupid, self-destructive thing I had just done, and I would renew my vow to attempt to hold it all together.

But even better than a solitary late-night walk through the campus was a trip into New York, a place where a lost soul could really get lost. The university has its own train station that runs a shuttle to the main line into New York. It takes about an hour, and in that time you can go from the most idyllic rural campus life to the middle of an absolute gong show in the darkest parts of Manhattan. I have always liked to travel and experience new things, perhaps because in a new place you have no past and there is always the potential for a new beginning.

I embraced traveling into New York, and I did it more often than most who knew me realized. In New York I would blow off steam, just walking the streets and soaking up the smells that are very much a part of the city. In my later years at Princeton, I had a girlfriend who lived in New York and so I spent even more time there. I loved the juxtaposition of Princeton and the Lower East Side—Princeton, a protected piece of perfection, up against utter chaos and the worst that the city had to offer only an hour's train ride away. "Alphabet City" is code for a lot, and New York in the early '80s was a very different place from what it is now, less sanitized, less Disney-esque, more, well, raw and welcoming for those who want to run from their emotions, to hide from their feelings, to numb themselves against the world around them.

I loved New York. I still do.

I don't miss Alphabet City one bit.

THAT VARSITY LETTER, proof that I could triumph over him? That dream was gone. As for academics, overall I did well, but not nearly as well as I could have and not nearly as well as I had proven that I could do. It was classic self-destructive behavior, the actions of someone crying out for help.

I had always thought that if I could keep fighting, keep myself occupied, keep pushing it down, keep running from the abuse and from Graham that I would eventually win. But I was never able to beat Graham. He had won. And in my moments of clarity, I knew it. My second set of roommates, friends who remain very close to me even after all these years, only saw a glimpse of what was going on—until the night they saw me for who I was when I was forced to confront myself in yet another moment of clarity.

Graduation is coming soon. My four years at Princeton are coming to an end. What have I achieved? What have I lost? What have I thrown away? What will I become now? What have I been ever since

*I first met him? I'm a complete and utter failure. I have no future. This
was never real. There is no future.*
It's over.

I couldn't hide my substance abuse that particular night. My
roommates had never known what went on behind closed doors,
but there I was, right in front of them, needing to let them into
my world, if only for a moment, to show them just who I really
was, what I was capable of. It wasn't their world, it wasn't their
thing. That night, sitting around the living room in our multi-level
dorm room right in front of them, I started and I just kept on
going and going. I saw the exchanged glances, the surprise, the
concern, the confusion. But I was done hiding, because in that
moment of clarity I knew who I was, what I had become, and that
I had lost, that Graham had defeated me, and that I was not going
to ever succeed or flourish, so nothing really mattered.

That night never ended for me. Long after everyone else had
gone to bed, I was still caught up in the aftermath of my moment
of clarity. There is nothing as sad as a spectacular sunrise and the
mellifluous chirping of birds when you crave darkness and silence.
I was hoping against hope that this would finally be the day when
the sun didn't also rise, and while it was pretty to think so, when
it did come up it brought with it only my darkness within.

I put on some shorts and running shoes and went down the
stairs and out the dorm. I started at a quicker pace than usual, my
body feeling no pain. The campus gave way to gentle green hills
and estates, sprinkler systems clicking as they moistened perfectly
manicured lawns amidst the long shadows of very early morning.
I picked up the pace further and started to feel a twinge in my
diaphragm, that familiar pleasant pain of exertion. I told myself
to go harder, make myself really hurt today, and when I did hurt,
I pushed harder still. I wasn't out for a run anymore, I was out to
hurt myself. And if I couldn't will the sun to not rise, then maybe,

just maybe, I could finally run away from myself, from him, from everything, from life itself, and it would all just end.

Albert Einstein did some of his best work at the Institute of Advanced Studies, a large, academic complex defined by Fuld Hall, a building with colonial columns set in the middle of a vast field with an imposing circular driveway in front. It's also the place I finally understood it was never going to end. I stopped running, I lay down on the cool, moist turf, and I went to sleep, until I was awakened several hours later by some gardeners.

IN THE END, I graduated with an A.B. (that's not a typo, it's the way the degree is styled at Princeton, an "arts baccalaureate") in Economics. I guess success and failure are always relative. My grades, though not what they should've been, were good enough to get me into Canada's most prestigious and selective law school. But I will always look at my undergraduate experience as a failure. Why? Because there are two scoreboards in life: the scoreboard that the rest of the world sees and judges you by, and the scoreboard inside your head. And no matter how things may look like from the outside, no matter how successful you may seem to be, if you haven't done the best that you can do, there is no hiding from the scoreboard in your head, the most important scoreboard of all.

Even today, even as I understand the forces that were at play, to me the end result was still failure, for it is actions that speak loudest. I had proven my ability to excel at Princeton, I knew I had that ability to succeed in me, but I simply could not follow through to the end.

My parents came to my graduation and met all of my roommates, all of my friends. They couldn't believe what they were seeing. I had forgotten the culture shock I had experienced on first arriving at Princeton, and I realized through watching them what it must have been like for me to have come from my home to a place like that.

After I had packed everything up in the rented car that would take us to the airport and then home, I went back to the simply amazing dorm in Little Hall, up to our room, to say goodbye to the rest, who were still collecting their things and hadn't yet left. And with tears in my eyes after our hugs and goodbyes, I walked down the hallway toward the exit and looked one last time into my bedroom. There, on my now empty desk, was my diploma. I had almost left without it. I had almost walked away without taking with me the reason I had gone there in the first place. It was almost, almost, as if I hadn't been there at all.

I couldn't tell you where that diploma is now. Several years ago, in an attempt to put the past behind me and move on, I threw out, ripped up, or destroyed so many things from my past, and my diploma was lost somewhere in that vortex.

AT FIRST GLANCE, a Rubik's Cube appears to be a nothing but an incredibly complex and unsolvable mystery. But pick it up and get to know it a bit better and it starts to reveal itself as a set of discernible patters. Apply the wrong patterns and you're left with a jumbled mess. Figure the patterns out and you can actually solve the puzzle.

I was a jumbled mess. Yet patterns were becoming clearly discernible.

SIX

THIS IS THE LAW

N SEPTEMBER 1986, I entered the University of Toronto Faculty of Law. I may have been a failure with no sense of self-worth, but I sure knew how to fail with style.

I didn't enter law school in any search for justice coming out of the abuse. I wasn't reacting to what had happened to me out of any desire to better understand a justice system that might eventually prosecute my abuser. And I was not driven to learn about the law as it applies to sexual predators in any devotion to the pursuit of justice for those who have been preyed upon by sexual predators. No, I chose to go to law school because when I was younger, before I had met Graham, I had wanted to be a lawyer. By going to law school I was attempting to reclaim the goals of my life before him.

The University of Toronto is an urban campus. The law school fronts onto a wide boulevard that runs north–south through the heart of the city, and it backs onto a park known as Philosopher's Walk. It is an appropriate setting: the thoughtful academic idyll sits alongside the rush of the city and its commerce. The law school had been established in opposition to the trade school approach of other law schools in the country, with an original mandate to be more scholarly, theoretical, and academic than the others. Law schools serve two purposes: to teach the law in a scholarly fashion and to prepare students to become lawyers. There is a tension between treating the law as an academic area to be studied and as a trade to be taught, and its physical location striding the line between the commercial and the philosophical was perfect.

My plan for law school was less than slightly half-baked. I had saved up money from a summer job as a counselor at the Manitoba Adolescent Treatment Centre, a facility for youth in crisis (I could also have been a patient, not just a counselor). I arrived in Toronto with no place to live, assuming I'd easily find a place to rent.

Unlike when I went away to Princeton, where everything— tuition, room and board, even a job on campus—had been arranged and financially covered beforehand, this was a different experience. This was really my first step into the real world, for now I had to find a place to live, acquire some furniture, get some dishes, and provide my own food.

I had arranged virtually nothing ahead of time. A Princeton roommate from Toronto, Michael Denham, was going away to the London School of Economics the very day I arrived, and he graciously introduced me to his family, who had offered me his room in his home until I could find a place to live. But it was a long way from the campus, and I quickly sought out alternatives, even as I looked for something more permanent.

I crashed on a few floors after meeting fellow students during first-week orientation. One student was living in his family home very close to the law school, and he took me in for a few nights. He put me into one of their extra rooms, one filled almost to its very high ceiling with museum-quality antiques and with carpets and artwork piled everywhere. I had to maneuver around stacks of woven rugs, vases, paintings, and sculptures just to find the bed. I was very concerned that I would stumble into something, that I would break something, or that I would throw up on or into something when returning from our law school orientation parties. That, and the fact that he had a twin brother wandering about who to this day I still can't distinguish from my friend Peter, made everything seem, well, quite disorienting.

Fortunately, I discovered that the law school had a meeting room with a couch that could, if I was careful enough, serve as an ideal base. I surreptitiously lived inside the law school for over a week, using the gym locker room at Hart House, the main building in the center of the massive University of Toronto campus, to shower. It was all I needed. One of the good things about believing you deserve nothing is that you need nothing, and I stayed there until I found a room to rent in a house with shared facilities on the Danforth, the Greek part of Toronto, close to the subway line and very accessible to campus.

The first year of law school is pretty much an all or nothing proposition. The curriculum was the same for all first-year students. We studied core legal areas of the law, and at the end of the year we wrote exams that were worth 100 percent of our grade. There were two exceptions to that grading system.

First, in one of the core subjects, our classes were much smaller and were conducted in seminar fashion, sitting around a table with our professor. These classes, referred to as "small group," were far more interactive than other classes, and the grades were determined in part by participation as well as by papers written throughout the year.

Second, there were several weeks during the year, "bridge weeks," during which certain classes would be suspended and the entire body of first-year students would study an emerging field in legal practice or theory, at the end of which a paper was assigned and graded. No other grades were issued for any students in the law school until the first bridge papers were assigned and graded, about two months into our school year.

The word that most aptly describes the law student population is "keen." I used many other words back then to describe my fellow classmates, but let's go with "keen" for now. Keen students tend to be very focused on grades. You have to be pretty focused on grades to get into law school in the first place, but once in law school, there was now a group of like-minded students looking at their doppelgängers and realizing that they would have to up their game to come out at the top of the class.

Some would say the same about what it takes to get into Princeton. But I found the students at Princeton to be, at least when I was there, much more well-rounded, more naturally inquisitive, more intellectual, and yet at the same time more grounded in the real world than were my new classmates. After having been immersed in an academically expansive and multidisciplinary environment like Princeton, I was shocked to see so many driven yet narrowly focused students in law school, most of whom seemed to read nothing out of class other than assigned coursework. I sensed immediately that, because of this, I had an advantage.

At the conclusion of our first bridge week, the faculty appeared to understand the "keen-ness" and grade-focused nature of the first-year students. So before making the graded papers available, the professors running the bridge week made a point of going over the grading system to ensure that mass panic did not result. They informed us that "there would be a number of A's, some B-pluses, many B's and B-minus/C-pluses, a good number of C's, and some grades below that. And oh, for a couple of you out there, where your work was truly exceptional, we agreed that we had to give you A-pluses."

I didn't rush to pick up my paper. I knew I had done very good work. I knew that whenever I did the work, I was among the best. I know how awful that sounds. But the scoreboard inside my head was fine with things, knowing that I had put in an effort.

A friend eventually grabbed my paper and handed it to me. I got an A-plus.

I followed that up with A's on my research papers for small group.

As at Princeton, I had shown immediately not only that I belonged but also that I could succeed at the highest level. But you already know where this story is going.

I don't deserve this.
I'm a fraud.
The person you see trying to look normal isn't real.
The real me is a failure.
You want to see failure? I'll show you failure.

So, me being me, that initial success immediately triggered a self-destructive response. I stopped going to classes. I stopped caring about school. I started to seek out ways to hurt myself. I explored Toronto and found it to be a most suitable place for somebody looking for ways to numb the mind, the body, and the soul. In contrast to Princeton, where I had roommates, a campus job, initially a sport, and a social structure that all required me to go to great efforts to hide my self-abuse, at law school I was on my own that first year, living by myself in a rooming house. That room became my safe place, where I stared at the ceiling and revisited the past, where I tried to make sense of what had happened and was still happening, and then tried to forget about it all.

I had so very little back then, a mattress on the floor of the single bedroom I rented, a desk, a chair, and an old dresser. Nothing on the walls. It was all I needed to get those early great grades, and it was all I needed as I slipped further and further into hell. I could stay there in my room and nobody, nobody at all, would care. And I did stay in that room. And nobody cared.

I would emerge for classes that interested me and for social events I thought would be fun, but I was having a harder and harder time engaging with the world outside my room. Self-doubt, the feeling that you're a fraud, the fear that people know you're a fraud, is debilitating. I wanted to hide. The more I hid, the less able I was to go out, because it had been some time since I had gone out. The fear of going outside grew. Withdrawal, living like a hermit, increasingly became my new normal.

I had less and less of the outside world and its reality to counter the reality playing out inside my head. The more I isolated myself, the more strongly I believed that I was a fraud. I spiraled deeper and deeper downward into depression, isolation, and the reality inside my head that kept me from engaging in life, until I just didn't leave my room, other than for brief trips to go to the corner store down the street, for about two weeks.

In my room I was all by myself with nobody to speak to, nobody to care about, not even myself. I wasn't lonely. I was where I needed to be, away from all of the energetic students with things to do. Oh, I wanted to be with them, but I needed to be with myself more. With them I had no control, by myself nobody could hurt me. The isolation was intoxicating. The things I took to go along with that isolation, they too were intoxicating. I lay on my mattress, closed my eyes, and the world disappeared. To get to that point I had to line up my supplies, and the juxtaposition between the panic and stress of being out and about in the living city and the serene isolation of being in my own room was immense. In my room, I could drift wherever I wanted to go. In my room, I was the supreme commander of my affairs. In the real world, I was terrified every single waking minute.

I would lie down on my mattress on the floor and wonder what was happening.

Why can't I just get over it and move on? Why can't I just accept that it happened, that I am still me, and nothing can ever change that? But what does that mean? The real me walked back to him over and over again. The real me is somebody who craved his attention, who got jealous when I thought he was with someone else. The real me is somebody who couldn't make it stop. The real me is somebody who hates himself for not being able to stand up for myself. The real me is somebody who wanted it, who needed it, who needed him. The real me is worthless, somebody he could just walk away from at the end. The real me is nothing but his discarded garbage. The real me wants, needs his affection, his protection. The real me misses him. The real me misses his attention.

And that is one of the scariest things I can ever admit.

BUT I AM much stronger than I sometimes give myself credit. I was able to eventually pull myself together and get myself out of bed and back to school. I just willed myself to push through it all and get myself going. I just knew that I needed to keep trying.

There were days when I would make it to the bottom of the stairs and then have to go right back up to my room. There would be times when I would get to the subway station and then go back home. I started making a game out of it, something I could win. I would promise myself that if I could make it to school, I would treat myself with this or that item of food, a chocolate bar, a meal at McDonald's. Food, always an issue with me, continued to be a coping mechanism, but I had figured out how I could use it to both make myself undesirable and safe and try to re-engage at school. As always, if I couldn't control anything else in my life, I could always control what I put in my mouth, as well as what

I would throw back up out of it. Bingeing, purging, gorging—it all helped.

And that's another thing about living on the Danforth—the markets are open twenty-four hours a day.

A good binge and purge required some planning and execution. When I was planning and executing, I wasn't thinking about him.

I always started with a good liquid base, usually a large bottle of Diet Coke, although not all upfront. It provided good lubrication, more than enough flow for the purge, and had the added benefit of being acidic and thus assisting with the breakdown of whatever I inhaled.

If possible, I followed that with ice cream, because it worked both as a liquid and a lubricant. Ideally, pasta came next, because it was soft and the warmth felt good, and because temperature transitions would allow me to mark where I was with my purge. Bags of potato chips were cheap, but I had to be careful to chew thoroughly and drink Diet Coke at the same time so they entered the system closer to a liquid sludge than a dry solid. Usually I topped it off with chocolate. For a successful purge I would never, ever use cheese or peanut butter—they put too much stress on you when you try to bring them back up, glomming onto whatever else is in your system as a type of glue. The only exception to this was if I was in a particularly dark place, when the pain of trying to regurgitate large masses was what I thought I deserved.

My heart would start to beat faster in anticipation of the binge. Once started, always in front of the television to distract me from the insanity of what I was doing to myself, the key was to never stop and to keep drinking liquids throughout. If I had too much food in front of me and hadn't budgeted enough Diet Coke, I would need to use water, though I can't stress enough how unsatisfying it is to have tasteless water in among the various flavors. Having to use water was always a letdown, as I thought better of my bingeing skills.

The feelings you get when you've ingested that amount of food and drink are intense pain and a need to purge. Your body is actually telling you it's at serious risk if you don't get rid of everything you've ingested. The faster I could get out of my room and down the hall to the shared bathroom the better. A shared bathroom in the rooming house was potentially problematic, but not as much as the large shared facilities at Princeton had been. Here all I had to do was chart an appropriate time when others were out at work or, if that wasn't possible, explain that I had the stomach flu. Again.

The sense of relief on purging that pain, on successfully making myself throw up, was indescribable. A sense of accomplishment at having planned and controlled everything at every step. Knowing that I and nobody else had caused my body that pain, and that I and nobody else had brought that subsequent pleasure. It's my body, not his, and I, not he, will do whatever I want to it.

"Purging that pain."

On some twisted level, it kind of makes sense now, doesn't it?

I ENGAGED SOCIALLY whenever I could, and my peers would probably even say I was well liked and popular. As long as I was strong enough to put on the figurative mask, hide what was really going on with me, and confront the world at large, I was fun to be around. The emotional late-bloomer I had once been was now somewhat more mature than most of his peers, having had experiences most of them could never have understood.

Whenever I showed up, I greatly enjoyed law school. I found the subject matter fascinating, especially given my circumstances. It was an interesting perspective to have while sitting through a criminal law class, delving into the proper way to approach sentencing. The thing that struck me most was how easy it was for academics to diminish or ignore the victim, for while the cases are studied as historical disputes between contrasting legal principles that emerge to develop "the law," the teaching of the law seldom, if ever, mentions, let alone focuses on, the victims.

It is a most inhumane way to look at things. The victims in all these cases were real people. Who were they? How did they live? How did the crime impact them? What were their struggles in the aftermath?

The legal system as taught when I was in school removed the victim from the equation. Thoughts of vengeance quite properly have no place in our judicial system. But at the same time, my peers and my criminal law professor seemed unable to consider that there were real people, victims, behind every case, and that there are indeed monsters among us for whom no sentence could ever be enough.

"MR. GILHOOLY. IT'S your turn today. Can you tell all of us what the rationale is for excluding this evidence in these circumstances?"

The details are mostly long gone. The example involved an offender who had committed a particularly heinous offence. The issue involved whether, to convict him, evidence could be introduced to show he had previously been convicted for similar crimes with similar sets of facts. Against that was a fear that such evidence of previous similar crimes would so cloud the judgment of anybody looking at this specific situation that the accused would suffer undue prejudice against him should it be introduced.

I started to answer with trepidation, because I was pretty sure I was about to disagree with my professor, who had already telegraphed his approach to the law. I believed he would focus on the need for the system to protect the rights of the accused, the crux of mainstream legal teaching, and that the evidence should be excluded, that only the specific facts from this specific case mattered.

I understood and agreed in theory, but at the same time I disagreed and suggested that there needed to be a better balance between the rights of the offender and those of the rest of society. I disagreed with the concept that once an offender had served his or her time, he or she had done all that was required, and I suggested that perhaps we as a society should understand that the criminal, in committing the crime, had also flagged a willingness to breach the social contract and was responsible for whatever else went with that. I said that we as a society could in no way ever determine whether or not that criminal had been truly rehabilitated and that, accordingly, it would be naive for us to discount or ignore the fact that the criminal had already shown a willingness to break the law. I noted that, absolutely, against this was an obvious need to allow the criminal access to fair treatment in the future. But, I asked, does fair treatment mean we're not entitled to draw inferences, especially where similar-fact situations warrant it? In the end, how do we find a balance? We can't always default in favor of the criminal, can we?

"And," I added, "what about the victim?"

The discussion was on. Of course the criminal deserves a second chance. Of course. Yet nowhere in the discussion was mention ever made of the victim other than to say that any talk of the victim invites vengeance. Not once did the professor or anyone in my class ever for a moment consider that the victim also needed to be rehabilitated, that the victim needed a second chance, that the victim needed to understand that society was taking steps to protect him or her.

I had made the point that the system needed to take into account the victim and protect society against the criminal, who had shown a willingness to break the social contract. By all means afford the criminal a second chance, but at the same time, let's not pretend that we don't now have additional information that allows us to identify one person as more likely than another to break the social contract. If we treat convicted criminals the same as everybody else after a sentence is served, we're assuming complete rehabilitation of the criminal. Yet there can never be indisputable evidence of rehabilitation, only evidence that the sentence has been served. How can we know, how can we trust that there has been complete rehabilitation? It would be illogical for our system to treat fulfilling a sentence as reason enough to justify equal treatment in the future.

My professor dismissively said, "Oh, so you believe in the scarlet letter."

He had no idea. Nobody in my class had any idea. Nobody could have imagined how loudly those words, his words, would ring in my head.

For an instant I thought of telling everybody right then and there what had happened to me. But Graham's secret was safe with me, because I was nowhere near ready to part with it. I neither pushed the matter further nor pointed out that the professor's use of the literary metaphor was not precisely on point. I resigned myself to the fact that he was neither receptive to ideas that might challenge his view of the world nor particularly well read, given his misuse of the metaphor. His name, however, remains on one of the leading textbooks in Canadian Criminal Law even after his death.

But the law eventually increasingly incorporated the rationale of what I raised in class that day. It's much more than applying a "scarlet letter." Next time a supposed giant in his or her field ever dismisses you, keep faith in yourself. Chances are their response might just be based on their unwillingness to accept that nobody owns the truth and everybody can benefit from considering different perspectives.

And, if Professor Mewett had been offended by the thought of figuratively applying a scarlet letter to an offender, imagine what he would have thought had he known about that very real skate that I wanted somebody to shove down Graham's throat.

I FINISHED THAT first year with what I imagine was one of the strangest transcripts ever at the law school. Some of my grades were higher than anyone could ever have imagined, and others suggested self-sabotage. It was exactly what you would have expected had you known anything about my past and what I was still dealing with or, more accurately, not dealing with.

I was thrown a lifeline at the end of that year. While traveling around Europe, a close friend from Winnipeg, Rod Pertson, had befriended the owner of a hotel in Brighton, England, and was now managing the hotel. He offered me a job for the summer. It was a chance to run away even farther, so I jumped at the offer.

The Queen's Hotel is located on the waterfront overlooking the Palace Pier and is featured briefly in *Quadrophenia* as the site of a fight between the Mods and the Rockers, just down the road from the Ritz, where Ace Face, played by Sting in the movie, worked. I spent the summer working as a porter at the hotel and as a doorman at its nightclub.

I had a great summer. After having continued to put on weight and fall further out of shape during my first year of law school, I began to run regularly again. It was liberating to be so close to the sea and feel the salty mist in the Brighton air, to walk along the shore and hear the stones crushing beneath my feet and the gulls calling as they hovered in place against the wind, looking for food. There was a certain freedom to being so utterly removed from everything. My good days outnumbered my bad that summer, though Brighton was a place where it was possible to be very, very bad.

At the end of the summer, Rod and I scraped together our limited resources and traveled through Europe, all the while living in a rented two-door Peugeot. Our strategy was to drive into a town, park near a central square, go out and drink ourselves silly, and then stumble back to our car and pass out. In the morning we would sneak into a hostel or public washroom to clean up and shower. Once again, I was getting by with almost nothing while on an adventure into the unknown with no safety net. It was heaven.

One morning in Switzerland, after spending a freezing night parked in a lot deep in a mountain valley near Täsch, we set out from our car, took the train into Zermatt, loaded up with supplies, and then hiked all the way from the village up to the Hörnli Hut, the base camp for the assault on the Matterhorn. We did it with no prep, wearing jeans and sneakers, and alternating responsibility for carrying not a backpack but a gym bag with a shoulder strap. We were fit.

Rod has since commented that he couldn't understand how effortlessly I tackled the high, thin ridges where the path fell off to nothing on both sides. Now, in my recovery, I have pointed out to him that back then I had no fear of death because it was in many ways the preferred outcome. That day I often confronted the simplicity of possible suicide, something that ever since the abuse started had always played on my mind to varying degrees of seriousness. All day long I thought about how easy it would be to take a single step to the left or the right and tumble several thousands of steep, rocky feet. But, because it was also one of the single best days of my life, I didn't.

I RETURNED HOME from that summer with a renewed energy for life. One of my friends at law school decided that he wanted to try out for the University of Toronto varsity hockey team. He had been an NCAA Division III (lower-level) U.S. college player as an undergrad but was looking for something to do to complement his legal studies. He suggested that I join him in going out for the team. While I had come to hate hockey and all that it stood for in my life, I did not reject the suggestion out of hand.

Could hockey be fun again? Could hockey help me? I had only the same old ratty equipment, and although my eyesight had only gotten worse and I was now wearing glasses in class, I did not yet have contact lenses. But the game still had a hold on me, so I agreed to join him.

My equipment was so old and worn out that, at the fifth or sixth tryout session, the heel of my skate separated from the blade when the rivets pulled the sole of the skate out the bottom of the boot. Because I'm so big, because my feet are so big—I wear a size fifteen or sixteen shoe, depending on the make—I can't buy anything off the rack, including skates. Replacement skates would have to be specially ordered. My friend had already been cut from the team, but I was doing well and having fun and was not willing to walk away simply because I had no skates. More importantly, the varsity coach at that time, Paul Titanic, himself a former U.S. college standout, had liked what he had seen and didn't want me to leave either.

The University of Toronto Varsity Blues hockey program is the most storied in Canadian university hockey history. The team plays out of historic Varsity Arena, an old rink with several rows of seating completely encircling the ice surface that eventually give way to a web of black iron and steel rafters. It is dark, somber, and imbued with the spirits of those who made the game what it is in Canada. The Blues had regularly featured former professionals and Olympians, as well as standout juniors, and over the years had achieved great success with coaches who went on to the NHL. And here I was, a guy with a broken skate who hadn't played any real hockey in four years, fighting an invisible battle.

It's only now, looking back, that I can appreciate that I must have had some talent to have been able to decide on a lark to put on the pads again after four years away from the game and do what I did. I certainly couldn't see that at the time. Back then all I could see is what I wasn't, not what I was.

Coach Titanic, a wonderful man with unbounded enthusiasm for the game, ran a hockey school each summer. During that time he had come to know a certain former NHL goaltender named Ken Dryden, whose child had been one of his hockey school students. After the equipment manager had called local stores and failed to find a new pair of skates in my size, Coach Titanic had an idea. He decided to ask Dryden, famous for how big he was, if he happened to have a pair of skates he could borrow for his new goalie. Coach Titanic thought that the fact that I was a Princeton graduate and law student might appeal to Dryden, winner of six Stanley Cups, five Vezina Trophies, a Conn Smythe, a Calder, and a member of the Hockey Hall of Fame. And that is how I came to try on Ken Dryden's skates—the skates that he had not worn since taking them off after winning the 1979 Stanley Cup and then retiring.

Coach Titanic picked up the skates at Dryden's house and brought them to the arena. He told me that Dryden had said we could do whatever we needed to get them to fit—wet them, stretch them, whatever. And so I sat down in the dressing room, took off my shoes, picked up the skates, and hoped and prayed a little bit that these skates would fit, that maybe, just maybe, Cinderella would get his happy ending.

I have very, very big feet. Ken Dryden, apparently, does not. Ever since I was about fourteen I had been wearing skates that were the biggest made but that were still far too small for me. I was used to skates that didn't fit me, but this was an even more extreme challenge. I tried curling my toes, twisting my foot, angling my ankle. I would have broken bones if it had meant fitting into those skates. But while Ken Dryden has big feet to fill in so many areas—hockey, politics, community activism, social commentary, and education—his skates just weren't big enough for me.

So close to greatness, but in the end, just a guy whose once "perfect" feet had let him down again.

I LOVED PLAYING hockey for the Varsity Blues, and in many ways it was a bigger achievement than playing at Princeton would have been. It's one thing to combine undergraduate schooling with varsity sports, but quite another to combine law school with varsity sports. While rediscovering a bit of myself in hockey improved my engagement with the rest of the world, my periods of self-doubt, self-loathing, and depression simply took on a different form and became far more intense when they did set in, occupying all of my time whenever I let my guard down.

But there is no question that hockey saved my life, and I am deeply indebted to the Varsity Blues for that. I finally made a varsity hockey team. I was able to overcome my demons for at least a short time. I had good times with the team. I have memories that make me smile in spite of what I know was going on inside my head behind those smiles in the pictures—memories of road trips, parties, practices and drills, team meetings that went off the rails, Coach Titanic wheeling a television set into the dressing room to show us a clip of Eddie Murphy in an attempt to loosen us up. And I proved to myself that I could still fight through even my darkest moments and accomplish at least one goal.

As before, there was always humor, sometimes dark. Given my height, the simple geometry is that my five-hole, the area between a goalie's legs, was quite possibly the biggest in hockey history up to that point. It certainly seemed that way given the number of pucks that found their way between my legs during practices. But whenever a shooter shot a bit high, there was, suffice it to say, pain. For a brief period I seemed to be feeling an inordinate amount of such pain. It was only at the end of the year that the guys let me know that they had been having a contest to see who could shoot the puck between my legs and over the net. Nobody won, with the closest shot having hit the crossbar.

Playing with the Varsity Blues also allowed me to add another name to the list of hockey players who would eventually form part of the intersecting set in the Venn diagram among "players who have scored on me," "NHL players," and "members of the Hockey Hall of Fame," a set bigger than one might imagine, as Rob Blake put one past me during our road trip to Bowling Green State University.

But as before, and for the same reasons, I played with poor equipment and without glasses or contact lenses, an unprotected goalie unable to see the puck. Nobody could figure out why I was so strong in certain drills around the net or on shootouts and then so brutally weak when the longer-range shots came. Of course I wanted to achieve and realize my dreams. Of course I wanted to fail miserably because I thought I deserved to fail. I was still a young man who knew what he wanted but because of his past couldn't see, literally or figuratively, how to get there.

In many ways it was frustrating to achieve a little success and then to trash that success just as quickly.

Why can't I function and succeed all the time? Success is clearly possible, so there mustn't be anything holding me back except my own short-comings. And if that's the case, then my past and the abuse really have nothing to do with anything, the abuse must be just an excuse. I probably always just wanted to fail and I was just going to fail anyway.

And it probably wasn't even abuse, it was probably something that
I wanted because I'm just that type of person, somebody seeking out
drama and other things to take attention off the fact that I'm just a loser.

For a victim of years of sexual assault who has lost all sense of self, there are no successes, simply defeats snatched from the jaws of victory. So, while achieving varsity hockey and good grades at law school would be something to be proud of to the average person, to me they were simply further markers of my own failure. I believed that I was worth nothing, that I deserved nothing, and so, without realizing it, I was taking steps to ensure that I would eventually fail yet again.

———————

I WAS A larger-than-life character at law school. I was the guy playing varsity hockey while going to law school. I was the one who played the role of Batman in the school production of *Batman*. I was seemingly laid-back and fun to be around. I was the one who secured a position as a summer student at what was then Tory Tory DesLauriers & Binnington, a leading firm with a reputation for securing the best and brightest out of law school. But inside, living in my own inner hell, I was no different from before.

My achievements were meaningless to me. I abused substances. I abused my body by cutting it and digging into it. In the face of wanting to achieve, I would repeatedly put on weight to make myself hideous, to ensure failure, to ensure isolation and avoidance, to ensure safety by avoiding attention. I tried to gain control over myself by bingeing and purging. I would fight through all of these self-destructive actions and still want to win. I would drop weight. I would train harder than anybody else to get back to a point where I could participate in hockey, where I could win the fight against my demons. I would wake early and swim laps at Hart House before classes, then after classes lift until my body ached beyond all imagination. Pictures of me from this period reflect incredible fluctuations in body shape as the desires to win and lose fought so hard against each other, the battle much like a tug-of-war where the ribbon first moves one way, then back the other, back and forth, and back and forth...

You know the pattern now. You know it well enough to finish every sentence I'm writing. And that's the thing, because if it's getting so predictable to you, imagine what it was like to have to live it. You can begin to understand my despair at even getting up in the morning, knowing that in the end the song would always remain the same. The miracle of it all is that I kept getting up to fight the good fight, day after day after day after day, hoping against all hope that things would get better.

They never did. But I did graduate from law school. At last, school was out. Forever.

––––––––––––

BUT NOT REALLY.

The world of a lawyer can look a lot like school. It was odd to see an adult in a suit sitting at a desk in the law firm library doing research. I don't know what I had expected to see inside a law firm. I mean, I knew that lawyers wore business attire to the office, but there was something jarring about that first day in the office, about seeing the exact same scene that had played out over years in school with only the clothing changed.

Everything about working in an office was new to me. It was exciting simply getting into an elevator to go to work. My life up until law firm life had not involved elevators, and it always felt like a bit of an adventure in those early days to have to take one to get to the office. Mine had been a life of stairs, of flatlands in the prairies where the only elevators held grain and where my life was not taking me anywhere near downtown. Oh, I had been outside of buildings with elevators, but those buildings seemed to be a club to which I didn't belong.

Princeton graduate, U of T law school graduate, guy in a suit excited to use an elevator.

After my summer job at Torys and the last year of law school, I returned to the firm for my articles, a required year of working at a law firm for practical legal training prior to writing the bar exams. I had been heavily recruited by Dale Lastman, a man I came to greatly admire, who had wanted to take me away from Torys to join him at Goodmans. I really liked Dale and his firm, and I sensed it would have been a far better fit for me. But I already knew enough about myself to know how things were going to turn out and that a bridge would be burned in the process. Better to stay put and burn the bridge I already knew was going to come down rather than start a bonfire on a new one. It was very hard to tell him that I would not be joining his firm.

Torys is based in the TD Centre, a collection of buildings designed by Mies van der Rohe, all in the form of his Seagram Building in New York. His mantra of "less is more" meshed perfectly with my view of the world. His entire body of work appealed to me. It did, however, always strike me as somewhat odd that there would be a collection of his buildings, all virtually identical but for height—more of less is more—on a single site. So beyond calling to my inner architect and designer with its sublime lines and modest, functional, and entirely appropriate glass, the TD Centre also offered me a daily smile. It was so Toronto, taking something from New York and, in wanting to make itself so much like New York, utterly corrupting the essence of things in a needless attempt to make itself more than it is, not seeing that it is already practically perfect in every way.

My year at Torys went as expected. I performed some outstanding work—one partner said I was among the best students he had ever worked with—only to sabotage it by not even completing other work that had been assigned to me.

My inner hell was only getting worse. I was able to hide it from most people, and to most at the firm I was sociable and fun to be around. However, one assignment found me off-site and working with an associate on a project in which we were integrated into a client's business affairs unit for due diligence. We had to work closely with each other while going through a company's legal paperwork to ensure things were all as described by the company. She couldn't quite put her finger on what was wrong, but I could tell that she knew that there was something not quite right with me and that I was struggling to engage properly with the outside world. Although I could put my mask on and hide my true self from so many around me, I knew she could see through the façade.

I loved so much about Torys. It was in many ways a very progressive law firm, and I especially appreciated the focus that it put on learning and research. The firm's library was given prime real estate in the office layout, with a wall of windows overlooking Lake Ontario and a view of a construction project of some notoriety at the time—SkyDome. Law partners usually fight over corner offices with more windows and the best views, while a firm's library is often relegated to a dark, interior space. I thought it was significant that the firm understood that the students and junior lawyers would be working so hard and so long in the library that that they, and not the partners, deserved the best view the firm had to offer.

———————

LAW FIRMS CAN be self-important places full of self-important people, and when you get up close and see how the sausage is made, a part of you wishes you hadn't ever seen it, for you can never look at it the same way again. In the end, though, people are just people, and most lawyers are like most people you would meet anywhere—kind, decent, and hardworking. But again, like almost anywhere else, there are those who are self-important and self-indulgent, who use their positions to try to control and bully others in the workplace. Torys had far more who were decent than not, but, like all organizations, it also had some who you wouldn't wish upon your worst enemy.

What I saw at Torys instantly resonated with me because of my past. Graham James on his own was a loser. Graham James employed by a junior hockey team became somebody with power who could control the futures of young men. Graham's position did not change who he was, it gave him cover to be more than he otherwise would have been, it gave him perceived status and qualities he himself did not possess.

I saw the same effect within the law firm. Torys is a law firm of the highest reputation. Yet despite its attempts to ensure otherwise, not all lawyers there are of the highest quality or caliber. The firm's reputation confers the attributes of excellence on all who work there, whether or not all are deserving. I instantly recognized that those who are truly talented and deserving are secure and don't need to rely on the institution for power—they have it independently of the institution. Those lawyers who were truly talented just were, and they were humble. They didn't have to go on about how the firm was this or that, they were just people who did their jobs very capably and would have been successful even if they had had to start all over again at a new place the next day.

There were others, though, who needed the cover of the firm to protect them from their own insecurities. Without the firm, their shortcomings would be visible to all. That insecurity pushed these lawyers to constantly bring up the firm's reputation and their own place in it, even with clients who questioned the wisdom of their advice. There was never a moment when these lawyers didn't remind you of your place relative to theirs, and this type of lawyer never hesitated to bully or condescend, just as Graham had done within the hockey community.

The truly talented would listen to any idea and consider any possible alternative, irrespective of who had come up with it or where it had come from. The insecure needed to silence the voices that might challenge their place in the hierarchy for fear of being exposed, stripped of the veneer of excellence.

My experience with Graham had given me a heightened sensitivity to manipulative behavior and greater insight into how people operate. It made me acutely sensitive to people's true motivations and the extremes they may be prepared to go to.

We victims of child sexual assault trust nobody. We trust nothing. We will be wary of what is right in front of us. The most important bonds may mean nothing to us, because we will try to look though everything, try to see through everything, so we can, while planning for the best, always be ready for the unimaginable worst, because we know that the unimaginable worst is possible.

This surprised me. Because of the abuse, I had acquired something that was helpful.

From the moment I set foot inside the firm, I could see the various power dynamics at play. I could see who was confident and who wasn't. I could pick out those who were truly helping and willing to share credit as opposed to those who were using the work of others for their own benefit. In meetings, I could sense when somebody was giving a real opinion or when somebody seemed to be tailoring a viewpoint to please a superior. I questioned everything, not in a cynical way, but to better understand who was motivated by what and what the various end games were.

The problem is that this "gift" was coupled with my need to self-destruct.

Because I understood immediately how the office worked, it was easy for me to do things to blow myself up in a way that nobody who understood how an office worked would ever consider. I would see an insecure lawyer bullying another, so I would go out of my way to speak over the bully in meetings and point to the bullied lawyer's work so that it was clear to people at the meeting that that other lawyer had done the work, not the bully. I had no desire to respect office hierarchy in the face of insufferable behavior by anybody, no matter how senior, for I wasn't a career-focused young lawyer, I was a warrior fighting against injustice, damn it, and if I couldn't confront Graham I sure could confront them.

Right.

Of course, my actions ensured that I would receive negative reviews and not be hired back at the end of articling. As always, I had cared, intensely, and had wanted to succeed. But at the same time I didn't care because I wasn't supposed to be there in the first place and had always deserved to fail. So, certain that I was going to fail, I chose not to play along in the first place.

That approach was wrong on so many levels, particularly in as much as everybody is entitled to your respect and it is up to you to maintain character and never diminish yourself. I was so wrong. But while I was going through so much inner hell of my own, I started thinking it was only fair to dole out some of my "justice" to people I thought were deserving. That pathetic grasping at whatever power I could put my hands on did, however, allow me to believe that there was purpose to my life, and in that way the disrespectful approach saved me. It burned a bridge, but it may have saved my life. Still, I know it was wrong.

When a somewhat pompous writing instructor showed up to teach us the basics of how to write clearly and asked for a sample of our writing, I submitted not my own work but a draft client letter prepared by a partner of some repute that had been given to me to fact-check. I thought it was poorly written, and I decided to give my view of him a fact-check. I changed his name to mine and submitted it. That backfired when the instructor called me in for a special meeting to set up times for remedial teaching. I, the student who supposedly wrote the letter, needed special help. I got cold feet about calling the partner out and explaining what I had done. It was easier to just go along with it than try to explain that someone else in the firm, a very prominent professional in his field, had written the draft and needed remedial training.

I did all of this not caring about whether I would be hired back, because I didn't deserve to live, let alone be hired back. But, of course, I had also desperately wanted to be hired back. Back and forth. The demon within. Over and over and over again. Once the self-sabotage is complete the young man instantly regrets what he has lost, resets himself, and moves on to fight another day against that internal demon.

But I was not the only one at the firm with demons. No matter how esteemed the company, firm, or institution may be, the city or town in which it is located has dark alleyways and doors that lead into places far removed from the magnificently appointed offices, places you couldn't ever imagine visiting, an underside that offers anything and everything to anybody in need. I saw them. And I was not the only one in pain or leading a double life of sorts.

Standing outside a bar after a firm event, a lawyer asked which way I was going. On finding out, he suggested we share a cab, and I thought nothing of it. Ten minutes later, after having rebuffed his numerous sexual advances while thanking him for his interest, I found myself in the middle of an intersection, trying to grab him and get him back into the cab after he had jumped out at a stop-light to play matador with the cars going by, and looking as if he was about to lose.

MY CONTINUING SELF-DESTRUCTION was getting worse.

I was abusing substances. It was becoming uncontrollable. It was happening at the office. I would sit inside my office with my door closed while other lawyers were holding conversations just outside, conversations that I could hear while I was trying to numb myself. Paranoia overcame me. The lawyers were taunting me, for we had a policy that our doors should always be open except under special circumstances. I believed they knew what was going on behind my closed door and were having a loud conversation just outside my office to make it clear that they knew all about me, about my past, that I was a fraud. I believed that they were laughing at me, knowing that I didn't belong. In my state I couldn't move my legs to open the door, but I wouldn't have wanted to anyway. All I could do was fall back into my chair and be taken to a place far, far away, a better place, a place where I didn't exist, where nothing that mattered existed, where everything made sense.

I didn't want to exist. So, I didn't. Goodbye, Torys.

I TOOK A job at an emerging firm. Actually, it was already well established in Quebec but was just emerging in Toronto at the time: Heenan Blaikie, home of former prime ministers Pierre Trudeau and later Jean Chrétien. But I knew from my first day that it was going to be a complete disaster.

The senior lawyer in the corporate group was a tall man who, like Graham, always had to be the smartest in the room. He called me into his office. When I arrived he, standing, waved me in, his phone held to his ear. I assume that what he was hearing wasn't good news, for, while I was sitting across from his desk, he turned suddenly, picked up a pen, and whipped it across the room, narrowly missing me but taking a chunk out of the wall behind me. Just what I needed: a stable, humble, and compassionate mentor.

I kind of admired him for being so patently ludicrous yet clearly transparent, me sitting there and being somebody unable to be anything remotely approaching transparent. But I also thought it was an incredibly immature act, especially as he had done it in front of somebody he was working with for the first time. Still, here I was judging him for throwing a pen while I was in the midst of destroying myself and doing far worse things in my own life.

It wasn't a good fit, but I worked at it for the sole reason that some very good people—Allen Garson, Norm Bacal, Joe Groia, Kip Daechsel, and others—were there. They were talented lawyers who were even better people, the type of people you aspire to become yourself. They renewed my belief in the goodness of things and the possibility of a future life for me. They believed in me and showed patience with me because, I suspect, they saw that I was dealing with something they just couldn't see. Without knowing it, their patience gave me enough of a window into what I was doing to myself—though I was far from being able to address matters head-on and get the help that I so desperately needed—that I was able to emerge from the deadly downward spiral I had been on at the time.

I WAS A Bay Street corporate lawyer making inroads into the broader business community. I had become a member of the Board of Directors of the Toronto International Film Festival. From Heenan Blaikie I moved on to a larger, more establishment law firm, Blakes, one of the so-called Seven Sisters of Canadian law, and my career was once again on the rise. This new opportunity was presented to me by a man who would become my mentor, close friend, and personal savior. David McCarthy, like me, had attended Princeton as an undergraduate, then the University of Toronto for law school, and he had played hockey at both. David is five years older than I am, so we'd never crossed paths until I was in law school, where he was helping with alumni affairs. David is now a senior partner at Stikeman Elliott, and to this day he remains a very close personal friend.

Things clicked at Blakes because of David's personal support and interest in me. Although the same issues plagued me behind the scenes, I was more successful there at compartmentalizing things and was becoming far more efficient at moving away from the past. It was so valuable having a personal connection with somebody who believed in me, somebody I didn't want to let down, somebody who supported me and took time to see the best in me, who helped me. I performed very well at Blakes, where my biggest misstep, to my eternal horror and shame, was that I once used the non-word *irregardless* in an internal meeting with another partner. It's a very big deal to certain people.

I never should have moved away from there, from the guidance and support David offered me. But me being me, no success should ever go unpunished. And because of his help, I was enjoying success that set up a move in 1994 to CanWest Global Communications Corporation, based back where it all started, in Winnipeg.

Only in my story could my biggest success involve moving back to the place from which I had run.

SEVEN

CORPORATE LIFE

ANWEST NO LONGER exists, a victim of changing dynamics within global media industries and its own over-reaching at the absolute wrong time. The company's demise came after I left. All I experienced while at CanWest's head office was success after success after success. It all went downhill for them after I left.

That's my story, and I'm sticking to it.

At that time, CanWest was Canada's leading media company, with additional international interests in Australia, New Zealand, and Chile. A Canadian publicly traded company, it was controlled, in terms of both equity and votes, by the Asper family. Israel Asper, known to one and all as "Izzy" (except to me, as I could never call him anything but Mr. Asper), was a larger-than-life figure. A lawyer by training, he was a former politician and an entrepreneur who had previously built and lost a corporate empire before making CanWest into the force that it was when I was there.

I had gone to law school with Leonard, the younger of his two sons and the friend who had dragged me along to try out for the Varsity Blues. He had applied to Princeton the same year that I was accepted, and he had also interviewed to work at Torys when

I was hired there. We had become close over the years, and I think that he, having grown up with so much, saw something in me with my dramatically different background that he admired and respected. For my part, I saw much good in him. Leonard was an heir who still worked hard, he was kind and gentle, and he treated everyone, absolutely everyone, with good humor and respect. As his family's corporate empire grew, and as he was being groomed to take control of the business, he asked me to come out to meet his father to see if I wanted to join the company.

It was the opportunity of a lifetime. CanWest was a fascinating company with assets and opportunities spread across a global playing field in a rapidly changing industry. The leadership group at CanWest was small and driven, and Mr. Asper was a dynamic and almost mythic business icon. It was a chance to do so much so early in my career, an opportunity to learn so much at the foot of one of Canada's leading business visionaries. How could I say no?

Yet, taking a job with CanWest would mean leaving David and Blakes, leaving Toronto and the practice of big firm corporate law, and taking a leap of faith with Leonard while having to return to Winnipeg, the scene of the crime. So many crimes.

It was very difficult to return to Winnipeg. No, that's an understatement. It was terrifying to have to return to Winnipeg. My immediate family had all moved away, my parents back to Regina, my brother and sister to Toronto and Hamilton, respectively. I thought I would never again have to go back there, no matter how much I loved it.

I worked hard to try to forget. I consciously avoided places from my past. I avoided people from my past, neighbors, old friends, in ways that must have seemed rude or arrogant or dismissive. But I just couldn't go back to anything to do with my past, and it hurt to shut out my past connections.

It was also too good an opportunity to pass up. Plus, if it blew up for the very reason that it wasn't the smart move, that the smart move would have been to stay with my mentor, well, that had the benefit of being entirely consistent with my need to self-destruct.

My time at CanWest turned out to be the most amazing ride of my life. I had no idea what I was getting myself into, and from the moment I got there, I did not have a dull day.

My office was situated between Leonard's office and his father's office. Leonard was being groomed to take over the company, something that had been evident from the moment I met him in law school. Mr. Asper was hard on his children, all of whom worked in the company, and he pushed them relentlessly. Growing up an Asper would have been difficult. That's not to say that there weren't benefits to growing up the way the Asper offspring did, and they certainly had advantages in life the rest of us can only dream of. But none of them were spoiled in the traditional sense of the word, for irrespective of whatever they may have received as a result of who their father was, there definitely was some bad that went along with all of that good.

They, like all of us, aren't perfect (well, actually Gail might be). Still, I can't overstate how much I like all three of them.

Because I wanted to do whatever I could to keep my mind off Winnipeg and what it meant to me, I kept very long hours at the office, often working deep into the night. Our offices were located on the top three floors, thirty-plus floors up, in the tallest building in the city, a sleek, modern tower owned by the Asper family. We were at the intersection of Portage and Main, one of Canada's most famous intersections, at the very center of the city. We had a 360-degree view through floor-to-ceiling glass windows and could see for miles beyond the city limits and across the flat, flat plains. If your dog ever ran away, you could see it running for days.

Mr. Asper also worked very long days, though he usually wouldn't show up until the afternoon. He and I were often the only two left in the office late at night, and we would spend hours talking about many things—business, politics, industry trends, the art of the deal. He was fascinating to talk with, and he loved to tell his favorite stories over and over again about how he had built the company, how he had wanted to be a successful politician and run the country. Perhaps because he grew up in Neepawa, Manitoba, a son of parents fleeing Russian persecution, he still identified with the underdog, an endearing trait given his wealth and status. He was then worth hundreds of millions of dollars and soon to be worth billions. But he didn't care who you were or how old you were or what you had done for a living. The only thing he cared about was your ideas. If a good idea came from the youngest, newest employee in the management group, he would run with that over the wishes of others who had been with him for years. He took a suggestion I made and acted on it during a contested acquisition over the advice of a leading Bay Street mergers and acquisitions partner, a specialist in the field, and made millions as a result. To Mr. Asper, what mattered was not who you were in the pecking order, but whether your idea was the best one.

I instantly loved working with him. And I instantly recognized a fellow broken soul who had been fighting his own demons for years, a man who had fought lifelong battles to maintain his sobriety and control his weight, battles that were widely known in the business community. He was still fighting those battles and sometimes still losing them late at night and into the early morning, when only the two of us inhabited the otherwise empty corporate hub.

I was immediately tossed into the deep end. I found myself traveling around the world, pursuing corporate development opportunities, scouring financials and spreadsheets, playing with financial models, teaching myself on the fly. Despite my relative youth, I was involved in extremely complex transactions with a level of responsibility that I never would have had while working in a law firm.

You name it, we did it, I did it: bank financings, refinancings, a U.S. offering combined with a listing on the New York Stock Exchange, corporate acquisitions, international acquisitions, submissions to local and international regulators, broadcast startups, lawsuits everywhere, corporate and industry strategic planning, internal corporate growth. I was the company's senior lawyer with responsibilities for corporate development, and I was having the time of my life. One day I would get on a plane to London, and a month later I would still be there in the midst of a bid for a new television channel. Then off to Australia and New Zealand to canvas radio opportunities. Later, I spent the better part of two years flying back and forth to Ireland while establishing TV3 as Ireland's first private television broadcaster, meeting and negotiating with government leaders, government regulators, and leading industry participants.

I sat on boards. I worked with our internal groups amidst the competing interests of a family-controlled public company. I worked with minority shareholders in a subsidiary spoiling for a fight. I balanced the line between newcomers to the corporate group and the old guard who had once been with the Aspers during the '70s and '80s and who now wanted back in with the corporate resurgence. My salary quickly escalated and bonuses regularly came my way as transactions were closed and goals achieved.

It was an extremely stressful life and I didn't have much of a personal life, but that suited me just fine because I was barely a person to begin with. No matter how much travel was involved to get our business done, all trips around the world, whether by commercial airline, private jet, or once even on the Concorde, inevitably ended with a return to Winnipeg, a place where I was always on edge. That leering face. Those groping hands. Those insidious threats. Those eyes. I knew Graham had moved on and was no longer in the city, his hockey career now increasingly public and on the rise, but his ghost was always present. I avoided dangerous places, trying hard to forget, but you can't always control what goes on in your head, as I well knew.

And CanWest gave me a good moment with my parents. When I took them on a tour through the CanWest offices, they never let on they were impressed. However, when I was returning from a detour to the washroom but still out of their sight, I overheard them talking with awe about the place. Of course, once they saw me and knew I was within earshot they became quiet again. But I knew, and later I sometimes heard from others, how proud my father was of me, although he never revealed that pride to me until just before his death.

CanWest was very good for me, and I was very good for CanWest. Its reputation was one of aggressive success and aggressive litigation. Anyone doing research on CanWest as a potential corporate partner would quickly learn about all of that, and as a result, we were often at a disadvantage when seeking to enter transactions or strike deals with potential partners. I was sometimes able to step in and smooth things over after the family had chosen more antagonistic paths.

I found the way around CanWest's reputation was to be exceedingly reasonable with potential partners or regulators about our interests. I would always ask, "What would you do if you were me?" to try to get the other side to focus on understanding what we needed to get out of any deal. Similarly, I would always step into their shoes and assess matters from their perspective and then pocket that understanding while never negotiating against myself, leaving it to them to see how much they were prepared to risk to push for their needs. It sounds obvious, but strategic role-playing isn't as common as you might think.

As somebody keeping dark, dark secrets and essentially leading a double life, I discovered that I was a good negotiator by being able to imagine the worst without letting it paralyze me. The easiest thing for a lawyer to say, whether to the other side of a deal or even to your own client or fellow executives, is "no," but I always wanted to try to find a way to get things done. Having to plan negotiations strategically appealed to me at an intellectual level and motivated me to craft deals around those risks. And I seemed to be very good at hearing not just the words being said but the meanings behind the words, the ulterior motives. I focused on facts and assessed behavior, I didn't get caught up in things people said or promised.

I want to live in a world where you can trust everyone. But being acutely aware that there are always inherent risks in trusting anybody sure had its professional advantages.

———————

HISTORICALLY, IRELAND HAD only state-owned television networks and commercial television from the UK. The Irish government issued a license in 1990 for TV3 to become the first private television broadcaster in Ireland. The local group holding the license had no broadcasting experience and was looking for an experienced media company to partner with to help make the network a reality. The Irish license holders were the business people behind U2: Paul McGuinness, Ossie Kilkenny, James Morris, and Paul Kelleher, all major figures in the Irish business and cultural communities. If they didn't meet their deadline for getting TV3 on air they would lose their license.

They had tried to make things work with several other partners, but for whatever reasons their efforts had failed. They were on their last chance to get it right when they came to us and struck a deal. But as soon as they signed, they wanted out for fear of having given us too much control. They, media giants in Ireland, had significant relationships with the Irish government and significant influence over the local regulator with whom we would have to negotiate the terms of business, a regulator regulating private national television for the first time.

It was a difficult year and a half. Each side walked from the table on numerous occasions. But, because of extensive efforts put in by me on our side and James Morris on theirs to develop a fundamental understanding of each other, James and I could always sit down and get things back on track when more volatile members of our teams had torn things apart.

I flew back and forth from Winnipeg through Toronto and then London to Dublin twenty-seven times in a year and a half to build trust where there was no trust. I immersed myself in Ireland, in Dublin, in the national culture, and in the end we came out of a situation that so many different times had been declared dead to CanWest with a deal that netted us many millions in profits. And when it was all over, James Morris, the man behind Windmill Lane, who ran The Mill and Shepperton Studios, the man who had worked more closely with me for an extended period of time than anybody else before or since, asked me to come to London and work with him.

Accepting the offer would have been a good decision personally for me. So, of course, I rejected it.

And while this Irish adventure may sound good, I was always still the same me. In Ireland I resumed old habits and discovered The Towers, in the north part of Dublin, a phalanx of semi-inhabited tombstones epitomizing the failure of a perfectly planned suburban apartment complex that had devolved into a glorified drive-through pharmacy. I understand that they have now been torn down. The world is a better place for that.

BUT MY PROFESSIONAL successes were always just footnotes in the far greater battle I was fighting.

Then, one night, on the CBC, there was Graham's picture. I hadn't seen anything of him for years. Now he was in the news. Sheldon Kennedy, a professional hockey player in the midst of his NHL career who was a number of years younger than I was, had come forward to disclose years of abuse by Graham. I stared at the screen but couldn't hear anything. I wasn't processing things properly. My body froze. I started to shake uncontrollably. Standing there, not knowing what was happening, I bent over and started throwing up.

Tangible evidence that Graham had abused someone else after me.

I'd believed that Graham had been in a relationship of some sort with someone I had played with all those years ago, but I'd never had any direct evidence. Now, however, not only was there confirmation that I hadn't been the only one, but Sheldon had come later. Because I hadn't stopped Graham when I had the chance, he had abused someone else.

I was responsible for what I was seeing in the news. I was the reason Sheldon was dealing with his pain. I was the reason Sheldon was living his own version of my hell. It was all my fault.

Any meaningful chance at a fully functioning life was all over. Graham was everywhere in the news, and not a moment went by without me thinking about it, about all of it, and wanting it all to be over. I was in no way ready to come forward. I wasn't even dealing with the abuse myself so I was in no position to tell anyone else about it. I couldn't try to help Sheldon or to join him in his suffering. And that made it even harder for me.

Who are you? Why can't you stand up? Why can't you step forward and deal with this? Why didn't you stop him when you had the chance? You knew he was going to do it to somebody else, you knew all along, you thought it had already been going on with others. This is on you. What right do you have to live?

I was deeply suicidal. I explored various options—jumping off a building, overdosing, hanging myself—and settled on jumping. I made plans, and several different times at the office I dropped out of sight during the day to test a plan.

If only I could figure out a way to unlock the exit door just down the hall around the corner from my office that opened on to a portion of the roof. If not that door, what about the one on the floor above, the very top floor that housed our corporate boardroom?

We were, after all, occupying the top floors of the tallest building in Winnipeg, each with access to different parts of the building's sculpted top, to high level walkways that would be perfect departing platforms.

I organized my belongings so that they could be easily delivered to my family after I'd jumped. I wrote a suicide note. I left a list of all of my personal contacts on my bedside table with instructions about which bankers and investment advisors to contact for which accounts, and where my insurance information was, in case one day I didn't make it home. These steps weren't cries for help, because nobody else knew about them. I took these steps to make sure everything was ready if I ever found the courage to jump.

I learned something awful about myself. The reason I didn't kill myself wasn't because I didn't want to, but because I was afraid I would jump but survive and be physically wrecked with no future ability to end it all, forced to continue living and in even greater misery. Given the hell I was already enduring, that would be a fate worse than death.

Imagine working in an office on the highest floors of the tallest office building in the city, in an office with floor-to-ceiling windows everywhere, expansive views of the world beneath you, when you've decided you're going to kill yourself by jumping to your death. It's slightly distracting.

FROM THE MOMENT Sheldon came forward, I could barely go through the motions of living. I knew that at some point I would have to either come forward and deal with things or else check out of my pathetic joke of an existence. I didn't know which would win out. I didn't really care.

Sheldon was incredibly strong. He stood alone and faced the world of hockey, declaring himself a victim at a time when the abuse he had suffered carried homosexual implications, which were distasteful to much of the general public and certainly to the macho sports world. He stood alone while many in the hockey community rallied behind Graham, who had been named the Hockey News 1989 Man of the Year after coaching the Swift Current Broncos to the Canadian Junior Hockey championship. Sheldon became an easy target for those who wanted to preserve their illusions about the nobility of Canada's favorite sport and Graham's role in it. And he stood alone because I and others weren't yet ready (in my case a nice euphemism for "too afraid") to come forward.

Graham pleaded guilty on January 2, 1997, to hundreds of sexual assaults against Sheldon and an unnamed player who came forward after seeing Sheldon in the news. In an attempt to lighten his sentence, Graham secured character references from respected hockey people and former players. He claimed he didn't understand that his relationships with Sheldon and the other player had been immoral. Whatever his lawyer said worked, as he received only three and a half years. I was ashamed that I lacked the inner strength to step out of my own hell to support Sheldon.

Nobody knew what I was dealing with, but I was rapidly falling apart. I was trying so hard to run away from who I was, what I had done those years ago, what I wasn't able to do now. I wanted to be anybody but me, I felt an incredible pressure to be anybody but me, better than me, different from me. I couldn't just be me. I tried to do everything at the office, to know everything, to be

involved in everything, to be essential to everything, bizarrely figuring that my only protection if everybody eventually found out
and scorned me was to be indispensable. It was the beginning of
a very dark time.

Yet, in many ways CanWest helped me cope. With so much
individual responsibility and so much traveling, I was often on
my own, and that allowed me to pursue my self-destructive habits
without fear of detection and to manage my work schedule around
my bad habits when I was away from the office.

Graham's sentence of only three and a half years was a mere
slap on the wrist. Even worse, he would eventually be paroled in
2001, having served only eighteen months, this for hundreds of
individual sexual assaults. Justice?

There was one glimmer of hope. On *Hockey Night in Canada*,
after Sheldon had come forward with his story, noted hockey
commentator Don Cherry was asked about the situation and what
he thought should be done. I sat there, watching with tears in my
eyes, already feeling responsible for everything. Yet Don Cherry
put the blame exactly where it belonged: on Graham. "I'd have
drawn and quartered the son of a bitch," he said. Graham was the
bad guy, not me. His words meant so much to me.

Graham, of course, sought advice on how to go about suing
Cherry. Poor Graham James, now a victim for having been called
out by Don Cherry.

I WOULD LIE in bed and stare at the ceiling, trying to figure
out if it was even worth getting out of bed. He'll always be there,
after all, meaning I'll always feel this way, he'll always win, and I'll
always be nothing more than his discarded garbage.

Stop thinking like that! Stop it right now!

If only I could sleep. But sleep meant nightmares, and he was always in them. I was always running from him, and those eyes, his dead eyes, his shark eyes.

Leave me alone! Let me sleep!

But if I sleep I lose control over what I can think of and he'll be there.

Oh, like that's any worse than now when you're awake, when all you can do is think about him, about it?

Please, let me sleep.

Please, don't let me sleep.

Please, I just want to live.

I just need to get through this, I just need to get through tonight and see what I can do tomorrow. Substances numb the pain. Food lets me control my body. Bingeing and purging let me think about nothing other than bingeing and purging. Cutting and digging into my body lets me feel what true pain feels like and takes my mind off him, off the past. Take. Drink. Gorge. Purge. Cut. Dig. Repeat.

I'm exhausted. I can't take it anymore.

WHILE I WAS at CanWest's head office we acquired Fireworks Entertainment, a small film and television production and distribution company based in Toronto with secondary offices in Los Angeles, and London. I was parachuted in to work with the management team at the head office in Toronto, a position nobody in his or her right mind would take, as I became the outsider inserted to report back. I took it so that I could leave Winnipeg.

The job itself turned out to be fascinating and intellectually rewarding, involving bank financings, production and co-production financings, sale-leaseback transactions, establishing an independent distribution company in partnership with other producers and distributors, studio co-productions, talent deals, a building lease and build-out in Los Angeles.

We had acquired Fireworks from an independent producer who had only recently taken his company public but who still controlled it and continued to act as an owner. I had met him while doing our acquisition of his company and knew it would be a rocky road given his chafing at thoughts of input or control from above. I was also suicidal and unconcerned about my own well-being. Working with him would be a perfect match for the state of my mental health.

When I left CanWest's head office, the company was valued at approximately four billion dollars and was virtually debt-free. The Asper family held approximately half of the equity value. We were planning to use the newly acquired Fireworks as a test vehicle for larger expansion into the film, TV, and emerging online content industries. I left head office with the idea that I would be a part of something important for years to come.

But I could also see that there were storm clouds on the horizon. The executives who had driven the recent growth in value were slowly losing ground to the old-timers from Mr. Asper's era who were coming back, all wanting in on the action. Leonard had been handed the reins, but Mr. Asper was still very much present.

Shortly after I arrived in Toronto the corporate strategy changed. An old-media view of the world took over back in Winnipeg as CanWest invested heavily in newspapers—in 1999. The model for a successful and vertically integrated media company with content creation and distribution across multiple platforms with content creators working for both old and new media at the same time had been the Tribune Corporation, based in Chicago. It sounded good in theory, but it was a step backward, an effective reinvestment in old media, not new. On announcing the deal, which was a very public and important moment in Canadian business history, Leonard Asper and Lord Conrad Black, then an international media baron, shook hands, and the image was splashed across media outlets worldwide.

Conrad Black shaking hands with Leonard Asper? My Spider-Sense started tingling. The Lord Black I had heard of would have insisted on shaking hands with nobody but Mr. Israel Asper (no matter that Leonard was now the head of the CanWest businesses), unless, perhaps, he was getting the much better end of the bargain? On seeing that handshake on the news, I immediately called my dad and told him that I thought CanWest had just been taken. That handshake told me all I needed to know about that deal.

CanWest's focus was now elsewhere. It was unhappy with Fireworks' management and quickly lost interest in it in the face of other deals it was chasing. Beyond newspapers, the company pursued bizarre corporate development opportunities that didn't seem to fit into any coherent plan of attack. I received a call from an old friend who had made his way to Turkey and who found himself on the other side of a deal with CanWest. He wanted me to try to help him understand what he saw as the irrational conduct of the CanWest corporate development executives he was dealing with. It wasn't a good sign.

CanWest was increasingly seeking out opportunities for cash, no matter where they were. As before, the company was making bets based on its ability to see what it perceived as opportunities being missed by others. Believing its phenomenal press from its past decade of success, CanWest thought that it was smarter than its competitors and that it would never make a mistake.

CanWest is no more—four billion dollars in equity value wiped out after I left. It didn't even last ten years after the second generation took power. And that makes me very sad, because it was positioned so well to take advantage of what was to come. But the world can change quickly. Tribune, the model for a modern entertainment company? Bankrupt. CanWest was far from the only media company not to make the transition into the digital era, but it had the misfortune to make all of the wrong moves at all of the wrong times.

I wasn't at head office for CanWest's demise, and I'm grateful for that, for it would have been too hard for me to witness. Things changed at CanWest after I left. Not because I left, just after. Still, I think having somebody like me there, somebody who could and would speak truthfully and clearly to power without thinking politically or with any self-interest, had been important. Some believe that in medieval times that role was played by the fool. At CanWest, nobody would ever deny that I was certainly a fool. CanWest benefitted when Mr. Asper sat at the table and encouraged people, anybody, no matter how young, to come at him with an opposing view. He didn't just love to hear different voices, he needed to hear them.

There are many lessons to take from what happened there, and there were many good people who worked very hard at CanWest who deserved better. Leonard deserved far better from so many of those highly paid professionals around him who in the end chose self-interest over the family that had given them so much. Leonard, like the rest of us, is not perfect, and like the rest of us he too made serious mistakes along the way, but he deserved a far better fate. I know he'll find great success again.

CANWEST WASN'T THE only one making bad choices.

Relationships? I had dated on and off and off and on again ever since I got to Princeton, amazing women, each of whom deserved much better than I could ever offer them. I cared too much for every one of them to ever bring them into my chaotic world of pain and self-abuse. Each and every one of them gave so much to me: they all tried so hard in their own ways to help me without knowing exactly what it was in me that needed fixing. Because I knew that, and because of their deep love and affection for me, it simply wasn't possible for me to sustain a serious relationship that I could take through to marriage.

But then through friends I met a tall, beautiful, strong woman, one who struck me as a sort of *über*woman—lawyer on partnership track, dynamic, and utterly charming, someone who seemingly had it all. And that single blind date led to our getting married several years later, in 2002, me now thirty-eight years old. We went to the Toronto City Hall and got married on a Monday over lunch, and we both returned to work later that afternoon after a celebratory lunch. I'm not one for being the center of any attention, so no wedding ceremony for me.

Part of my reluctance to celebrate was that deep down I believed that she had no idea who I really was. She had only seen the me you see when you look at my résumé. She hadn't seen the other me, the me who was troubled, who self-destructed, who lacked any sense of self-worth, because I hadn't shown that to her. But she wanted me, and that was good enough for me.

Amidst all of this personal upheaval and in the midst of my increasingly worsening state, it was difficult for me to maintain consistent employment. As CanWest crumbled I took a position with an emerging children's television production and distribution company as its senior lawyer, again involving myself in the business end as well. We made acquisitions. We expanded into product licensing. We became an industry leader. We acquired a historic Los Angeles–based competitor and expanded our market presence. Initially I did very well, but from the moment a senior executive reneged on a promise that I thought had been made to me, those fears latent inside of me raged. I felt exploited and betrayed. I no longer cared, and although the job called on only a small amount of my skillset, I now gave it even less than that.

None of this really mattered anyway. Ever since Sheldon had come forward and I hadn't, my life had had no meaning. And with each day, things got worse. New job? New wife? New life in the suburbs? They barely registered and hardly seem worth mentioning because in so many ways I wasn't present to experience them myself.

I was still alive, but I wasn't living.

Who are you? You know exactly who and what you are. And you know that none of this is ever going to change. This is your life. There's no escape. You deserve this. You did this to yourself.

I tried very hard to connect with my community. I was coaching minor hockey, but I wasn't really in the moment. I was commuting into work and then coming home consumed by thoughts of failure. I kept trying so very hard to lead a normal life while skirting around my emotional black hole. We had a nice home in a sought-after neighborhood. We vacationed overseas with friends. Yet all of this meant nothing to me, this false dream, none of it made me feel any better about myself. Forget about what we have. We only are who we are, and I knew exactly who I was.

I was, of course, tormented by what I saw as my life's wasted potential, the professional price I had repeatedly paid through my bouts of underperformance, my inability to enjoy any success, my loss of friends because they couldn't understand my actions, my bloated body abused through overeating, a new and already faltering marriage. Everything I ever had that was good in my life I had broken. Everything.

There was no room in my life for success. Anything good I destroyed. Anything bad I fed. And this relationship, this marriage, was bad for me from the start, bad for both of us from the start. My wife was in many ways that *über*woman, so beautiful, strong, and accomplished. When she met me, she saw only my good. But when she found out everything about me, her first instincts were to protect herself, and I don't blame her one bit for that. I wasn't good for her, for what she wanted out of life, and that's fine by me.

I COULD SEE what was coming. We had drifted apart. My dad's death in 2003 gave me increasing perspective on the life I had lost, my own life. In many ways his life ended the day he dropped out of school after Grade Eight. I could see with greater clarity just what I had lost through the abuse, what it was doing to me, what I had done to myself. The more I thought about him, the more I missed him, the more I understood him. And the more I understood him, the more I worried about what kind of impact I would have on those closest to me.

My father died just after my wife and I had married. Although my dad and I had always fought, he was still my dad, and I knew he was, at heart, a sweet man. We never really connected until he was on his deathbed, when, fortunately, we had a chance to say all the right things to each other. I was so sad at not having had him by my side throughout my life, so sad we couldn't have had a loving relationship during all those years when I was growing up, when it would have meant the world to me, when I needed him.

My dad couldn't help me with the same old questions that had haunted me for so long, that continued to haunt me. They would awaken me in a sweat, making it impossible for me to fall back asleep. They would come up while I was working on a legal file. They would be front and center during a handshake or a seemingly normal conversation. They would be there during intimate moments with the one I loved.

Why did he pick me? He must have seen I was weak. People must see me as weak. I must be some sort of joke.
Why didn't I stop it? I must have wanted it. I deserve what I'm feeling now. I deserve to feel like his leftover garbage.
How could somebody like him control somebody like me? I'm worthless and weak. I'm not the strong, tall, intelligent, athlete people see on the outside. I'm a fraud.
Who am I? I'm his garbage, his enabler. I'm somebody who doesn't deserve to live.

I knew that I had killed myself many times without actually taking my life. The only thing left to do was to complete the job, one I had been working so hard on ever since the abuse. Enough was enough. It was time to end things.

EIGHT

CHOOSING TO LIVE

NOTHING FOCUSES YOU on life like the reality of death, and I was about to die.

I hadn't circled a date on my calendar. I hadn't made any personal deals with myself like "If I can make it until Wednesday and still feel the same way on Thursday, then Friday will be the day," something I had done before to get through rougher periods of time. I just got to the point where I was in too much pain and I knew that it was time, that things had finally deteriorated to the point where I couldn't deal with life anymore, that I was too tired to fight on.

So, one night—a night just like so many others, a night in August 2008—I crawled onto the edge of the bridge over Sixteen Mile Creek in Oakville, Ontario, the safe suburb just outside of Toronto where I was living, with the intention of ending my living hell by jumping.

I was incredibly calm and ready, ready in a way I'd never been before. I'd researched suicide and made plans many times, and I'd even taken steps to act on those plans. The suicidal thoughts tended to come in waves. I was in the midst of another such wave and had been searching out alternatives. I'd narrowed my choices down to this bridge, another bridge, and the railway tracks.

There is an art to figuring out the best way to kill yourself. With trains you have to study the schedules to determine when the faster trains will be coming through without stopping. Some spots along the tracks have better hiding places than others, cover you need so the engineer won't sound an alarm and slam on the brakes, lessening the chance of a successful death but increasing the chance of an unsuccessful maiming. In fact, you always think of the negatives, as living in the aftermath of a failed attempt can be much worse than succeeding.

I finally decided that jumping in front of a train was too risky. Given my immense size and the shape of the front of the trains, I was afraid that I would just end up seriously injured, and I couldn't take that risk. Jumping off a bridge made much more sense to me—my size and the increased force of hitting the ground on contact would improve my chance of "success."

Try explaining that thinking to your therapist.

In some ways, making the decision to die gave me peace of mind, a sense of control over my own destiny. I carried on for a while longer, fighting the hardest I'd ever fought, without anybody ever knowing or even suspecting that there was a fight going on. I carried on as best as I could until I couldn't carry on anymore. And when I couldn't carry on anymore, when I couldn't fight anymore, and when I knew, absolutely knew, that things would never change, a calm came over me. I was fine with things. I accepted defeat. I was ready to die.

I didn't say any goodbyes. There would be no note this time, nothing. It was impulsive in the moment, but it wasn't impulsive in concept. Simply stated, I had an opportunity—it was late at night and everybody else was asleep—and I took it.

I left the house in running gear. I was horribly overweight and was not doing any running at the time, but that's what I put on that night to leave the house and take my own life. Read into that whatever you will, perhaps a cry out to the lost athlete within, maybe a twisted homage to the poem "To an Athlete Dying Young"? Whatever it was, I tiptoed through the house as quietly as a morbidly obese giant could and made my way out the door.

It was a quiet, still night. I lumbered slowly down the street, down the hill, and then over to the bridge crossing Sixteen Mile Creek. My thoughts were all over the place as I approached the bridge. Although I had been planning for the event and had dreamed of the release I would get from ending all of my pain, I hadn't ever thought through the very act itself, the climbing up, the pushing off, and the letting go.

I crawled up and balanced myself on the guardrail, which was in itself a most indelicate act given my size. I imagine that it would have been amusing to watch but for the fact that I was in the process of killing myself.

As I looked down, I did indeed feel the anticipated rush of freedom. It was so close to being all over.

Freedom.

I was as lost as I could possibly be, desperate, hopeless, believing I had no other way out. I sat there rocking back and forth on the rail, considering the pros and cons of life. I sat there for hours. It was a beautiful night, the trees dark against the night sky. I was as awed by nature's beauty that night as I had been awed by the Princeton campus. Memories flowed, memories of dreams, of laughs, of joyful moments. Then reminders of the horrible moments, dark moments, where life failed to have meaning. Back and forth, in my head, my life played out before me. Great memories, phenomenal memories, then crushing defeats, moments of having been shunned, shamed, of having lost at life. Life's great pageant played out upon the midnight sky of my mind while death beckoned below me, not for the first time, but this time more loudly than ever before.

And then suddenly, a moment of clarity. One so intense that it was, as it had been with the one I had at Princeton, as if I were separate from my body. A wave of emotion grabbed me and focused me on one thing and one thing only. I needed to live. I took one long last look at my world, at my life, at my past, at the abuse, and at what had become of me. I cried even more deeply than I had after first being abused. And in crying so hard I realized something very important. I still wanted to live, to live my life, but not the life I had been leading. I had lost track of what it meant to live and be me. I had no idea who I was anymore. I wanted to live so that I could find out who I was, I needed to find out who I really was. I was able to choose life over death because I could see that in spite of it all there remained something in my life that needed to be developed, nurtured, coddled, and loved. In many ways I had stopped growing and living all those years ago when the abuse first happened. I needed to meet, understand, and accept myself and then bring myself back to life. In effect, I had to bring another human being into this world, teach him all of life's important lessons, provide him with all of the support necessary to sustain him against outside threats. I had a reason to live—to love this other person—this new me—as much as possible.

I slid off the rail and crawled back to a safe spot. I sat there for a while and then walked home and went to bed, exhausted. I felt no sense of salvation. I felt only that I'd failed. I had lacked the courage to jump, had added one more failure to my long list of failures, displayed my weakness and my unworthiness again. But those feelings gave way to an incontrovertible awareness that I had made a choice. I had chosen life over death.

I PROMISED MYSELF that things would be different this time. I was prepared to confront my past head on. I would tell those closest to me. I would seek out help. I had something in my corner even stronger than me. I had something to live for, this newfound me.

I prepared to explain to those closest to me all about who I was and what had happened to me. I hoped they would understand. After all, they had seen firsthand the tensions at play within me, my unexplainable behavior. They must have suspected something like this. But not everyone was prepared for what they were about to hear. One of the first I told was stunned.

"I've got something I need to tell you, no, something that I want to tell you."

"What is it?"

"Well, I, uh, it's like this..."

I dove in and described all about what had happened to me and how it had affected me. I made clear that I knew I needed to get help.

First there was shock, then confusion. After an awkward silence, the first words in response were, "That's a little old to be abused, isn't it?" Our conversation was effectively over. That response caused even more pain for me, and to this day I don't believe that the person understands the pain that the response caused. To me it seemed that the person saw me as being broken, defective. Instead of being a first step to recovery, coming forward had just reinforced all of the internal questions and self-doubts I had carried with me for so many years. Coming so soon in my process of coming forward, it was like being immediately slapped back into the past. Maybe I was broken and defective. Maybe I was wrong to try to confront my past.

At the same time as I was coming forward about my past, my marriage was increasingly falling apart. I had let down my wife, and my inability to be all that I had appeared to be had no doubt disappointed her. My failure to address my past had left me as emotionally unavailable and prone to self-destruction as I had been before I had met my wife.

With everything crumbling around me, with me coming forward it not going as well as I had hoped, I worried that I might again be tempted to kill myself. I knew I had to keep moving forward.

I contacted a medical doctor from my past, a friend in Toronto whose old-style family practice meant that he worked virtually around the clock with a packed office. The day I showed up to see him was no different—his waiting room was full of patients. He called me in, we chatted briefly, and he clearly realized that whatever I wanted to talk about was serious. He sent all the other patients home, and we spent the remainder of the day talking.

This time things went far better than I could ever have hoped. Dr. David Greenberg saved my life that day.

Speaking with Dr. Greenberg made subsequent disclosures easier. When I later revealed my sexual abuse to my brother, my sister, and my mother, all were supportive. I was surprised to discover just how much I was loved. Even my mom was there for me, as much as she could be.

As for my wife, our relationship had become increasingly difficult long before I finally got around to telling her my secret.

———

DR. GAEL MACPHERSON'S OFFICE was on the third floor of a medical building in Oakville. It had a slow-moving elevator that took more time to get to the third floor than it would have taken for me to walk up the stairs, which I could never seem to find. The carpeting in the building was bland, the paint was bland, and the whole place smelled of disinfectant cleaning supplies, typical of a building dedicated to dealing with the diseased. But when I entered the doctor's office, I stepped into a different world, one of color, warmth, and nurturing.

I sat down in the waiting room Dr. MacPherson shared with another doctor. There were reading materials for patients of all ages, toys to be played with by bored children. My first decision of the day: do I go with adult reading material or children's toys?

When I called to make my appointment I had not mentioned sexual abuse. I had said that I wanted to become a better partner in my relationship. I wasn't able to just walk into a therapist's office and start spilling my innermost secrets. I, a person who trusted nobody, needed to find someone I could trust to help me.

About five minutes in, I sensed that Dr. MacPherson was going to be somebody I could trust, but even then it seemed premature to get into anything of substance. Almost at the end of our hour-long session, almost as if it were a teaser of sorts, I let her in on why I was really there: "But the thing is, if we're going to get anywhere in figuring me out, we're probably going to have to talk about the years I was sexually abused when I was a kid."

After a slight pause, she slowly and clearly responded: "Yes. I think that would be a very good idea."

I got up, put on my jacket, and asked if I could see her the following week at the same time. Without batting an eye, she said, "Of course." I knew that she knew that was the real reason I was there.

At the same time, I was also continuing treatment with Dr. Greenberg, who was introducing antidepressants and other medication to bring me into a more engaged and responsive state. To me, accepting medication carried a stigma, even though I was deeply depressed and struggling to recover. Through proper treatment coupled with psychoanalysis, I have become a convert, but I initially struggled very hard to accept medical intervention in addition to psychoanalysis.

And so, not that long after the night on the bridge, I had, just like that, assembled the makings of a team that would work to support me in my recovery. I had my psychologist and my medical doctor. A psychiatrist would be added later.

I could only ask myself why I had waited so long to get the treatment I so badly needed. I had to keep reminding myself, and my doctors had to keep reminding me, that it wasn't as if I had ever rejected treatment. I had simply been unable to assess and accept that I both needed treatment and, more importantly, deserved treatment and recovery, a better life. For me to see that I deserved a better life, I needed to accept that what had happened to me wasn't my fault, that I was a victim, and that I was now choosing to be a survivor.

I struggled over the fact that I had voluntarily gone back to him time and time again for something I thought I should have been able to control outright. The grooming didn't make sense, the abuse didn't make sense, and my life thereafter didn't make sense. It was embarrassing for me to admit weakness, to admit that it had all happened, that I had succumbed to him and his advances, and yet somehow had been rendered powerless in the face of his actions. It just didn't make sense to me. And because it didn't make sense to me, I had assumed it wouldn't make sense to anyone else either.

———————————

"DO YOU WANT to tell me more about it?"

"Not really, Gael, not yet."

All I could think about, as I wondered what I could say and when I could say it, were his eyes.

His picture is in the media more than you might think. Whenever I see him in a media report it looks like he's trying to hide. He turns away from the cameras, sometimes covering his face by pulling a scarf up or a hat down, or by sticking a hand out in front of a camera. But look again. He looks like he's trying to hide, but he never really succeeds, because a part of him, even now, wants to be a star, a celebrity. He can't resist being the center of attention. He can't look away from the cameras, from the limelight, and so we see his eyes one more time. I see his eyes. I see them over and over again. I see them even when I don't see them.

Take a good look at his eyes. His eyes, those eyes, look right at you through the camera. Or maybe they don't. Maybe you see his eyes the way he wants you to see them, the eyes of a nice man, a helping man, the eyes of a caring mentor, the eyes of a good man who can be trusted, the eyes of a man who surely through no fault of his own finds himself in a situation he never intended, the eyes of a man who is just a bit misunderstood, the eyes of a man who could contribute so much if only he could put this bit of trouble behind him.

I saw his eyes like that right up until that first night it happened. I saw all of the good in him that he wanted me to believe was there through those eyes. Until then, his eyes had been eyes that would reflect upon me my future dreams for myself, eyes that could see what was best for me, eyes that would search out a path for me that would bring me all of my dreams and everything I had ever wanted. His eyes reflected the best me that I could be while showing a kindness and concern for me that I had never seen before.

But look again at those eyes, just a little more closely this time and imagine them behind closed doors. Now they no longer reflect anything back at you, now they absorb all light coming their way, dead black eyes sucking the light, the life, out of everything before them. Eyes that take whatever they want without discretion. Eyes that grab and bite and suck to feed the hunter within. Imagine those eyes on you, covering you, locking in on you, taking you in. Imagine those eyes on you, getting closer and closer as the hunter hunts its prey, as the shark feeds itself what it needs to live in the frenzy of the kill.

"Maybe next week, OK?"

"OK, Greg, that's OK. Whenever you're ready."

RECOVERY DOESN'T HAPPEN just because you finally decide that you want to recover. There's no magic wand that can be waved to make everything go away. Instead, in session after session with my therapist, we would discuss what I was doing on a daily basis simply to keep going.

At the outset of therapy I was still married, and I was still working and had a significant amount of responsibility at the company. On top of all that, I was supposed to be rebuilding myself and everything that had gone into shaping who I had been during the past decades. That's a lot to have on your to-do list.

My wife and I separated within a year of my seeking help. We finalized our divorce as quickly as possible.

Even if Dr. MacPherson and I just talked about nothing, we were talking about something important, because talking to her helped me establish trust with her. Trust, something I had been incapable of ever since the abuse, was the first goal. I had to find a safe place, something, somebody, I could trust.

Some days were better than others. I worked hard every day to follow up on what I had discussed in psychoanalysis that week. I was diligent about taking my medicine. I had done as much as I could within a crumbling marriage, but now I was on my own. I continued to work long hours at the office as we fought through the acquisition of a major competitor and attempted to integrate it successfully into our operation.

I discovered that I was not equipped to deal with all of this at the same time, and the positives to be taken from instigating a formal recovery process were often negated by the stresses of everyday life. This reinforced the doubts I had about myself while confirming everything I had been carrying with me since the abuse. It was not long before I gradually began to shut down under the weight of it all. I binged and purged increasingly at night, my weight fluctuated wildly, and I was digging into my body again, ripping at my toenails.

Yet unlike before, now I had hope. I knew I had to continue to recover, that there was no alternative this time. Even if it was one step forward, two steps back, I had to at least keep moving, because I knew what awaited me if I didn't. And that was a bridge I never wanted to cross again.

NOT EVERY DOCTOR or every therapist is right for every victim. Much later, after my story had become more widely known, I was referred to a psychiatrist who heads up the psychiatric department at a major downtown Canadian hospital.

She was far more aggressive than my other doctors had been. She questioned every answer I gave to her questions and challenged me on everything I said. This wasn't therapy, this was a debate, and I found it very difficult to open up to her. She was, to be blunt, very blunt. And while she was extremely off-putting given where I was at in my recovery, and while I thought she thought I was wasting her time, she did show great interest in me and my medical case. Our sessions continued, though I was reluctant to discuss in detail what I needed to discuss, as I was finding it virtually impossible to get out of bed and face the day and had yet to establish a relationship of trust with her. I was clearly frustrating her, and my guess is she was doing what she thought best to rejuvenate me.

She was also aware of the notoriety of my case, and one day she asked me if we could have our next session in front of other doctors and students in her group. They would watch from a room next door through a one-way mirror and could use our session as a learning experience. "Fine by me," I said.

Our next session was held not in her office but in a larger, nicely appointed room. We sat on plush chairs, with flowers on the table between us and a one-way mirror behind us. And just as the setting had changed, so had she. Gone was the aggressive, almost terrifying psychiatrist I had been dealing with. Here instead was the nicest, most respectful person you could imagine. It was jarring. What happened to the frustrated, almost dismissive psychiatrist who thought that I was wasting her time? Oh wait, I get it. There was an audience. I suspected that she couldn't approach me in the same manner as she did behind closed doors. She seemed to me to be using me and the notoriety of my situation to attract interest in her teaching methods. But she was treating me very differently from how she had treated me when we were alone in her office.

Like other victims of child sexual assault, I believe I have been used and discarded as somebody else's garbage, and I never want to be used again. I resent anybody who takes advantage of me, though I often still comply with them. That's what victims do; that's our learned behavior. All I could think was that she was using me for her own advantage, and I decided that I would take a stand.

As our session continued, I acted as if I were engaged, but mentally I had checked out. We went back and forth, seemingly making progress, until she asked me what I thought I needed most to move on to the next level of my recovery. That was my chance.

"Supermodel dog walkers," I answered.

"What?"

"Supermodel dog walkers. Think about it. I am severely depressed and am having trouble finding meaning in life. If I could have a group of supermodel dog walkers show up at my front door several times a day to walk me instead of a dog, I'd be cured. I'd be motivated to wake up and get out of bed, because who doesn't want to hang around with a group of supermodels? And I'd have great incentive to re-engage in life, because who doesn't want to impress supermodels? And not being in shape, I'd have to get in shape, because right now I'm clearly not attractive to any supermodels. So, supermodel dog walkers. I think that would help."

All I could hear was laughter through the one-way mirror from the supposedly soundproof viewing room adjacent to us.

THE MORE I dealt with the abuse, the easier it became for me to explain what was going on behind the scenes. Still, there is a stigma around mental health issues. From the moment I came forward at work about what I was dealing with, things were never really the same, although I was extremely lucky to have an employer I could speak to about it all. I'll always be thankful to Michael Hirsh (and the rest at Cookie Jar Entertainment, but especially to Michael) for all that he did for me. Although we had many successes together, he deserved better than I was able to offer him at the time, and I know that I'm lucky to have had his presence in my life.

Recovery can often be one step forward, two steps back. But you simply cannot give up. Failure along the way is an essential part of recovery. Sheldon Kennedy describes his own recovery as truly kicking in only after he had failed about seven times in rehab. And Sheldon is no failure.

Initially, I believed that I would be able to make the past evaporate. I believed that my running away from Graham was itself a type of recovery that I had been doing on my own. What I came to see was that pushing the past down while internalizing guilt, responsibility, and shame was only creating a greater problem as I myself became an even worse abuser than Graham had ever been.

TO OPEN UP in therapy is to begin a new life, one that requires trust. You have to trust your therapist or you will be unable to share everything about yourself, and if you can't share completely, the therapy will be of little use. Therapy requires a completely honest and open subject. It took me some time, but, unlike with my psychiatrist and the supermodels, I was getting there with my psychologist, and I was able to find out more about myself and how the process of abuse had operated and controlled me.

So, with that understanding, things should have started moving quickly, right?

That is, apparently, what many people think. "Just get over it," they say. "You need to move on and put it behind you. The sooner you just start living your life, the better things will be for you."

I desperately wanted to just get over it, to just move on and put it behind me, to just start living a life. It's the obvious first answer, and something I had been telling myself for decades. So many told me to do just this, thinking they were helping, but it was so hurtful to hear it, as if people thought that I hadn't been trying to move on, that I didn't already know that I should be trying to do that. I didn't need to be told that I needed to move on, I needed to figure out why I couldn't.

In therapy we used the words *victim* and *survivor*, and I use both here. I do not want to pressure anybody who has suffered sexual abuse into thinking they have survived anything if they don't yet feel ready to think that way while their struggle to recover continues. I do not use *victim* to stigmatize anybody who has suffered from sexual abuse. I use it to provide comfort to those who do not yet feel—and believe—they are survivors.

THE PAIN THAT goes on inside a "broken" brain can be devastating.

*I ache to be understood. I want to be appreciated. I need to be helped.
I love to be loved in spite of having done everything in my power to
make myself unlovable. I desperately want to live a normal life. But I
know I'm letting others down. I know I'm hurting the ones I love most.*

Hurting the ones you love and need the most makes everything worse, so you think even less of yourself, so you hate
yourself more, so you have even less desire to interact with the
outside world. Having commenced therapy, I was now on a downward spiral. I had alienated many friends over the years, especially
following my inability to come forward after Sheldon had. I repeatedly made plans and then canceled, not because I didn't want to
be with others, but because I couldn't leave the house because of
my panic and fears of self-doubt. My friends initially referred to
me as "Gil No-Show" until they just stopped referring to me at
all. I missed them more than ever, I needed them more than ever,
but all I had ever done was put up walls between us, effectively
shutting them out of my life.

In my mind, I was a unique patient with the most bizarre story
to tell, one nobody would ever understand. I'd believed for so long
that I had been suffering alone and in my own way, one nobody
else could ever possibly understand. Yet my doctors instantly
knew all about me, they were now telling me that my actions
during and ever since the abuse were virtually textbook, entirely
predictable, and easily understandable.

So, I wasn't unique. I was a victim like so many others, a survivor who had been strong enough to make it through and get to
the point where I could engage in recovery, a recovery that would
take time but that in the end might lead to an understanding that
would allow me to accept that I had been a victim and was now a
survivor. To my surprise, the doctors could explain me to myself.

It was readily apparent to my doctors that I was suffering
from extreme clinical depression, a common result of abuse. I

was also diagnosed with post-traumatic stress disorder (PTSD), an injury to the brain that negatively impacts the way in which the brain processes emotional responses and responds to stress. In my case, it arose from the intense stress inflicted on it by the abuse.

Slowly, we attempted to answer the questions in therapy, with the answers to the questions always leading to more questions. Going through therapy meant reliving the inner dialogue that had been playing in my head year after year after year.

Why couldn't I stop him?
Why did I keep going back to him?
Why can't I just get over it?

Except now there were people providing me with something other than my own twisted perspective.

Who were you before you met him?
Why do you think you first met with him?
Who was the adult with power back then?
Can't you see that you could never stop him?
Did you know that most victims like you suffer as you do?
Did you know that your self-abuse and destruction is perfectly textbook?
Do you know you're actually an amazing survivor?

It's easy to speak the words, quite another to live the answers. It's easy to research the issues and understand at an intellectual level how everything works. Living that new reality, however, is a different matter entirely.

Why can't I just move on?

I discovered early in my treatment that I may never truly understand how somebody seemingly so smart could have let the abuse happen and persist for so long. Despite the therapy, it still doesn't make sense.

I was starting to better understand that Graham held all the power, that he was lying and manipulating me when he said I was gay, that I kept going back to him because I didn't think I had a choice, that he was also the only person I had to talk to in my darkest moments, that he had me right where he wanted me—in awe of him.

I saw that although Graham had committed the abuse, I was left to punish myself for it. I had to forgive myself. My therapist assured me that cutting, bingeing, purging, and other forms of self-abuse are common among those who have been abused. They were ways of showing that I could and can do things in addition to what Graham wanted. They were also subliminal cries for help.

Being overweight is also common among those who been sexually abused as children because it makes us feel safe. This has been a big problem for me. My issues with body image and the association of physical fitness with danger has time and again left me grossly overweight and out of shape. After having tried so many ways to self-destruct, I found that not only did weight gain offer safety from abuse, it was also the best way to remove myself from the mainstream of society and find the ultimate self-destruction I had been seeking.

I've seen the world from the perspective of both a fit athlete and an overweight recluse who wants to dissolve into nothingness. Being overweight is without a doubt the most effective way to kill yourself without actually dying. Not dying in the physical sense, but in the way that the world looks at you, or rather doesn't. People look away. They don't want to see you. They make assumptions about your personality, about your character. You want to self-destruct? Put on weight.

That can be a problem in recovery. I have said for years that an alcoholic on his or her first day of AA presents to the outside world as a "normal" person. The morbidly obese person on his or her first day of recovery presents as, well, a morbidly obese person. For a person whose mental state is so fragile, who is in the midst of a reprogramming that will supposedly open up a new future, the mirror is an enemy. Even worse, while the plan is to re-emerge and once again live a real life, who wants to present to the world as somebody morbidly obese, who wants to make first impressions, or renewed impressions, as their very worst physical version of themselves?

I wanted to emerge, re-engage, and yet I also wanted to hide from view. And so, while I was in recovery, I reverted to old habits, old behaviors. I tried so hard to break the pattern, yet I was reminded of my past mistakes because I was still living them. One step forward, two steps back.

Through treatment I gained a new perspective on my failed relationships. I had to admit that it must be difficult to be in a relationship with someone like me who was dealing with what I was dealing with and who self-abuses and self-sabotages. I also had to admit that, because I believed that I didn't deserve to be with good people, I often ruined very good relationships with very good women.

I discovered that, because I had no sense of self and believed myself unworthy, I was actually more comfortable in situations that were bad for me than in ones that offered me the possibility of real success.

My healing began not all at once but with an odd good day among the usual bad days where all I could see was futility. Incrementally I was getting better, though it took a while before I could see it. It's a long road back. You don't just show up, have the carnage explained to you, and then say, "Well, I'm better now."

Nevertheless, I was on my way back when it happened once again. One evening in 2009, there on the television was a story that Theo Fleury, of the Calgary Flames, was retiring from hockey. Except it wasn't just the usual press conference announcing a retirement. He was also announcing that he had written a book detailing the sexual abuse he had suffered as a young hockey player at the hands of Graham James.

Graham's picture was once again all over the news. The same pictures, his dead shark eyes once again looking back at me.

But unlike the moment when Sheldon Kennedy came forward, I didn't bend over and throw up. It was jarring to see Graham's face again, but this time I was already dealing with him every day and in my weekly sessions.

I had gone to my doctors to fight for my future. In my mind, all I had ever wanted since that night on the bridge was to live again. I never thought of doing anything other than working hard, in private, to secure my own recovery.

I had regretted for years that I had not come forward when Sheldon had. I wasn't going to let anybody down this time, no matter how unready I may have been for what was about to follow.

My recovery was about to take a bit of a detour. This time I wasn't going to remain silent. This time I was going to stand up to him. This time I was going to take my power back and assert myself.

This time I was going to live again.

NINE

COMING FORWARD

HAD ALREADY BEEN in therapy for almost a year when Theo came forward publicly. Once again I was required to confront the reality that there was yet another victim who had come after me, another victim who wouldn't have been hurt had I stood up to Graham.

The timing couldn't have been worse. I was alone. While therapy had allowed me to manage the past on my own timeline, Graham's face was now everywhere pushing me to act, while deep down I knew that I wasn't yet strong enough and still wanted only someplace to hide.

Graham had long left the public eye, so the only pictures of him were from the past. They showed a pudgy, shortish, disheveled mess. Back then, I hadn't seen that. Back then, I had seen a powerful, intelligent man who held the key to everything I had ever dreamed of. The disconnect was startling.

The focus in therapy was for me to try to understand things from the viewpoint of the young boy who had first met Graham so that I could learn to forgive myself for what had happened and to understand that it wasn't my fault. This was very difficult now that

Theo had come forward, as I was caught up once again in blaming myself for what had happened to those who came after me.

But in contrast to when Sheldon came forward, I had now emerged from my night on the bridge and was in recovery, taking steps to become stronger.

I had always intended to conduct my recovery in private and just try to move on with my life. The thought of going to the police or anybody else about Graham wasn't ever on my radar. My only goal was to try to live again. However, after Theo came forward there were rumblings that a police investigation was underway and that new charges might be laid against Graham. This presented a new problem for me.

Recovery would be much more possible for me if I could work with my doctors and professionals without interference, on my own timeline, and in a way that respected my relative abilities at the time, given the inevitable ups and downs recovery involves. At the same time, I knew how damaging it had been for me when I didn't come forward when Sheldon had. There was no good option. I could either come forward and risk my recovery, or remain silent and risk becoming suicidal again.

After hearing that the Winnipeg police were investigating and considering what to do, both alone and in therapy, I made multiple tentative approaches to the police. I say "tentative" because, as with my experiences with a new doctor or therapist, I couldn't simply open up and discuss my innermost secrets with strangers until a certain trust had first developed. My initial approach was less than direct, and I was nowhere near strong enough to think that I would be believed. I went back and forth with the police for a few months before I let them know that I was ready to come to Winnipeg and give them a formal statement.

While I was debating whether to make a formal statement to the police, I discovered that Graham had been pardoned by the National Parole Board of Canada. Pardon me? Yes, Graham, having received a ridiculously short jail sentence after Sheldon and the unnamed other had come forward, was now not only out of jail and a free man, but he had also received a pardon.

His pardon wasn't widely known and it didn't make sense. How could a sexual predator convicted of hundreds of individual sexual assaults ever receive a pardon? I was angry. I knew that if this was true, and if word of this ever got out, there would be immediate political fallout. How could a pardon for a convicted child sexual offender ever be considered just? I knew there would be enormous pressure on the government to make immediate changes to the law if the public ever learned of his pardon.

His pardon offended me to the core, so I wanted to come forward with my story. But I also knew that I was not ready to do that, that my recovery was still in its infancy. I started to regress. The situation was getting the better of me—until strength came to me from the strangest place.

Princeton's official motto is *Dei sub numine viget* (Under God's Power She Flourishes). I've never been religious (though I remain open-minded and support all who are, provided they respect all others' beliefs), and with the mention of "God" I had always looked past it while preferring the second, unofficial motto: In the Nation's Service. As I mulled over what to do next, for some strange reason that second, unofficial motto came to me over and over again. I have no idea why, given that the definitive article "the" likely meant it referred only to the U.S., but it gave me strength when I had none. I came to believe that I had to live up to it and come forward and tell about Graham's pardon and my abuse no matter how unprepared I was for whatever would follow.

Why did I happen to think of that unofficial Princeton motto just then? Well, maybe I was wrong about the official one. And, in another twist of fate, the unofficial motto was subsequently expanded to cover not just the U.S. but all of humanity.

I took a leap of faith and opened up to Gerry Arnold, a friend from the local Oakville minor hockey coaching world who held a senior position at the Canadian Press. He was both sympathetic and helpful and put me in touch with two writers. There was only one condition: I was to remain anonymous. I had no interest in ever going public with my name. I just wanted the story of Graham's pardon revealed. I did not wish to have anybody but close contacts ever know what had happened to me. Throughout the process, everybody at the Canadian Press was extremely diligent and respectful of me and my privacy.

I didn't want the government to be embarrassed or caught unawares by my disclosure of Graham's pardon. It would be best to bring the government up to speed so that it could respond in a proactive rather than reactive manner. I was not coming forward so that somebody could scoop anybody or make the government look good or bad. I was coming forward because I had discovered something that distressed me. I thought everybody should know about it so that the right thing could be done irrespective of political stripe. I was upset that Graham had been pardoned, and I wanted that corrected.

A former colleague from law school, Nigel Wright, was at that time Chief of Staff in the Prime Minister's Office. I gave him a heads-up as to what was about to happen. Nigel is a very good man, and I am proud to call him a friend.

I told my mom, brother, and sister what was going on. They responded perfectly, taking time to listen, saving questions that I know they must have had until later, when I would release more and more information to them slowly, over time, at my own pace.

The story of Graham's pardon and its impact would be told in reference to me as an unnamed victim. I was clear that I never wanted my name to be publicized in association with Graham. The story was simply to be that Graham James, my abuser, had been pardoned, and that he was out there, somewhere, living just like the rest of us, as if nothing had ever happened. Nobody seemed to know where he was. Nobody was shining a bright light on him.

That was about to change.

On Easter Sunday, April 4, 2010, the Canadian Press published a feature article written by Bruce Cheadle and Jim Bronskill. It was picked up nationwide and then internationally.

The article was explosive. It began:

> *Graham James, the junior coach convicted of sexually abusing his players in a case that rocked the hockey world from house leagues to the* NHL, *has been pardoned by the National Parole Board, The Canadian Press has learned. Though the pardon was granted three years ago, it comes to light only now as a result of a previously unknown accuser contacting Winnipeg police.*

The Prime Minister's Office was ready. The pardon was "a deeply troubling and gravely disturbing" development that demanded an explanation from the parole board. The Prime Minister, "while noting the independence of the parole board, expressed shock that the government is learning of the pardon only three years after the fact," and he "has asked for explanation on how the National Parole Board can pardon someone who committed such horrific crimes that remain shocking to all Canadians."

I, the anonymous victim, was very clear in my comments that the authors chose to quote in their article:

> *"To say that the parole-board process has been abused would be a grotesque understatement. Here you have an incredibly high-profile pedophile—and there's no other word to use to describe him—who clearly has not been able to take responsibility or show any accountability for his actions." The man said he considers the mere act of seeking a pardon as an illustration of Mr. James's absence of remorse. That it*

was granted, he said, is like a fresh wound. "I can't explain in words
the extent to which this just cuts right to the heart of the pain again, in
terms of who he is and what he did."

Graham's story was, of course, placed in its hockey context.
He had been "a smooth-talking, savvy rising star in the Prairie
coaching ranks of junior hockey when he committed the crimes
for which he's been pardoned." In 1983 (shortly after I had left
for Princeton), Graham had recruited "Fleury and Kennedy, both
of whom would go on to NHL careers." The piece reported that
Theo's recently released book relates that "James began molest-
ing him at age 14" and describes one "occasion when James
drove Kennedy and Fleury to Disneyland for a vacation, allegedly
assaulting the pair on alternate days."

Notwithstanding the hockey context, to me he was just my
abuser, no different from the all too many others out there you
never read about. His hockey story is fascinating, but he really was
nothing more than a previously convicted child sex offender being
called out once again for his sins.

———————

THE FALLOUT WAS predictable. The story of Graham's pardon
was on all the front pages, it was the lead story in all of the newscasts, and it was featured on all major sportscasts. Had I wanted
attention and fame, I could have put my name forward to claim
credit for disclosing the pardon and for allowing the government
to prepare itself for that disclosure. I could have taken some credit
for the eventual change in the applicable legislation and regula-
tions pertaining to pardons generally so that people like Graham
could never again receive one. But I wasn't doing any of this for
attention or fame. I was anonymous and wanted to remain that
way. I was already in therapy, I was already taking steps to get

better, and I knew that I still had a long, long way to go to get there, if I ever could get there. Coming forward anonymously was already so stressful that it was jeopardizing my very survival, let alone my recovery. It was unthinkable that I'd ever be able to go public.

But I also sensed that I was no longer running from him and that he could no longer run from the law.

———

THE STORY OF Graham's pardon kicked things into motion. While the police investigation continued with heightened energy, media outlets tried to find Graham. Born in Prince Edward Island, raised in Winnipeg, coached across western Canada, jailed and then released, tracked down coaching minor hockey (unbelievable, I know) in Spain, and then rumored to be living in Montreal—nobody really seemed to know where he was.

The CBC and the *Globe and Mail*, working together, eventually tracked him down in Guadalajara, Mexico, where an investigative journalist from the CBC's *The Fifth Estate* discovered him leaving his apartment, apparently for the first time in several days, to go to the laundromat.

Self-described Shakespearean expert and former Man of the Year as selected by *The Hockey News*? Out, damned laundry spots, out, I say.

The interview, conducted as they catch him on the street, is fascinating. Graham sort of pulls a hat down over his face, looking as if he's trying to conceal himself. He turns from the camera to hide, but it appears that the natural instincts of a practiced con-artist, a master manipulator, kick in. He continues to engage while trying to remain pleasant. He appears to be known in the community and responds to a local passing by. He doesn't run, and he doesn't keep his mouth shut. Being Graham, he cannot help himself, he must engage, he must try to win you over. Being Graham, he tries to be polite and charming.

Well, as polite and charming as a previously convicted serial child sexual predator found carrying his laundry to a laundromat in Guadalajara can be. Guadalajara has been reported as infamous in certain circles for its place in the world of pedophiles and hebephiles. The same has been said about Montreal. It's likely just a coincidence that Graham was said to be based in Montreal before leaving for Guadalajara and that he again lives in the Montreal area. But if it is a coincidence, it is one that any self-professed Shakespearean expert should be able to appreciate as divine.

That interview captures everything about him. Even when he has absolutely nothing going for him, he's still trying to win everyone over, still trying to let people know that he's just a good guy, that he really wishes he could talk, that he's very sorry the reporters came all that way to see him, but that they should contact his lawyer and he wishes he could talk but he can't, that he's very sorry for that, but do have a nice day now.

So says the pleasant man who brandished a weapon in front of young boys to scare them into silence about the sexual abuse he was inflicting on them, the nice man who taped over his windows so that nobody could look in and catch him performing his despicable sex acts on his victims.

Have a nice day.

BY AUGUST 2010, after months of dialogue with the police, and after working hard to prepare myself for the moment, I was finally ready to go to Winnipeg to give an official statement.

At least, I thought I was ready.

The night before my scheduled appointment, no matter how hard I tried, I couldn't fall asleep. My mind racing, I lay awake in my bed, thinking and worrying, unsure of how I would react, not knowing if I would be able to go through with it. Unable to sleep, yet craving at least a short nap, I left things until the last possible moment before I accepted failure and finally got out of bed, readied myself, and left for the airport to catch the morning flight to Winnipeg. Now grossly overweight, I was a sweaty, disheveled mess of a man, apprehensive and unsure of the day I had ahead of me.

The Winnipeg Police Department is located in a concrete bunker of a building deep within the city's core. It is not a warm and fuzzy place. The Public Safety Building, as it's named, has a heavy presence and in no way provides any feeling of safety. Instead, there is an overriding sense of power and control that saps the life from you. When I entered the building, my heart immediately sank as I confronted a very real fear that I would not be able to make it through my interview.

After checking in at the front desk and meeting the detectives who were responsible for the investigation, I was escorted up to an interview room. At least, I think we went up a level or two, as my recollections from that day are anything but clear. I was under so much stress that it was as if I were floating in a bubble, immune to the outside world.

I was left to myself in the interview room while the detectives prepared for what was about to take place. There was a couch for me to sit on along the wall opposite a one-way glass or mirror. I recall the mirror as being somewhat elevated so that people in the adjacent room could see me over the detective who would be interviewing me and who was sitting just below it. There was nothing on the walls and nothing in the room to occupy my attention but for a bottle of water the detectives had given me.

I'm a lawyer, but I'm a corporate lawyer, not a criminal lawyer. My only experience of being in a police station was when I'd toured one as a young kid in the Cubs or Boy Scouts, I can't

remember which. I'd never given a formal statement in anything other than civil litigation proceedings. This was a very new
experience. And although I couldn't see the camera through the
one-way mirror, I assumed that everything I did from the moment
I entered that room would be recorded. I was also aware that
anything that was recorded would at some point be available to
Graham and his lawyers. Knowing he would again be watching
me made me feel sick.

During my flight to Winnipeg I had made up my mind that I
was going to do my absolute best to ensure that at no point would
I display any sign of weakness to Graham. I was determined to
show him that I was not the victim he had last seen all those years
ago, but instead a survivor who was now capable of seeing this
process through to the end. I believed in my heart that Graham
would still see me as somebody weak and would assume that I
would quickly fall by the wayside should he put up any resistance
to my efforts to take back some of my power. I wanted to show
him he was wrong—but I was neither physically nor mentally at
my peak. No matter how hard I tried, he would still immediately
be able to see the mess that I was at that time.

In spite of that, I had to try not to let him think that he was still
getting the better of me. I had to at least try to show the best me
possible that day.

On entering the room, I did the only thing that I could think of
to look as blasé as possible while I was waiting for the interview to
start. I read the label on the water bottle. And then I read it again.
And again. And again. I tried my hardest to appear as if all that was
about to happen was not getting to me at all. I tried to appear calm
and collected in the face of the camera. I was virtually imploding
inside, but I didn't want him to see that. I didn't want anybody to
know that this ordeal was as traumatic as being abused itself.

I was sweaty. I was disheveled. My hair had not been cut for
months. I was wearing whatever limited clothes I had that would

fit me in my heavy, bloated state. I was not the athletic and academic star Graham had first encountered all those decades ago. I was a shell of a man who had been broken and who was trying to pick up the pieces while trying to hold onto whatever sense of self I still had, however little that was. And I had nothing to do but read the label on a water bottle.

And even after staring at that water bottle for what seemed an eternity, I couldn't tell you the color of the label, the brand of water I was drinking, the rough size of the bottle, or whether the water was warm or cold.

Stress does strange things to you.

Detective Ken Ehmann came into the room to start the interview. Having done my best to look as if I were completely calm, I immediately betrayed that false veneer by blurting out a question: "Should I look at you or look at the camera? I mean where should I look?"

Rookie error.

"Ignore the camera," he told me. "Just look at me."

I remember very little about the details of that interview except that time seemed to pass far more quickly than I had anticipated and that I answered the questions in a somewhat disassociated state. I sensed that I was trying to distance myself from the reality behind the answers to avoid breaking down. The answers were just words that masked all the pain from what I had endured so many years ago, nothing more than words.

I've never seen the tape of that interview, and I've never wanted to. Not only do I have no desire to see the bloated man I was at that time, but I'm also certain I wouldn't recognize myself or anything I said that day. To say that I was in a fog would be an understatement. I was there in that room and I was doing my best to convey as much information as possible in response to the questions presented to me, but in no way was I a fully functioning human being.

My recollection is that I was almost able to hold it together. It seemed to me that I was being responsive and coherent in my answers, for the most part, until a single simple question cut me to my soul. Detective Ehmann asked me a question, something simple:

"So, when was the last time he abused you?"

For the first time ever, it dawned on me that while I had always looked back on the abuse as having been something inflicted upon a boy, a young man, I had also been abused after my eighteenth birthday. I had been a man.

I immediately shut down. I was no longer there in the room but deep inside my mind, my memories, my assessment of my own self-worth. I had not once, ever, realized that I had been of legal age, a fully grown mature man of the age of majority, during my abuse. Had I blocked it out? Had I known but just pretended to myself otherwise? Had I just wished it all away?

I didn't know how to process that realization. For decades I had lived with my abuse, I had recently begun taking positive steps to recover, and there, in the midst of what should have been a bold statement of my newfound strength, everything was starting to fall apart again, right in front of him. A sound inside my head started pulsing through my ears, louder, rushing, roaring, until the question came again, with awful answers.

Who was I?
You were a man.
You weren't abused.
You were a man who consented.

I barely made it through the rest of the interview. I remember nodding in agreement to some questions, giving answers when asked, and being asked some questions after I thought the interview had ended and then answering them as we were leaving the room. But after that, I really don't remember thinking anything except that I just wanted to get back on a plane to fly home so that I could crawl into my bed and cry myself to sleep, a sleep where, if I was lucky, I'd be able to lose myself in dreams, but more likely a sleep that would hold the usual nightmares.

I just wanted it all to be over. Everything. Over.

The detectives walked me out of the building and we said our goodbyes. I held it together long enough to walk around the corner out of their sight. Then I fell to the ground, exhausted, tears in my eyes, knowing in my heart that I had failed in my attempt to show no weakness and stand up to Graham. He had beaten me one more time.

———————————

THE POLICE WERE interviewing others throughout the summer and into the fall. I was kept abreast of their investigation and told that there were follow-up questions for me. I knew that they were in discussions with the Crown prosecutors and that it seemed certain that Graham would at some point be charged. But victims are nothing more than witnesses in the judicial process. I had no formal place and was not formally involved in anything to do with charging Graham. All I did was tell my story and give my evidence. Beyond that, I was nothing, nobody.

It was a complete surprise to me when, one night in October 2010 when I'd gone back to pick up mail at my ex-wife's house— my former house and the last residence I had been linked to in publicly available records—I was met with the news that members of the media had been calling there. They had been trying to reach me to get my comments on the news that Graham James had been formally charged for his abuse of Theo Fleury and two other victims whose names were protected by a media publication ban. They knew I was one of those victims.

Victims can have the courts place a ban on the publication of their names. But anybody can go down to the court offices and find out who the victims are. The media are required to protect your anonymity, and they will. But they will also know who you are.

It was a most unfortunate way to find out about what was happening.

GRAHAM, STILL IN Mexico, had been formally charged. He agreed to return voluntarily for his bail hearing. He did everything in his power to present himself as a helpful accused. His lawyers pointed out to the court that he could have resisted and forced the Canadian government to extradite him back to Canada to face the charges. Because of his voluntary return, because he had no record of reoffending since his previous jail term, and because he had fulfilled all the conditions of his earlier release from jail, Graham was granted bail.

Our legal system doled out a gold star to a previously convicted serial child sexual predator who had agreed to come back and show up in court on more charges. Oh, to be back in my first-year criminal law class.

And so the legal game commenced.

The decision to grant bail facilitated all the posturing and positioning that would take place over the next thirteen months. That decision to grant bail seemed to most to be something innocuous. Frustrating, yes, but just a minor blip in the face of a proper and just system that worked for most. Who could object to a system that rewarded an accused for good behavior, that saved the citizenry the time and expense of having to bring him back under duress?

Except we were dealing with a previously convicted child sexual predator.

So what? you might say. Surely our system should not presuppose anything. Surely our system should afford the accused as much justice as it would anybody picked up for the first time. Surely it would be both unwise and improper to keep the accused behind bars pending trial after he had gone to the effort of coming back voluntarily. Further, wouldn't it be wrong to hold the accused's past against him, given that he hasn't reoffended and thus clearly poses no risk to society at large? Surely only a Neanderthal would insist that we put Mr. James back behind bars pending his trial, right?

That's all well and good in a classroom. And it may even be appropriate in the world in which we live for most charges an accused may face. But by not looking into things a bit more deeply beyond those theoretical presumptions, several important concepts were missed.

First, all we can ever know is whether Graham has or hasn't *been convicted* for reoffending, not whether he has or hasn't ever reoffended in the community. The legal system can't ever see what happens outside the courtroom.

Second, in letting a previously convicted serial child sexual predator out on bail, the system left itself at the mercy of the accused giving up the only leverage it may have had by having him in jail while he decided what he was and was not willing to plead to.

Absent a confession by the accused, how could anyone ever prove beyond a reasonable doubt a sexual assault that is decades old? There may be little or no physical evidence. Witnesses? People around Graham who may have known of a relationship between the accused and the victims may themselves be victims, and the Crown does not like to compel victims of sexual assault to testify. Further, it's not as if anybody actually witnessed the assaults. Would the Crown ever take these charges to trial? The Crown knows how difficult it is to prove allegations beyond a reasonable doubt on only "he said, she said" evidence at the best of times. Given no physical evidence, no witnesses, and the extensive time that had passed since the alleged assaults had taken place, "difficult" was now looking highly unlikely.

The only leverage the Crown would ever have had (and it would have been limited leverage at that) would have been if the court had denied Graham bail and had he been placed immediately behind bars pending trial or resolution of the matter. In granting Graham bail, the court left him free to come and go as he pleased until the Crown either accepted or rejected whatever he was and wasn't willing to plead guilty to. Unless, of course, the Crown decided to call his bluff and take matters to trial—but again, highly unlikely. The Crown didn't even have this limited leverage.

The prosecution knew this going in. The Crown fought as hard as it could for months. During that period, the three of us whose complaints had led to the charges against Graham were kept abreast of matters in general terms, but not in any specific detail. At one point the Winnipeg police called and asked me to provide pictures of myself from those days, which the Crown would deliver to Graham and his lawyers. I did as requested, but I think it was lost on all involved what was happening. Although the photos might have helped in the proceedings against Graham, I was providing pictures of myself that I knew my abuser and his lawyers would look at, pictures of me as I was back then. I scanned and sent the pictures. And then, in what was becoming a familiar refrain, I bent over and started throwing up into my office wastebasket.

In the end, the Crown realized it could only do so much in the face of Graham's willingness to plead guilty to only two of three charges. On December 7, 2011, the Crown formally accepted Graham's guilty plea on the charges in respect of Theo Fleury and the then-still-anonymous Todd Holt, while staying the charges in respect of the third complainant, me. A stay effectively means a halted prosecution, with the Crown agreeing not to move forward absent egregious action by the accused.

The agreement between the Crown and the accused was entered into court. Graham was ordered to attend court in person on February 22, 2012, at which time both the Crown and Graham's lawyers would make submissions to a judge regarding what each believed would be an appropriate sentence in the circumstances. The judge would hear those submissions and make a decision. Done deal.

The lawyer in me reluctantly agreed with the Crown's conclusion that accepting Graham's plea on only two of the charges and not fighting any further on the third was prudent. This would secure immediate convictions and avoid a trial, and there was no guarantee a third conviction would bring about any materially longer sentence for Graham beyond what he would get for the two convictions. Real life isn't like television, where justice is served up in an hour. Trials are ugly and uncertain. Sexual assault trials can be the ugliest and most uncertain of all.

As a lawyer, I understood the Crown's acceptance of Graham's limited plea, but as a victim, I was devastated. After all the pain of coming forward, I had now been dismissed from the process and rendered nothing and nobody simply because he'd decided he wouldn't plead guilty to my charges. That's no fault of the Crown, that's just the way things work. But all lawyers, prosecutors, judges—anybody involved in the legal system—should remember that just because something makes sense as part of the legal system doesn't mean it actually makes sense. Once you focus only on the legal system, you lose your connection with the real world in which we live.

From that day forward, Graham, his lawyers, and any future lawyers he may ever need, could speak as if I didn't exist. If any further victims came forward (and they eventually did), it would be as if I had never existed. It would appear as if Graham had admitted to all of his victims.

Once again, Graham had won. I was never going to get anything remotely touching on justice. Not only had he defeated me, but this time he had absolutely destroyed me. Once again, I was nobody.

My guess is that Graham thought he would never hear my name ever again. At one time he would have been absolutely right. But no more. Enough was finally enough, and I was not going to let Graham have this one last victory over me. I advised the Crown that, at the same time as the guilty pleas that Graham had agreed to were announced and entered into court, the Crown was authorized to release my name publicly as the victim whose charges had been stayed.

I may still have been nobody, but I would be anonymous no longer.

TEN

JUSTICE FOR NONE

"This is a complete gong show."
　　—(Whispered to me during court proceedings.)

Y OU DON'T HAVE to be a lawyer to perfectly understand legal proceedings.

GRAHAM'S SENTENCING HEARING was set for the morning of February 22, 2012. Even though my charges had been stayed, I wasn't going to miss it.

Nor would I be entirely silent. After my name became public, Roy MacGregor of the *Globe and Mail* gave me a voice, writing a feature story about me that included the victim impact statement I would have read at the sentencing hearing had I still been a part of the process. My statement may not have been delivered in a court of law, but it was delivered to a far more important audience: the public.

This court appearance, now his second for sexual assault, had always been Graham's ultimate destiny, the realization of his true self. His defining moment wasn't ever going to be achieving coaching greatness, hoisting the Stanley Cup, basking in the glory of having revolutionized the sport of hockey, or winning accolades for developing boys into men. No, it was always Graham's destiny to be in court as a convicted serial child sexual predator facing sentencing, this time with the Honorable Justice Catherine Carlson presiding, in Winnipeg, my hometown, the place where I had grown up, the place where it had all happened.

Me? I was there to bear witness.

ROD PERTSON, AND Brent Littlejohn, friends I'd played hockey with while growing up, had traveled to Winnipeg to support me and make sure I wouldn't be alone, and I met both Sheldon Kennedy and Todd Holt for the first time. I'd exchanged emails with both and had spoken with both on the phone, but it was my first chance to see them and look into their eyes. Their eyes reminded me of my own, the ones I see whenever I find the courage to not look at away and instead glance at myself in the mirror. They are eyes that are just a little distant, eyes that have seen just a bit too much, that are just a little sad.

Todd had decided to release his name from the publication ban, and he was about to encounter the public glare that went along with that. Theo Fleury chose not to attend and instead read his victim impact statement at a media conference in a show of strength while also sending a message that he had moved on far beyond Graham's influence on him. Different people react differently, and I commend Theo for the strong messages he delivered that day both in his statement and in the symbolic distance he put between himself and Graham. To this day I have never met Theo, though he has provided much emotional support to me via text and phone.

The four of us, and the unnamed other victims out there, are all very different. We have all reacted differently. We will all have different paths forward. I like to think we have all survived. Except I can't say that with certainty.

THE LAW COURTS Building in Winnipeg is an amalgam of old and new. In the small plaza that fronts onto the modern entrance that has been tacked onto a historical building of some note, there is a large, abstract sculpture made of polished steel that, depending on who you talk to, represents a bison (the symbol for the province of Manitoba), a mosquito (Manitoba's quasi-official bird), or the scales of justice. I'm going with the scales of justice, and I applaud the sculptor for either his sense of irony (like justice in all matters pertaining to Graham James, the sculpture is absolutely indecipherable) or acute social commentary.

Because of Graham's notoriety, the hearing was to take place in the largest courtroom, located in the older part of the building, a courtroom constructed back when justice was a grand concept and no expense was spared to give the judicial process a level of gravitas it seemingly deserved. The courtroom had high ceilings and decorated arches, with grand sculptures and artwork on both the walls and the ceiling. It featured a large gallery for visitors, a carved wooden bar to be passed only by those called, and an elevated bench from which a judge presided. Contrasted with the courtrooms of today—tiny hovels lit with fluorescent light that reflect the industrial process that modern justice has become—the grand courtroom was glorious. Yet it was in stark contrast to the justice actually now being doled out, a justice more akin to the manufacturing of a low-grade appliance produced on a barely functioning assembly line staffed mostly by machines, with whatever grossly overworked, overstretched workers were still left on the job wondering why anybody would even care about the crappy product being produced in the first place.

The grand, more traditional setting was enough to take you back to a different time and almost, just almost, make you forget that judges are only real people too, and that nobody holds the absolute truth or all the correct answers.

I KNEW I would be in for a rough day. It would be the first time in decades that I'd see Graham in person, for he too would be in the courtroom. I hadn't seen him in more than thirty years. A virtual lifetime had passed since then. Walking into the Law Courts Building amidst the media frenzy outside, I could think of only one thing:

I should have put him, put all of this, behind me years ago.

Should have, should have, should have. There I was again, beating myself up over something I had tried so hard to succeed at over and over again only to fail at over and over again. I was thirty years removed from the abuse. I lived far away from him in a modest, safe house in a modest, safe neighborhood in a modest, safe suburb just outside of Toronto. Everything in my life was safe. All that was unsafe was far in the past. Except it wasn't. And it still isn't.

I'd promised myself that I would look him straight in the eye and let him know by my very presence that I was still alive, that I was still fighting, and that I had never deserved what he had done to me. I was going to stare down all of it—the abuse, the pain, the failure, the self-harm, the self-sabotage. I wanted to look into those dead shark eyes of his and let him know I was still alive and kicking.

Graham and his lawyers had been granted early access to the courtroom, so he was already in the room by the time the rest of us entered through the public entrance toward the back of the room. He was seated at the defense table in front of the viewing gallery, facing forward, but looking down, as if he were staring at his shoelaces. We were only able to see him from behind and so we couldn't see his face or any emotion he might be showing. It was clear that he was doing whatever he could to make himself look invisible, humble, small, inoffensive, and certainly no threat to anybody. I couldn't stare him down.

However little we could see of him, his looks were still shocking. It was only natural that he would have aged dramatically over the thirty years since I had last seen him. But it was his presence, or lack thereof, that startled me. He had lost so much weight and looked so small, so insignificant, a shell of his former self. I didn't really believe that I was looking at my abuser. It was as if I were looking at a complete stranger.

Except he was, still is, and always will be Graham James and all that is tied to that name. Even if he now goes by Michael, his middle name. Michael James is Graham James.

Michael was also my father's name.

"ALL RISE FOR the Honorable Justice Catherine Carlson."

I kept looking at him from my seat behind him, hoping that at some point he would turn around and look back, affording me a chance to stare right back at him. He never did, coward that he is. He hid all day from me, from everybody but his lawyers and the judge, never daring to look our way.

Graham has never gone to trial on a question of guilt or innocence. He has always avoided trial by working out an acceptable
guilty plea with the prosecution to avoid one. His only appearances in court have been for sentencing. Sentencing hearings are
not trials but are where the appropriate punishment for the crime
is determined. Graham has always avoided any detailed public
presentation of the facts and evidence against him.

At a sentencing hearing, the prosecution and defense each
attempt to describe the offenses in general terms, they each
review the sentencing law and precedent they see as applicable to
such offenses, and they each then attempt to define for the judge
why the sentence they are proposing is appropriate in the circumstances. The prosecution goes first, followed by the defense.
There is no direct testimony on any of the details, as guilt has
already been established.

Colleen McDuff was the lead prosecuting attorney on this
matter. She ably presented the overview of the charges that had
been laid against Graham and for which he had been convicted.
She presented her analysis of the applicable law relating to appropriate sentencing for offenders for these crimes. The arguments
are legal ones, based upon an interpretation of both the *Criminal Code (Canada)* and sentences issued in previous sexual assault
cases that serve as precedent.

The prosecution represents no client. The prosecution's only
interest is to see that the law is properly applied. Crown prosecutors, the actual lawyers representing the state in its prosecution of
a criminal, do not represent the victims. They are only responsible
for upholding the law on behalf of the state. Victims give evidence
on behalf of the prosecution of the criminal, nothing more.

A defense lawyer, however, has a client and must give that client the best defense possible within the rules. A defense lawyer
presents both a legal argument as to appropriate sentencing and
a sympathetic explanation of the convicted's place within that

law, trying to show why the client is deserving of less punishment than the prosecution is seeking by positioning the client's crimes within the body of sentences previously handed out in similar situations. Graham's lawyer did what any defense lawyer would do—namely, attempt to present his client in the best light possible. He was just doing his job.

Still, it is hard as a victim to sit in court and watch a defense lawyer operate. I can never get that day back, nor will I ever be able to forget some of the things Graham's lawyer said in court that day. Though I have no animus toward Graham's lawyer, I do not believe it appropriate that he receive any recognition in my telling of my story, as his efforts that day did not aid in my recovery. Accordingly, I will not use his name here. At the same time, I want to be absolutely clear that he was just doing his job—one essential in our legal system—and he was doing it well.

The problem with our legal system is not that Graham was afforded a strong legal defense. The problem is that there are people who are prepared to listen to the defense and accept it as fact, forgetting that the submissions presenting Graham in the best possible light have never been tested, point by point, for truth. People confused Graham's sentencing hearing with a trial. It was nothing of the sort.

There are more problems with our legal system: a lack of sufficient appreciation for the atrocity that sexual assault is and the carnage it leaves with its victims; a shortage of understanding as to why victims may take so long to come forward and may be afraid to open up to the police; and often a failure to see how and why victims may try to cope with the abuse by suppressing detail or attempting to normalize the relationship with the abuser. All of these issues would soon be evident.

Most troublesome, however, were the potential sentences being debated. Graham's lawyer argued that Graham should serve only a conditional sentence of twelve to eighteen months, to be served in the community under supervision—this for the hundreds of individual acts of sexual abuse he had admitted to, never mind the abuse he had not admitted to with the stayed charges. To even think that such a proposal could be put before a judge was in my view simply incredible—and I am lawyer. But it certainly did move the goalposts, because it left everybody hoping for a victory by the prosecution, which was seeking a jail term of six years.

In the United States, when a sexual predator such as Jerry Sandusky, assistant coach for the Penn State football team, is found to have sexually abused a number of boys and young men, he goes to jail for the rest of his life. That's just the way it is. It seems fair. It's not seen as vengeance, but as something right, just, and appropriate. In Canada, the prosecution was seeking a further six years in addition to time already served on Graham's previous conviction.

I'd like to think there might be a happy medium somewhere in between. Then again, I also believe that Jerry Sandusky got exactly what he deserved.

GRAHAM'S LAWYER PRESENTED him as an ideal product of the correctional system.

After all, as his lawyer set out, Graham, previously convicted for hundreds of individual sexual assaults, had participated in rehabilitation programs during his incarceration. He had taken steps to understand more about himself, and he had come to learn more about his earlier mistaken understanding of having thought that his victims had consented. He had once thought that consensual sex with underage boys was natural and that he had not done anything wrong. Now, having learned more, now understanding he had been wrong about their consent, now understanding that his sexual pursuit of underage boys was wrong, he was, well, rehabilitated. He had not reoffended, and he would never, ever, ever reoffend again.

It wasn't that he had ever been a bad person, but simply that he'd never understood that what he'd been doing was wrong. Yes, these were new offenses being presented in court, but they didn't relate to the man here today. This was all a remnant from his past life, the life before he had been successfully educated and rehabilitated.

Right.

Once again, that logical fallacy that the legal system skips over. All we could ever know was if Graham had or hadn't been subsequently convicted for reoffending, not if he had ever reoffended. Yet over and over again references were made to the "fact" that Graham had never reoffended.

This is of particular concern when looking at historical child sexual abuse. It can take years, if not decades, for victims to come forward. I did not go to the police for thirty years. How can we ever know what Graham did after his first stint in jail when the time between offense and reporting can be so long? Based on my own timeline of abuse and reporting, he could have reoffended in 2003 and we wouldn't find out about it until sometime around 2030.

Because a previously convicted abuser can never prove a negative (it's impossible for him to prove that he's never reoffended unless he has a recording of every minute of his life showing he hasn't reoffended), the legal system uses a shortcut and looks to whether the abuser has been subsequently *convicted* for further crimes. There is a risk inherent in not being aware of a possible time lag in reporting offenses. The system, while it should certainly take note of a lack of subsequent convictions, should under no circumstances ever see rehabilitation as a "fact."

GRAHAM'S LAWYER TRIED to present Graham as a man who was far better than the public understood, a man who had been wrongly and unfairly seen as being worse than he truly was. He went all in to tug at the heartstrings right from the start. From the transcripts of that day:

> *I want to share with you the man, because with the greatest of respect,*
> *having sat here all day and having been Mr. James's counsel for some*
> *two years now or so, I can tell you it's like representing young women*
> *in Salem, Massachusetts, centuries ago who had all been accused of*
> *being witches.*

The Salem Witch Trials are well known both historically and in literature for two reasons. First, those women accused of being witches, well, they were innocent. Second, there are no such things as witches.

Unfortunately for those of us living in the real world, there are such things as previously convicted serial child sexual predators, and Graham James had already admitted his guilt.

Graham's lawyer didn't stop there.

> *We can, if we choose to, look back at every action that an individual*
> *takes if we know that that person has committed acts of some crimi-*
> *nality and start tying all of those actions back to the criminality, if we*
> *choose to. You can make it seem sinister. You can hear the music in the*
> *background. But that doesn't make it so at the time.*

"Acts of some criminality"? Hundreds of sexual assaults already admitted to by Graham were "acts of some criminality"? The sexual assaults were far more than that. Plus, they had all required planning, preparation, and a grooming of the victims. Everything he did back then was indeed "sinister." And yes, there was always music playing in the background as he tried to muffle the sounds of his actions.

Graham's lawyer attempted to present Graham as a man who had done much for the betterment of the game of hockey.

Listening to him reminded me of the man I had first seen, the Graham who had done so much to achieve significant status in the Winnipeg hockey community.

Graham's lawyer noted that Graham had been a leading advocate against bullying and hazing in hockey. Great, except he left out that Graham was, at the same, doing things behind closed doors to young hockey players that made hazing rituals look trifling.

His lawyer touted all the steps Graham had taken to campaign against violence in hockey. Yet he conveniently left out that Graham had a previous conviction for assault, committed with a hockey stick. And he also left out that Graham had used a firearm to scare young victims into complying. I do not disagree that hockey can have a problem with violence, but I've never seen anybody bring a gun to a hockey fight.

Graham's lawyer noted that Graham crusaded against alcohol and tobacco use, and that Graham had his junior teams refuse sponsorships from such companies. However, he failed to mention that one of Graham's methods of securing compliance with his sexual wishes was to get us drunk, and he showed utter indifference when his victims got high or abused other substances.

Graham worked hard to make sure that people saw him as a progressive role model, but his private reality was dramatically different. Advocating against bullying and hazing, campaigning against violence in hockey, crusading against alcohol and tobacco use, his choices of causes to publicly champion were always diametrically opposed to the things he was actually doing or facilitating in his private life through his position in the hockey world. This was no coincidence. Those public causes gave him cover for his private deeds. Who would ever believe he was capable of doing the very things he stood against?

Astonishingly, Graham's lawyer pointed to an incident in which four of his players tragically died in a bus crash as an example of some good that Graham did:

[On December 30, 1988] the Swift Current Broncos were in their first season as a franchise. He was managing and coaching and they had a bus accident. Four players were killed including a 16-year-old. The coverage was extensive and it was a complete and utter tragedy. But he remembered thinking what if he hadn't banned beer from the bus and as pictures and photographers showed up there were cases of beer strewn about the crash site on the news? What if anybody suggested alcohol had been involved?

I am sure that the parents and loved ones of the deceased extend their heartfelt thanks to Graham James for having saved the Swift Current Broncos the potential embarrassment of alcohol having been involved in those deaths. I'm certain that the town of Swift Current credits Graham for its ability to retain its hockey franchise and thanks him for preventing any backlash that would have arisen had alcohol been seen at the scene of the accident.

Graham as hero of the tragic bus accident for having banned alcohol? That on its own is patently ridiculous and tells all you might ever need to know about Graham and how his mind operates, he being very much at the center of a Graham-centric universe. Yet, his lawyer left out an even more important point about the bus crash—that after the accident, Graham denied his players access to specialists who had been offered to the team to aid in their recovery from the deaths of their teammates. Graham said that the team would handle it internally, that it would strengthen the boys and the team. The real reason was most likely a very real fear that those of his players being abused might open up and tell the psychological experts about the sexual abuse they were suffering at his hands.

Graham's lawyer tried to present Graham as a sympathetic, lonely man who, because of his homosexuality and resulting isolation in macho conservative hockey outposts, turned to young players because he had no other sexual outlet. Graham was indeed lonely, and I myself felt sympathy for him. But homosexuality and loneliness have nothing to do with the psychopathy of serial sexual abuse and issues relating to the need to exploit, control, and dominate. Nothing. It was an abomination that this was even mentioned in court.

His lawyer even presented Graham's unwillingness to admit to his crimes unless his victims first came forward as a virtue. Supposedly, this showed that Graham was sympathetic to any pain a victim might suffer should Graham disclose any abuse that a victim might prefer to remain unknown. In this telling of the story, Graham had been doing his victims a favor by not admitting to all of his crimes up front, and this further reflected Graham's rehabilitation, for he now thought of his victims first and himself second.

Except that Graham could have gone to the police at any time and given a complete statement of everything he had done, including a complete list of those he had abused, the number of times he had abused each, and the nature of the abuse of each. He, and at the very least his lawyer, would know full well that the prosecution rarely, if ever, moves forward absent cooperation from a victim, and that if a victim wished to remain anonymous and not move forward, nothing would ever come of it and the victim's name would never be disclosed. But Graham could never do that, for if he is like most sexual predators, the list would in all likelihood be far longer than most people could ever imagine and he would never, ever again spend a day outside of jail.

For everything that Graham's lawyer raised that seemingly made Graham worthy of the court's sympathy, there was a response of equal or greater impact against him, one grounded in the reality of who Graham was and what he had been doing. But this was not a trial, and there was no detailed point-by-point rebuttal of the story told by his lawyer.

Graham was a fraud back when I knew him, he was a fraud when he was abusing the others, and his lawyer did nothing but try to perpetuate that fraudulent version of Graham.

Lawyers are paid to tell a story. That doesn't mean anybody has to believe it.

"GET OVER HERE, he's coming!"

The staff inside the courtroom understood what was at stake. I had made clear to various security officers in the courtroom that I wanted a chance to look him in the eye so that I could put all of my years of suffering back onto him while showing him that he hadn't crushed me.

"The piece of shit will be coming down this hallway in a couple of minutes. Be ready!"

Graham had left the courtroom during a break in the proceedings and was now being brought in from the back of the room down a hallway next to the viewing gallery, separated only by a small divider. Knowing that I had wanted to look him in the eye, one of the bailiffs motioned for me to come over to where I could do so. My heart was pounding. The moment I had been waiting for.

And then there he was, coming down the hallway, surrounded by security on each side.

I was ready. I had been repeating to myself over and over:

I'm now a fully grown man. I am ready for this. He can't hurt me anymore. Here is my moment. I have waited a lifetime for this. Do it.

I looked at Graham and immediately recoiled. It took only a glimpse of the front of him coming toward me, his eyes locked to the floor, for me to quickly turn away. I panicked. I couldn't look at him. I was terrified. I couldn't breathe.

I felt humiliated and wanted to run away. I sank back into myself, as if I were sixteen years old again and in the middle of the abuse. It felt exactly like it did back all those years ago when he was sexually abusing me.

I had thought I was ready. I wasn't. All these years later he still had so much power over me.

In his presence I was nothing but the same fearful, sexually abused teenager I had once been, who I had been ever since.

NEAR THE END of the proceedings that day, Todd Holt, who had endured hundreds of sexual assaults over a five-year period, delivered a powerful victim impact statement. Fighting to hold back tears, he talked about how he had lost his innocence, his sense of trust, his soul, his motivation. He talked about having drowned his pain in alcohol and how that had impacted his marriage. Todd was the most fragile of us all that day for the simple reason that he was just that day going public with his story. The strength and poise he showed was unimaginable. His words cut me. I couldn't hold back my own tears.

As noted, Theo Fleury's impact statement had been filed with the court. Theo read it at a media conference held far away from the proceedings, to show how far he had come and how far he had moved on. I loved the powerful image of being far away from Graham, far away from the charade playing out in the courtroom.

Graham was then given an opportunity to speak. He stood up slowly, head down, and read a prepared statement, never turning back to look at any of us. It was really quite something. He apologized to his friends, to the Canadian hockey public, to the institution of hockey, and to "the many good people who work only for the betterment of sport and those under their care." He apologized to everyone in the communities where he had coached and to those involved in his teams and league. He apologized to people who were inconvenienced by having been asked questions as a result of his actions. He apologized to his players and their parents, and then finally to Todd and Theo.

Graham likes to quote Shakespeare. His apology was a tale told by an idiot, full of sound and fury, signifying nothing.

And yet, it left me feeling empty. I never got the apology, however meaningless, that the others did.

Sitting there all those years later, I actually still craved Graham's attention, his respect.

———————

JUSTICE CARLSON ENDED the day by saying that she was reserving judgment and that we would reconvene just less than a month later, on March 20, 2012, for the reading of her verdict. It was a cliffhanger of sorts, everybody leaving the courtroom wondering what would happen next. But the lawyer in me knew, for ours is a system with much to learn about child sexual predators and the impact the crime has on its victims.

When the court reconvened in Winnipeg, in the Law Courts Building, in the very same courtroom where we had been just weeks earlier, everything was the same as we'd left it. Everything, that is, except for one person in the room who was acting in a most different manner.

When we entered the courtroom this time, Graham was not seated and he was not looking at the floor. The previous month, when he'd been looking for sympathy, he had been hiding and had presented himself as meek, harmless, remorseful. Now, knowing the judgment was written and there was nothing more he could do to influence what it might be, he was standing up with his hands on his hips, stretching, moving about, speaking with counsel. He was strutting as much as man in his position could strut.

"All rise for the Honorable Justice Catherine Carlson."

And with that she began to read her decision.

There is no sentence this court can impose that will give back to Mr. Holt and Mr. Fleury that which was taken from them by Mr. James. The court expects that there is no sentence it can impose that the victims, and indeed many members of the public, will find satisfactory. But the court is confident that the victims of Mr. James' offences, and the public, appreciate that what is a fit and appropriate sentence for Mr. James for these offences, must be determined based on the application of sentencing principles that have been set out by Parliament in the Criminal Code.

And with that, you knew instantly where this was going.

That paragraph is perfect. Nobody, absolutely nobody, could ever disagree with a single word of it. But decoded from legal-speak, it is an aggressive statement, effectively saying: "Disagree with this if you will, but this is an appropriate and rational sentence based on solid intellectual arguments. If you disagree, you would only be advocating for a sentence based on vengeance resulting from a visceral reaction to circumstances that make you too emotional to see things properly."

It was first-year criminal law all over again. Once again, permit me to disagree with the lesson presented in that class. Objections to insufficient sentencing can be based on concepts of appropriate retribution, not just vengeance.

THE JUDGMENT REGURGITATED much of the information submitted by Graham's lawyer detailing his contributions to hockey.
Judge Carlson paid particular attention to Graham's rehabilitation
and credited him for the sincerity and dedication he had brought
to his counseling sessions while he had first been imprisoned, all
thirty-two sessions, noting that he had deferred early parole to
complete his program.

Thirty-two counseling sessions. If only I could recover that
quickly.

I was sitting in the gallery in bemusement, having expected
this all along but still in shock at the reality of how the words
sounded. I wanted to yell out from my seat:

*You just don't get it. You're being conned by the ultimate con artist, a
man whose life has been dedicated to fooling all of us. For his entire life
he has taken advantage of the weak while making himself appear as
the victim. Rehabilitated? Contrite? Aware of the damage he has done?
Accepting responsibility for all that he has done? Dedicating himself to
therapy? Apologizing? You've been had! I have looked deep into his eyes,
the cold, dead eyes of a shark stalking its prey, and I have seen who he
is and I know in my heart exactly what he is. Those who agree with
this have all been fooled. Our system is ensuring that this monster will
soon be back among us—again.*

I had had over thirty years to prepare for this. But when Justice
Carlson was handing down the sentence—a sentence that related
to several hundred individual acts of sexual violence, sexual aggression, sexual exploitation, sexual whatever you want to call it—it was
too much for me. How could she even begin to understand a man
like Graham? She couldn't, for if she could, she never would have
been able to utter a single good word in court about him. Yet here in
court I was hearing about the goodness in Graham. What else can

be said other than that our legal system simply does not understand repeated and systematic serial child sexual assault?

Not only was Graham about to get an inadequate sentence, it would be reduced even further, for Justice Carlson was pointing to a provision of the *Criminal Code* that worked in Graham's favor:

> *Mr. James has experienced an extreme degree of public humiliation. Indeed Mr. James' career and reputation have been ruined. He is, of course, the author of his own misfortune. But, while publicity and stigma are ordinary incidents of the criminal justice system, and are not always cause for mitigation of sentence, the fact that the intense media scrutiny of Mr. James has lasted for such a prolonged period of time, and has been relentless, is a factor to consider. Public humiliation, beyond what is ordinarily incidental, may be considered in mitigation and may provide a degree of denunciation and deterrence. In this case, some mitigation is warranted.*

That's right. The public outcry against Graham for his crimes could be considered to be part of his punishment, meaning that the judge could properly reduce his jail sentence as a result of the pain he had already suffered.

Judge Carlson then analyzed Canadian precedents and the history of sentencing for child sexual assault generally. She noted that a case referred to as the *Stuckless* case, another high-profile case of child sexual assault inextricably linked to hockey, appeared to be most relevant. Gordon Stuckless had been an employee at Maple Leaf Gardens in the '70s. He had used his position there to access and groom victims. Stuckless and others working behind the scenes as ushers or in equipment and maintenance had granted children access to one of hockey's shrines, grooming them and then later sexually assaulting them. Judge Carlson used *Stuckless* to guide her in her sentencing.

What wasn't mentioned in court is that Martin Kruze, a victim in the *Stuckless* case, jumped off the Bloor Viaduct in Toronto and killed himself on hearing his abuser's ridiculously inadequate—even after it had been increased on appeal—sentence.

Stuckless had originally been sentenced to two years, increased to six years on appeal, reduced by one year to five for credited time served. Remember those numbers.

OUR WORLD IS far smaller than we know.

The year before I met Graham, when I played Minor Bantam hockey in Winnipeg, our team hosted a team from Toronto during a spring tournament. One of the players from the Toronto team who stayed with me in our house, an amazing hockey player named Tim Cole, would later join me at Princeton. But something else from that weekend was even more of a coincidence.

We, the hosts, set up a road hockey game against our visitors. During the game, one of the guys from Toronto was going on about how we should come to Toronto because he and some friends were able to get into Maple Leaf Gardens and get used hockey sticks from the Leafs, and they were allowed to come in and watch practices. I didn't think about that for years. But when news about *Stuckless* came out, I realized that was exactly what the pedophiles at Maple Leaf Gardens had done to attract their prey. I didn't think anything more of it until I heard about Martin Kruze's suicide. His picture was in the news, and the accompanying article mentioned that as a young boy he played for the Dorset Park Bruins. I stopped dead when I heard this. The team we had hosted all those years ago was the Dorset Park Bruins, but several years younger than his. Boys from the same area and same hockey association, talking about all the same things, all the same cool, amazing things about their hockey idols.

I don't want anybody to commit suicide. But I understand Martin Kruze. If you'd been through what we've been through, you'd understand him too.

———

AFTER CONSIDERING EVERYTHING that had been presented by both the prosecution and the defense, Judge Carlson held as follows:

> *The court has determined that a sentence of two years' imprisonment going forward, one each for the two offences, is appropriate. Giving recognition to the principle of totality, so as to avoid what would be a crushing sentence, the sentences for these offenses, which would, but for the principle of totality, otherwise be consecutive, will be concurrent to each other. The two-year sentence is a penitentiary sentence. It acknowledges the seriousness of Mr. James' offences. It means sending back to jail someone who has not reoffended in the last fifteen years and has done all society has required of him during that time.*

Two years.

This is our justice system at work when dealing with an admitted and already convicted serial sexual predator? This is why we all came forward? This is supposed to encourage other victims of child sexual assault to come forward? This is supposed to send a message that we as a society will not tolerate those who prey upon our most vulnerable?

I say this with the utmost respect for judges and lawyers and commentators and other deep thinkers who are somehow able to reduce matters like these to academic discussions of the delicate balance between rehabilitation and the need to denounce and deter, to protect society, to promote a respect for justice. I can go on for hours with the best of them about the legal theories of crime and punishment. I can cite Michel Foucault on *Discipline and Punish* in a way that can end dinner parties.

My personal objections to Graham's sentence are what they are. But, as a lawyer, I was and remain appalled. It has nothing to do with vengeance. It is about respect for the legal system. It is about recognizing the severity of the damage inflicted upon those who are sexually abused. Our courts have punished those who have stolen from banks more severely than they have punished Graham James. How is that even remotely appropriate in an advanced society?

I knew it was coming, but I was shaken by actually hearing it. By the end of the reading of the judgment I was shocked by the extent of my own rage. But I knew once again that I couldn't let Graham know that he had won. As Sheldon and I made our way out of the courthouse we were immediately met by a throng of reporters. Stay positive, stay positive, we had agreed. As upset as we were, we didn't want to do anything that would dissuade anybody else who had suffered from coming forward.

We put on a brave face in front of the media, saying to one and all that we were happy that Graham was going to jail, that if you come forward you will be heard, and after all, what was important wasn't what happened to Graham, but that we all now focus on our own rehabilitation and on making things better for other victims out there.

And with that my nose grew more than just a little.

I cut my interviews short, for I had a class to teach. I had been invited to give a lecture to a first-year criminal law class at the University of Manitoba being taught by Professor David Asper, my former colleague at CanWest. Suffice it to say that my lecture was firmly grounded in reality, not theory.

THERE WAS AN appropriate amount of outrage at the verdict. At the same time, some commentators stated that the judgment had achieved an appropriate balance. As always, the debate played out between "appropriate rational sentencing" based on the "intellectual" and "good" versus "sentences which are based in vengeance," which are "visceral" and "bad." The usual suspects could be found in their usual places in the discussions.

The Crown filed an appeal, which would be heard in the Manitoba Court of Appeal on December 12, 2012. Once again, I flew back to Winnipeg to be there for the hearing. By that time I just wanted it to be over. We all just wanted it to be over. I was the only victim to show up this time, and according to the legal process now playing out, I wasn't even a victim.

But that day, sitting there again in the gallery, something happened that renewed my faith in the legal system. No matter the outcome of the appeal, the process had finally introduced some humanity into what had otherwise been an extremely frustrating process. During the proceedings, the three justices from the Manitoba Court of Appeal serving on the panel asked difficult questions of both sides, and I was growing increasingly frustrated. But then one of the justices, Justice MacInnes, interrupted the proceedings and asked bluntly, "Why aren't we looking at even more time than the Crown is asking for?"

Somebody finally appeared to understand the horror of what Graham had done.

In March 2013, the appellate verdict was delivered. Judge MacInnes, writing on behalf of the Manitoba Court of Appeal, overturned Judge Carlson, ruling that she had erred in applying the sentencing rules. Graham's sentence of two years was extended to five years.

In interviews we hailed the decision. But what, exactly, were we celebrating? Five years? For all that he had done? We still had shattered lives to look back on and futures to salvage. But five is better than two, right?

Once again, I understood Martin Kruze more than anybody should ever have to understand him.

IN LAW SCHOOL I learned all about the theory behind the law and how and why our systems developed the way they did and why they operate in the manner that they do. I can answer the legal questions on the issues from both sides. I can go on and on about the theories of incarceration and rehabilitation and sentencing. Nobody need ever try to explain to me why the anger I have about what happened is misplaced. I understand the arguments in response to what others may see as my visceral, less intellectual discourse on these points. I get it.

But make no mistake about it. We have a legal system, not a justice system. Justice is not guaranteed in a legal system. It is a system that yields legal results in a game played between prosecution and defense with its own set of rules that is in no way related to the reality of what did or did not happen. A judgment comes long after the offense has been committed, and a judgment does not prevent the crime from happening in the first place. A judgment is just a result, no different from a postscript attempting to describe a bit of recent history.

One person's vengeance, or excessive and emotional sentencing, is another's retribution, and another's appropriate sentencing consistent with legal principles. There is no objective standard, only a difference of opinion about what is appropriate in the circumstances.

The difference between how Jerry Sandusky was treated in the U.S. and how Graham James has been treated in Canada presents a stark difference in approaches taken to sentencing child sexual offenders. I am not a "lock 'em up and throw the key away" type of person. I believe that we over-incarcerate for so much, that we underrehabilitate, and that in the process we cost society dearly. So many who advocate for progressive reforms within our legal system have my ear, and I most often find myself nodding in agreement. But when it comes to many who commit serious crimes, I believe that we get it wrong by failing to accept that there really are sociopaths and psychopaths who are incapable of full rehabilitation. I believe this is especially so when it comes to sexual predators, and even more so when it comes to child sexual predators.

People need to better understand what child sexual assault is. Simply stated, child sexual assault is the killing of a victim's sense of self, a taking of the child's life as he or she knew it. A life has been taken. It should be recognized as such a crime, and it should be penalized as such a crime.

Yet, the severity of the crime is often not recognized in a legal system based largely on precedent, where decisions made in previous cases can control or guide decisions to be made in new cases. Decisions made when there was an inadequate understanding of the severity of a crime can last forever within the body of precedent. This is a problem, for sexual assault is only now increasingly being seen for the serious crime that it is. Previously it was seen in the context of a time when women were considered property and sexual assault wasn't a crime.

Our views on what is and isn't a crime can change, and our ideas about how such crimes should be treated by law evolve. Child sexual assault is one crime for which the law has evolved and must continue to evolve. The historical case law and the sentences handed down to those who have committed child sexual assault neither reflect the severity of the crimes nor adequately capture the gravity of its impact on society and the extent to which lesser punishment diminishes the respect that society has for the legal system.

At least in Canada, that is.

And so, several years later, when I was in Ottawa appearing before the government's House Standing Committee on Justice to deliver my view on Graham's sentencing, my answer was, shall we say, to the point. I am not proud of what I said that day, something that will live forever in the government records. But it needed to be said. If Graham's sentencing represents the best that our legal system has to offer, if it is the best that the courts can do to understand an offender like Graham, then, well:

"Fuck the Manitoba Court of Appeal."

ELEVEN

RECOVERY

R *ECOVERY* IS A wonderful word. It sounds so bright, so hope-
ful, so full of a sense of accomplishment and a chance for
rebirth after a triumph over seemingly overwhelming odds.
Yet anybody who has ever had to try to recover from anything traumatic knows that recovery can be anything but wonderful. It isn't
easy, it isn't linear, it's never certain, and things can often become
much more difficult before they start to get better.

I thought that things would start to get better for me the
moment I became strong enough tell others about what had happened to me. I couldn't have been more wrong.

We were deep into one of our weekly therapy sessions:

"When you think back about it, what do you remember most,
what do you see?"

"I see his eyes, always his eyes. I see my shoes, a blue binder, a
field, and stairs. I remember his breath, terrazzo flooring, a ratty
beige sling, metal wire, and his breath. I think of carpeting, a
hallway, and hockey books. I see orange signs on the bridge to
the restaurant, mud, a mess. Cold nights, warm summer ones. I
remember never wanting to play hockey again."

"Anything else?"

"Nothing, you know, nothing important. Can we, look... I don't know, can we maybe stop now and just talk about something else?"

"Sure, that's fine. How are you sleeping? Any improvement?"

"A bit, I guess. I had a few nights where I had some real sleep, but it's still bad. I was able to make it in to work every day, but I'm not getting any deep sleep until the sun starts to come up. When I finally wake up and get in to the office I'm exhausted, my mind is elsewhere, I'm not into it, it's like I'm not even there."

"How are the nightmares?"

"Nightmares? Better than before, not as often."

And by "nightmares," I meant "thoughts of killing myself."

I often used the word "nightmares" in therapy because of my more than passing familiarity with the legal obligations I could trigger for my therapist should I be brutally honest about my suicidal thoughts. I did not want to be institutionalized. So, as long as I was comfortable with my ability to manage such thoughts and not act on them, I usually thought it better to just leave them out of our discussion.

"But what I don't get is how come I have so many nightmares now that I'm finally doing something about all of this. Why aren't things getting better now that I'm dealing with this? Why are things worse?"

"Well, when you were running from things, hiding from things, were you dealing with the abuse? Or were you doing everything in your power to avoid having to deal with the abuse? Sure, running from it created its own problems, but doesn't it make sense that it's harder to confront something than to run from something?"

SO OBVIOUS, BUT so impossible to see while living in the midst of it. Like a drug addict who first has to suffer through the hell of withdrawal before getting clean, I was facing my own living hell while fighting to emerge from the other side. Not only had I finally started to deal with the sexual abuse, I had also become enmeshed in a legal process that ultimately yielded nothing remotely close to justice, a legal process that in the end saw me as nobody.

It was all so overwhelming.

My recovery had started with my night on the bridge. I don't like thinking about that night, but I thought that night had been my hell. Suicide is tragic. It is incredibly painful for those who are left behind and have to deal with the aftermath. It is to be avoided at all costs. But I wasn't thinking of taking the easy way out. I was thinking of doing something very hard that would leave the world and those around me much better off. I believed that by killing myself I would be doing everybody a favor.

When I walked along bridges now I would see the fences, the barricades. To me they looked like bars of a jail cell, barriers protecting me from myself but keeping me locked in a solitary confinement of my own creation, my own living prison, my own living hell.

I needed to summon all of my strength to find someplace safe to go to be heard, to be understood, to be helped in my fight against the inner voice telling me that I didn't deserve to be helped. I needed to choose life over death before I could move forward. Maybe I was just one of the lucky ones who, upon facing death, was fortunate enough to realize that I deserved and could seek out help. All I know is that I didn't kill myself and that I'm still here.

Yet, having chosen life, I was now worse than ever. Several years removed from the bridge, in the midst of therapy and having come forward and gone through the legal process, I was no longer living a life.

I wasn't working and was on long-term disability. I dropped out of sight for several years and cut myself off from all my friends. I didn't know that I was doing that, it just happened as I increasingly saw myself as unworthy because of my depression and PTSD.

Like many others who have suffered mental health issues, I was often antisocial and difficult to be around. I could appear to be selfish and unappreciative, generally receiving a one-way stream of emotional energy directed toward me with nothing coming back from me in return. To like me, to help me, was to take on an obligation that on its surface came with no rewards. It required people to leave their comfort zone, ignore normal social cues, and accept that the normal rules didn't apply. I was suffering from a disability, and while I was desperately trying to get better, I was not always getting it right.

Recovery was difficult because I could now look back with greater insight. That embarrassed me, because I knew how I had acted back then, how I couldn't be myself when I was running from myself. Looking back forced me to confront all of that behavior once more. When I saw somebody from my past, I knew, thanks to this greater clarity, that they must have thought I was a dick, a jerk, a loser, because that's what I could be when I was unable to just be myself, when I was self-sabotaging to make myself less than I was. I knew they had no idea who I really am, because it's only now that I'm more comfortable being me, that I'm not trying to be somebody else, somebody who wasn't broken, defective, responsible for it all. So, I couldn't face people from my past. I skipped reunions. I isolated myself from friends from the past. And it only got worse, because then I worried that they all thought I was just blowing them off and not making an effort, I worried that I was not worthy of their friendship. And by then I just might have been right.

But nothing I did was ever about anybody else but me. My failures, my rejections of invitations, my hibernation—it was all about me. I wanted so badly to be normal, to be able to be with others, but I just couldn't. I rarely left my house. I spent days in bed. And after spending days in bed, I was too tired to do anything but go back to bed. I was numbed by my medication. I remained a bloated morbidly obese walking corpse.

But I was alive, and I was going to therapy.

Slowly, very slowly, the clouds started to lift. No longer was every day intolerable. Some days I made it outside to my back yard. Other days I celebrated making it to the shower. On a very good day I would get up and take my accumulated garbage to the dump, a task imposed on me as I usually didn't have the strength to actually get up and take it to the curb for pick-up on garbage day. Princeton graduate, lawyer, international business executive, now celebrating my use of soap and shampoo and dumping the garbage. Clearly my "Best Trash" award from Princeton hadn't been won lightly.

But I was still alive and I was still going to therapy.

There remains an unwarranted stigma attached to mental health issues as being akin to laziness or lack of effort. Depression and PTSD are both very real and extremely devastating. I would wish neither on anybody. I don't want anybody's best friends to be the checkout people they only see when they go to their local grocery store, no matter how nice those people may be.

"WAS I JUST unlucky and in the wrong place when a grenade exploded, or was I a target, a victim of a planned hit?"

"What do you mean?"

"Well, was Graham an attacker who lobbed in a grenade and scooped up whatever he could? Or was he an assassin who carefully selected his target while carrying out his mission?"

"Why do you think it matters?"

"If a grenade caused the damage, the abuse would have just been bad luck. If he was an assassin, why me? Did I do anything to cause the abuse?"

Behind my questions were the same fears. I must have done something wrong. I must have invited this. I must be weak. I was stupid not to protect myself. I was stupid to put myself in that position.

The therapy meant I was increasingly able to answer my own questions. I knew that Graham had been a sniper. I just wanted to hear it from somebody else, I wanted to tease out that metaphor and explore its impact on my psyche. I was coming to the realization that the process I was going through bore all the hallmarks of grieving a loss, with all the various stages that entails. I was in the process of grieving the loss of a loved one—except the loved one was me.

SEVERAL OF MY nightmares happen more frequently than others.

I'm in a corporate business tower. I can never see outside the building, as it's enveloped in a dark gray fog. I'm always trapped inside, unable to get out. The look everywhere is tasteful elegance. I'm the only one in the elevator. Every time the doors open I see a different law school classmate or a lawyer I once worked with. I'm ignored, I don't fit in, I'm unwelcome. I see others I know, perfectly dressed and smelling of scented sophistication. "Call security. Now!" somebody eventually shouts. And then it's some variation of the usual tirade. "Stop following me! Stop talking to me! You're insane! You never worked here. You don't even have a law degree. You don't belong here. You need help. How could you ever think you could work here?"

A second nightmare happens more often than the first. It's the same theme, different setting. I'm in Baker Rink at Princeton, but I'm wearing all of the proper equipment, I'm ready to play, and I have my varsity jersey on. Except I can't find my way to the ice surface. Like a band that can't find the stage, I'm desperately running in my skates and full gear down hallways, up stairs, into dressing room after dressing room, looking for somebody, anybody, to help me find the way to the ice surface. This isn't the real

Baker Rink but an unsolvable puzzle. I join my teammates just as we're about to go on the ice. The arena is packed. I'm last in line. Then, just as I'm about to step on the ice, Coach Delventhal yells to me, "Where do you think you're going?" "Higgins said he wanted me to..." "Your jersey, take it off! You will never wear that jersey on this ice surface, ever."

At night, when my thoughts are on their own, I am grieving the life I lost. But unfortunately, neither of these nightmares is the nightmare I have most frequently, the nightmare I fear the most. I can describe this third nightmare in one short sentence that sums up all you need to know to understand just how horrific my nights can be.

Graham repeatedly sexually assaults me.

I can't control the nightmares. They can happen frequently, and after so many years of having so many nightmares, eventually my memories are more about my nightmares than about the actual abuse they are based on.

I spent decades first trying to run from the abuse and then trying to put the abuse into context. To survive, I have done my utmost to try to forget everything about the abuse. Yet, no matter how hard I try to put it behind me, certain things have stayed with me, and even if I could forget everything, my nightmares can always bring it all back in their own peculiar way, whether or not I am prepared for it.

Therapy helps with the nightmares because it helps me better understand the abuse. I still wake up in a sweat, heart pounding, whenever I have one, but now I can see the nightmare for what it is—simply a part of my past.

THERAPY DOESN'T ANSWER all of my questions about who I was, who I am, how it happened, and who I can be now. Instead, it gets me to understand that I have to challenge the assumptions built into all of my questions. It gets me to ask different questions. It is an interactive process in which the asking of questions prompts further questions, which themselves prompt reflection and understanding in a way that was previously unthinkable. All of this leads to more questions, and then to still more questions.

My assumptions, my questions, my perceptions, and my answers often change depending on the day and the mood I am in, and the answers to my questions often prompt more questions and greater understanding. In the beginning, negativity ruled. Over time, I became far more positive.

Before entering therapy I had been looking back from the perspective of an adult with life experiences. Therapy showed me that I needed to remember that when I was fourteen or fifteen years old I didn't understand the world the way that I do now. Therapy enabled me to see things from the perspective of who I was back then by getting me to ask different questions than before:

> *Did I believe that Graham was more powerful than I was?*
> *Did I believe that Graham had power over me?*
> *Did I believe the threats he made about me not being believed?*
> *Did I believe that I would lose everything I wanted if I didn't comply?*
> *Did I think that I could talk to my mom or dad about this?*
> *Did I know enough about who I was to understand that he was manipulating me when he said that I was homosexual like he was?*
> *Did I understand that just because I responded physically, that didn't mean I was gay?*
> *Did I even really understand what being gay meant back then?*
> *Did I think I had a choice?*
> *Did I believe what he was telling me?*

By coming back to these fundamental questions over and over again, I could start to see that it made sense that I could want the support of somebody like him in his position, that he would do whatever he could to get me to think less of my physicality so that he could take advantage of me mentally and control me, that it would become worse for me when I most desperately needed somebody to talk to, to support me, to get me through my darkest moments, that I would see that all I had was him, and that once I realized that, and believed his threats, I would think there was no way out.

I was increasingly able to put my interaction with Graham into context. Even when I knew that sexual abusers are sociopaths, psychopaths, I had been unable to apply that intellectual knowledge to Graham because of my beliefs about my own weakness, responsibility, and participation in the abuse. Slowly, I managed to shift my focus away from my own participation in the abuse to see Graham more clearly as a typical abuser.

This was an essential part of my recovery. The more I understood about Graham and how he and his type operate, the easier it became for me to understand my part in what had happened and where responsibility properly rested.

Sexual abusers possess a chilling skill-set that can lead to horrifying results. Graham is somebody focused on maximizing his own interests, needs, and desires without regard for the welfare of others. In the face of a purported apology by Graham, another of his victims said that it was meaningless, that Graham was incapable of telling the truth, that everything Graham had said to him or stood for since they first met was a lie designed for the sole purpose of facilitating Graham's sexual desires.

Graham's lawyers have had him evaluated by professionals who have taken a different view of him and who see him as rehabilitated. Graham has by all accounts been a model participant in any counseling or therapy program he has gone through. There are, no doubt, doctors and others out there with many degrees hanging in their offices who would testify that Graham is not a psychopath, not a sociopath, and that he poses no risk to society at large.

With respect, they have no idea who they are dealing with. They have never seen his particular and specific true character, they have never seen him in full attack. While they may be able to place him, in an academic manner, within a class of offenders, they can't begin to understand exactly how *Graham* operates, just how easy it is for *Graham* to manipulate, how *Graham* knows exactly what to do or say in any situation to get exactly what *Graham* needs, and how *Graham* preys upon others. No matter how many degrees in psychiatry or psychology, or how much experience in the field one may have, nothing can ever match direct contact with the sexual predator in action.

Victims know their predator. I could see Graham for who he truly is, not for what the textbooks say he likely may be.

Therapy helped me to better understand all of this, to trust my instincts, to believe in my own perceptions and not the thoughts of others further removed from the situation. Still, recovery was difficult, because while my abuser had set the trap and committed the abuse, he had also left me to punish myself. Having punished myself, I now had to accept that I had incorrectly viewed the world and my place in it in order to recover. That's progress, but it also required a reprogramming of how I think about everything. That required me to forgive myself. And somebody who still sometimes deep down wonders whether he might still be responsible for everything that happened? That's not somebody fully prepared to forgive himself.

THE ONGOING LEGAL process didn't help my recovery.

It was no surprise when in June 2015, several years after Graham had been sentenced, yet another victim came forward. The victim, still at this time anonymous, had been coached by Graham in Swift Current. Graham's lawyer and the prosecuting Crown

Attorney worked out a recommended sentence of another two years in jail, to be added to the five years he was already serving. Seven years for hundreds of sexual assaults against three acknowledged victims.

It appears that the Canadian justice system has set the market rate for repeated sexual assaults against a single victim by Graham James at about two years, offering him, in effect, a significant volume discount. This volume discount appears to be understood by Graham himself. When asked whether he was concerned that more of his victims might come forward, Graham testified to the National Parole Board that while this was a possibility, all of his major, longer-term victims had now come forward and he remained a good candidate for full release.

First, I don't believe anything he says. Second, Graham was implying that even if another victim came forward, such a victim would "only" have been sexually assaulted once or twice, or maybe just a little bit more, and relative to his other convictions it would be nothing significant and should therefore be of no concern to the parole board when considering granting him full parole. His response should have surprised nobody, for when you give inadequate sentences in response to hundreds of individual acts of sexual abuse, single acts of sexual abuse become meaningless in the eyes of the abuser.

Graham served only a portion of those seven years behind bars. He served almost four and a half years in a minimum security retraining center before being granted full parole on September 15, 2016. He is now a free man, subject only to some minor official conditions, including a restraining order in favor of his victims, including me.

From the National Parole Board decision:

Your case meets the serious harm criterion. The physical and psychological harm caused to the victims is undeniable. Your file reveals 6

official victims, even though you have already admitted to have had
[sic] sexual intercourse with around 20 hockey players you were coach-
ing. You were using manipulation, control, and your position of trust
and authority to facilitate the assaults.

Twenty. It's not widely known, but in therapy Graham admitted to sexually assaulting approximately twenty boys. In court, he
has admitted to sexually abusing only six. But his number is about
twenty—and that's according to him. Who knows what the real
number is?

Yet the National Parole Board noted as follows:

According to the latest update of your Correctional Plan, you present a
low risk for reoffending, and your level of accountability, motivation
and potential for social reintegration are all evaluated as high.

In light of the above, The Board concludes that you have made
significant, observable and measurable progress during your period on
day parole with respect to the objectives set out in your correctional
planning. This process contributes to the reduction of the risk to society
that you pose.

With respect to your release plan, the Board is of the view that it is
well structured, responds to your needs, and represents the next logical
step in your process of social reintegration.

Is this justice? Graham spent very little time behind bars in
Canadian "correctional facilities," the official Orwellian term that
is used for Canadian jails. I'd like to be able to say that all I had
to do was, like Graham, spend a certain number of years working through things, complete the required number of hours of
therapy, and then be free to go. But life doesn't work that way,
abuse doesn't work that way, and recovering from the aftermath
of sexual abuse doesn't work that way. Graham? He got off easy,
so to speak.

Therapy helped me see to see all of this for what it was, to see him for he who he really was, and to remain calm in the face of the way in which he tried to play the crowd at his parole hearings. Graham could say in remorse that he had learned that he never should have been a hockey coach, yet upon his first release from prison he went right back into coaching, in Spain. Graham told the parole board that he was so sorry for what he had done that he was apologizing too much to his victims and had to be told to stop apologizing. He told the parole board that he didn't see himself as a criminal and had never so much as had a speeding ticket, conveniently forgetting his assault charges and his use of weapons to terrorize victims.

His entire life was a fraud, nothing more than a series of choices and events designed to feed his desires to obtain whatever he wished, be it power over a victim, control over a victim, sexual release and domination at the expense of a victim, or defeat of a victim.

Graham is not the university graduate he pretended to be, at least he wasn't until he completed a degree behind bars. He was no intellectual, and he was no former elite athlete hobbled by the unfortunate luck of physical frailty. He was a short, soft, pudgy, plodding high school graduate with a part-time job teaching, a job that let him hang around kids. He had few friends and lived vicariously through boys and young men while they played hockey. He, their coach or mentor, imagined a bright future for himself as a leader within the game of hockey. Remove hockey from the equation and he was little. Remove boys and young men from the picture and he had nothing to live for.

Fundamentally, Graham is a pedophile, or more accurately a hebephile, with a foot fetish. He is attracted to feet and sees them as if they are sexual organs. He loves feet, he loves looking at them, touching them, rubbing them pressing himself against them. He loves having his own feet looked at and touched and played with. I had thought that I was in the presence of a very smart, very concerned hockey coach. Instead, I was in the presence of a psychopath with a foot fetish. I can only imagine how hard it must have been for him not to give it all away when he first massaged my feet.

It wasn't that everything he said was without merit. It's that what he was saying was always tailored to his specific audience. He was, and likely still is, a master salesman, one who can both charm and con at the same time while getting people to forget about putting their own interests first and instead buy into his version of things, a version that serves his interests.

He has always needed as many others as possible to help, knowingly or unknowingly, as part of the fraud. He needed cover, he needed safety, and he needed protection. Those who are not his victims are nothing but pawns he is playing with to help him achieve his ends. He is no doubt smiling when others buy into his explanations, his covers, his rationalizations, his supposed rehabilitation, for in the predator's world there is him and there are his victims—anyone else is just there to be manipulated to allow him to achieve his ends.

Whenever he is back in the news the same issues come up and the same questions are asked of our legal system. People are up in arms about inadequate sentencing, nobody understands the process, and Graham, either directly or through his lawyers, is given another chance to try to distance himself from any responsibility for the carnage he left behind. After Graham's 2015 sentencing, his lawyer noted that Graham wanted to assist the educational system by working within it to help identify pedophiles and hebophiles like him. At his 2016 parole hearing, Graham seemingly showed remorse, yet he couldn't resist pointing out that he had been instrumental in making Todd Holt, someone he had assaulted well over a hundred times, into one terrific record-breaking junior hockey player.

I believe that Graham actually craves the attention that his periodically renewed place in the spotlight offers him. I'm sure that having a public profile as a several times convicted serial child sexual abuser brings its own challenges, but Graham had always badly wanted to be a star like the hockey players he coached, who he had "created." He was very proud of the ones who went on to achieve success in hockey and he believed that their successes were his successes. To this day he points to their successes in an attempt to reduce his overall net negative presence in their lives.

Because of that, I don't believe that Graham truly understands who he is or what he has done. And if that is true, it can never be said that Graham has been rehabilitated. And because of that, I fear I may not have heard the last of Graham.

There are people out there who still support Graham, people who try to find flaws or shortcomings in his victims, who to this day question whether we really are victims, who think that perhaps some of it may not have happened, or, if it did, maybe it wasn't as bad as we made it out to be, or that we were his friends and it was consensual. Sometimes this information reaches me indirectly, sometimes directly. After I went public, one of his closest friends from junior hockey in Winnipeg contacted me and told me that he thought that all of this had actually worked out well for me, that I was a celebrity now. Pardon me?

Other people want to believe that Graham can be rehabilitated, that he has been rehabilitated. They want to believe that Graham can be said to have paid his debt to society and that he now deserves to be treated like the rest of us. I too want to live in a world where that is true. Except, I have seen too much. I know that Graham can never, ever be trusted. "Sexual intercourse" with about twenty boys? He is just wired differently. Nobody wants to say that, but our inability to contemplate that, to accept that possibility, makes us all vulnerable to him.

I don't blame anybody for being conned by Graham. Nobody was conned by him more than I was. I get it. I understand how you can come to see the world from his perspective.

What I do find difficult, and what has interfered with my recovery, has been the crushing disappointment I go through when encountering people who still choose to see things from his perspective after having been awakened to the reality of who he is: judges who issue inadequate sentences, columnists who write legal treatises arguing that the sentences are appropriate, lawyers who support the rights of the convicted while dismissing the rights of a victim, hockey people from his past who cling to old friendships with him, a hockey publication that passes up opportunities to take a stand against him rather than writing about the good he has done while accepting responsibility.

> *You haven't been listening. Can't you see who he is, what he's done, what he's still capable of doing? Don't you care enough to look more deeply into the facts rather than accept his story, his steps to further con you?*

Not caring about what other people think about him is something I continue to work on. Still, the next time anybody considers helping him or giving him a second chance or saying that he has paid his debt to society and that he should face no further consequences, please also think about those he has left in his wake. The legal system has treated him far better than it ever treated any of us.

RECOVERY ITSELF NEEDS to be put into perspective. It's not like going into a hospital with a broken arm, getting a cast put on it, and then emerging a month or two later with an arm that's as good as new. Rather, you develop a means not to eliminate the past but to cope with it, to incorporate it into who you are as you move forward with your life.

Recovery is about learning and developing coping mechanisms that put the past into a perspective that allows you to live a life that will not be dictated by that past. You simply cannot make the past go away, as good as that would be to happen. The past will, unfortunately, always be a part of the tapestry that is your life. Recovery teaches you that the rest of your life remains to be woven into that tapestry and that you can choose what to weave into it.

As good as things are now, I still have some days where I start thinking about the past and about how stupid I must have been, how weak I must have been, to let this happen to me. I tell myself to suck it up, I remind myself that it's over, that he can't hurt me anymore. I tell myself what I've learned in therapy—that the grooming process is complicated, that I was young, that I'm not responsible, that I couldn't have stopped it given what he was doing to me.

And I can say those words. But I know deep down what is wrong. My feelings have nothing to do with him. They're all about me. How did I ever let this happen to me? Seriously, how did I let this happen to me? With hindsight it's all so obvious, so clear. Just how stupid was I? The answer I give myself is ugly. I must have been so weak back then and I must have wanted it to happen. Nobody will ever believe that he controlled me. Nobody.

But unlike before, the moment passes. Because, after years of therapy, I am indeed better. I remember that I didn't do anything wrong. He did.

TWELVE

MOVING THE LAW FORWARD

I N AN INTERESTING way, the worse the legal system performed throughout Graham's trip through the legal process, the more of an opportunity it presented for possible positive changes. Rational reforms to the parole and pardon systems—rational at least as far as the reforms applied to the very worst of offenders such as Graham—came about quickly following the outcry after word of Graham's pardon was made public. Similarly, awareness of the inadequacy of the current sentencing provisions for sexual offenders increased as a result of the publicity arising from the national outcry at the minimal sentences given to Graham.

Greater understanding and positive change can grow out of horrible decisions and, in this case, out of an inadequate understanding of the impact of assaults on victims.

___

SEVERAL YEARS AGO, the NFL suspended a star player, Ray Rice, after investigating reports that he had hit his fiancée. The NFL suspended him for two games, but later increased it to six games as a result of public outrage. The NFL was applauded for correcting a mistake, two games having been too lenient and six games seeming about right.

But then a videotape of the assault emerged, and people were horrified that missing six football games could ever be considered an adequate sanction for what they saw there.

Why did it take actually seeing a tape of the assault for people to understand its seriousness? Because it's too easy to hear the word *assault* and skip over the details. The word itself allows you to compartmentalize and intellectualize what happened. It doesn't force you to think about what Rice's fiancée's face looked like as his fist smashed into it. You didn't have to hear her bones as they cracked, you didn't have to consider the drops of blood, the brain inside her skull jerking wildly, the immediate lifeless fall to the ground.

What goes through your head when you hear the term *sexual abuse*?

I believe that one of the reasons our system does not properly assess the harm associated with sexual assault is the term *sexual assault* itself. It covers so many different physical acts that it has ceased to have meaning. It's a term used to remove the stigma from a victim, a term designed so that a victim doesn't feel violated all over again whenever it's mentioned. It was designed to protect the victim.

However, in protecting the victim, the term dehumanizes and diminishes the crime. It does not carry an appropriate level of animus against the perpetrator. My guess is that Graham would still be in jail if there were crimes for "digitally raping a young boy," "sticking your penis in a young boy's mouth," and "ejaculating on a young boy's body."

The problem is that the terms we use to describe the crimes don't convey the horror of the acts, and so the sentences given to those who commit such acts deviate from what would be just and appropriate for the carnage they leave behind with the victim.

I understand that any move away from the term is virtually impossible in the current environment given the proper sensitivity we show to victims. But because the term doesn't convey the pain and suffering that victims experience, sentencing tends to be inadequate, causing more suffering to the victim, who then believes that nobody understands the impact of the crime.

People thought Graham's initial sentence of two years for hundreds of acts of sexual abuse was too short. Some of them were placated when the sentence was successfully appealed and increased to five years. But as with Ray Rice and his one punch, if you had seen the actual abuse, if you had experienced the actual abuse, if you had looked more deeply into the details of what he had actually done, the reality would have been too ugly for you to have ever imagined.

Graham James is lucky there is no videotape of his actions, or he would never spend a single day of the rest of his life outside a prison.

OVER THE PAST several years I have been asked on numerous occasions to give evidence to committees of both the House of Commons and the Senate on matters relating to criminal justice reform, with a specific focus on the place of victims, especially victims of sexual assault and child sexual assault legislation, in our legal system.

· There are no easy solutions and no absolute right and wrong answers.

· I believe that we over-incarcerate for so many crimes but still under-incarcerate our worst offenders.

- I believe that we under-rehabilitate not only criminals but also victims too.

- I believe that victims are not sufficiently recognized in our legal system. I believe that it is possible to include victims in the system not out of vengeance but to ensure appropriate denunciation of the criminal act. Victims' voices can have a positive impact on the administration of justice by humanizing the process and reminding all involved that lives have been affected by the criminal and maybe also by the court process.

- I believe that legislation as such need not be determined as constitutional or unconstitutional, but rather that we should try to make the best laws that we can and then implement them, knowing that we would always apply a judicial review of the application of that law in the specific instance when assessing whether an individual's constitutional rights had been infringed.

- I abhor mandatory minimums and prefer sentencing guidelines, as I believe that there should always be room for exceptions. At the same time, I believe that judges should be required to respect legislated sentencing guidelines and only deviate from them in the most extreme of circumstances and that it is essential that such guidelines respect the severity of the impact of the crimes.

- I believe that education and training are essential and that judges should be given tools to better address issues that may arise in sexual assault cases, such as deferred reporting and ongoing contact with an accused.

- I believe that we should revisit the right to remain silent in sexual assault cases. Such cases so often revolve around issues of "he said, she said," and that cannot be a fair process when one of the parties has the right to remain silent.

- I am happy that pardon and parole changes were made in response to my disclosure that Graham had received a pardon. I am not happy that the changes have adversely affected those who have committed lesser crimes, where the focus should be on increased rehabilitation, not less.

MY EXPERIENCE WITH the legal system was that it did not adequately consider victims, let alone protect them. It has not traditionally recognized the severity of sexual assault and its lingering damage and instead shows far more concern for fair treatment and rehabilitation of those who commit sexual assault than those who suffer the abuse. We do a good job of trying to rehabilitate the criminals. We do a terrible job of rehabilitating the victims. This needs to change.

As I have noted, sexual assault is a crime that is often a case of "he said, she said" with the most problematic legal issue being that very often "he" gets to hide behind his lawyer. Absent any corroborating physical evidence, such a case, by definition, becomes all about the credibility of the complainant, as the only thing being tested in court is the complainant's evidence.

And that is as it should be. All evidence that goes into court must be tested for credibility. This can become a difficult issue, however, when an alleged victim has acted in ways that seem to show a lack of candor, which might lead one to assume a story is being made up. Consider an alleged victim where there is a time gap between the actions in question and when the victim reported them to police, or when the victim may have continued to interact with the alleged abuser, or when the victim may have left out embarrassing facts or given incorrect details to the police. All of this will be brought up by the defense in court and the alleged victim will be made to look like an unreliable witness at best, a liar at worst.

Yet is it reasonable to expect that all victims will be able to be perfectly candid when giving statements to the police about their abuse? Or are there other issues that might reasonably be expected to impact an alleged victim? How much can one remember from an assault? What process does a victim go through to attempt to rationalize an attack to allow a victim to go on with life? How much can a victim admit to one's own self, let alone to a stranger at a police station, about actions that the victim may have taken with an abuser? How long can it take a victim to understand that no matter what they may have done, an attack is an attack?

That is not to say that an alleged victim's statements and actions are not to be fully tested in court, that questioning an alleged victim should in any way be restricted, that an alleged abuser should be entitled to anything but the best defense possible. Absolutely the alleged abuser must have these rights for our system to work. However, for the system to work we must also understand why alleged victims may respond in ways that might seem to imply a weak story but which might just be perfectly rational and normal ways in the aftermath of an assault.

Most importantly, when the only evidence for whether or not an assault took place is a set of competing stories, is it fair that one of the parties is permitted to remain silent? We see how the alleged victim looks when the unverified story is put to the test in cross-examination by the defense, a process that can destroy an alleged victim. Meanwhile, the alleged abuser sits quietly beside a lawyer. Perhaps the alleged victim wouldn't look so bad if the alleged abuser also had to face cross-examination?

Credibility is difficult to establish when there are competing stories and no corroborating evidence. I would never advocate for a system that would convict anybody on the basis of a story told by someone who has been shown in court to be less than credible. At the same time, I believe that it's important to better understand just how and why a victim might be unwilling to disclose all of the details of his or her actions as they relate to an alleged assault. I believe it is also important for the courts to gain a better understanding of how victims may respond to their alleged abusers and how they may take steps to preserve some self-respect both through continued interaction with an abuser and throughout the legal process.

Is a purported victim not credible because he or she didn't report the alleged abuse immediately or maintained ongoing contact with an alleged abuser after the incident in question? Or is she blaming herself, thinking she is weak and stupid? Is the victim ashamed and trying to show that she didn't fall for a predator, that the predator really is just a nice guy? Is she trapped with no way out, afraid of the consequences of trying to get out of the relationship?

The answer usually is that we have no idea. But that very answer of not knowing also means that the fact that the incident has not been immediately reported, or that the purported victim maintained ongoing contact, does not mean there was no sexual assault, it does not make the purported victim anything less than credible or any less of a possible victim without people on the outside knowing much, much more about what did or did not happen.

Not all victims will respond the way we think they should. Not all victims are prepared to report an incident immediately. Not all victims are comfortable disclosing all that happened. Not all victims are willing to disclose actions that may embarrass them. For these reasons, such victims can be terrible witnesses in sexual assault cases. But while they may be terrible witnesses, and while convictions may not be possible, it is still possible that the alleged abuse took place. A higher level of expertise would be welcome in our court system so that the actions of the witness could be better understood within a broader context.

There would be an unconscionably serious problem if we ever moved beyond the concept of innocent until proven guilty. Nobody wants to move beyond this concept. Well, I don't.

At the same time, however, a competing assumption that the witness is telling the truth until that statement has been shown to be false would be welcome. Do not ever convict on that assumption—this is not for the courtroom but for the court of public opinion, something very important in these matters. Nobody should ever be convicted on anything but proof beyond a reasonable doubt.

But for our legal system to work more fairly for an alleged victim in a sexual assault case it could be more effective if both parties were required to present evidence. I believe that the time has come for us to consider removing the right to remain silent in cases involving sexual assault so that things truly become "he said, she said."

The important thing to a victim isn't necessarily a guilty verdict. It can be more important simply to be heard. It's one thing to have a system designed to attack credibility to the point where there are insufficient grounds for a conviction. It's another thing if that system leaves the accuser looking bad without being able to put any such attack on credibility in the context of what the accused's denial would look like after a similar review of his credibility in the circumstances.

Again, and to be perfectly clear, nobody should ever be convicted on anything but proof beyond a reasonable doubt. Never. The point I am trying to make is that in the case of sexual assault, unlike other crimes, an accuser can feel repeatedly abused by the legal process.

Think about how the legal system processes murders, for example. With a murder there is almost always evidence that a crime has been committed by somebody—there is a dead body—and the issue goes to "who did it?" With the equally serious crime of sexual assault, a possibly guilty party is often free to go about his daily business, in front of the alleged victim—something we as a society would never tolerate with a possible murderer—for the very reason that with sexual assaults, the issue is often as basic as whether a crime was even committed in the first place.

In the difficult circumstances of sexual assault, a type of time-out may be appropriate.

Imagine a world where a hockey team responded as follows:

Today we received word that Player X has been accused of sexual assault. This is a serious accusation, one the local police are investigating as we speak. We stand one hundred percent behind Player X, and we remind everybody that he remains innocent of any such crime until proven guilty in a court of law.

At the same time, given the severity of the accusation and an initial assessment that the accusation is not merely frivolous but one requiring further investigation by the police, we equally support the accuser and stand behind her as well until more is known.

Accordingly, and without any prejudice to Player X, but in recognition of our equally important obligation to our community, it would not be appropriate for Player X to participate in any league games until more is known about this accusation. During his absence Player X will be paid in full and the NHL will not count any salary paid to him during this time against our salary cap.

We trust and expect that both our fans and our community will understand our decision and will support both Player X and the as yet

unnamed accuser until more is known. We love our fans, we love our
team, and we love the game of hockey. But we also understand that
some things are more important than hockey, and this is one such thing.
We will have no further comment on this matter until further notice.

A man can dream.

––––––––––––

THE LEGAL SYSTEM will likely change only as fast as society at
large is able to understand more deeply the real damage inflicted
on a victim of sexual assault. We are, however, making progress,
as both the medical community and society as a whole are coming
to understand that sexual assault involves much more than the
physical assault itself.

Things are starting to change. Education is the only way things
will truly improve, and sentencing will only become more appropriate once the rights of the accused and convicted are met with
an understanding of the true impact of the crimes committed
and a need to respect the impact that the crimes have on victims.
Simply stated, everybody in our system needs to understand that
victims need to be rehabilitated too.

––––––––––––

AS A LAWYER, I am well aware that all the issues I have noted
above are in play anytime an accuser comes forward with an alle-
gation of sexual assault. As a victim, I wanted justice. As a lawyer,
I knew only a legal result was at stake, something that would be
rendered by the courts from far above long, long after the actual
events had taken place.

I also made it clear to anybody who found out that I had been
abused that I had no intention of suing anybody for anything. I

just wanted to get better. The damage had been done. There was no justice system for me to access that would allow me to get my life back.

Hockey Canada heard about me during the police investigation and reached out to me, and the people there were supportive throughout. Hockey Canada showed me an element of humanity that the legal system never could. This is likely because Hockey Canada is a world leader in how sports organizations can take steps to try to prevent and protect against sexual assault, and it has developed a deep understanding of such situations when they do occur. Hockey Canada implemented positive changes in minor hockey as a result of Graham's first convictions, including background checks to flag dangerous offenders and prevent them from being put in positions of trust with young boys, as well as other programs to heighten awareness of risks.

The only group I ever contacted for help was my local school board in Winnipeg, for Graham, as a substitute teacher, had abused me at the school once and had used his position as a teacher to win me over as much as he had used his position as a hockey coach. I approached the school board only after the legal process had played out and my name was public, when I was at my absolute lowest and worst. Still, I made it clear up front that I was not going to commence any litigation, that I was just offering them a chance to do whatever they thought was appropriate in the circumstances. In the end, I requested compensation for therapy and medication that I was paying for out of pocket. They declined, pointing out, among other things, that any money paid to me would come out of resources that would otherwise go to teaching young children. Fair point. I felt bad for even asking.

SO MANY COINCIDENCES. As a young, tall goalie who excelled at both hockey and school, it was only natural that people would often bring up Ken Dryden in connection with me while I was growing up. Then, while in law school, I was able to try on his skates to see if they would fit. Things then came full circle when Dryden wrote an article in the *Globe and Mail* about the time when, as president of the Toronto Maple Leafs, he had received a letter from Martin Kruze, the Dorset Park Ranger, before Kruze killed himself as a result of the sexual abuse he endured at Maple Leaf Gardens.

It was because of that article that Roy MacGregor at the *Globe and Mail* wrote a feature about me and gave me a voice. And, while it was difficult at the time to speak loudly, that voice has made all the difference for the positive outcomes in my recovery.

Dryden's article fascinated me because of how exceedingly human he revealed himself to be. In that article, and in interviews since, Dryden has been open about his initial inability to respond to Kruze's letter, how he left it sitting on his desk until it was too late. But he didn't hide. He stepped up and admitted right away that, with everything going on around him, he had missed that the important thing would have been to simply respond as a human being. He owned it, he was never going to make that mistake again, and he made amends. In the end he did the human thing.

One of the things I have encountered repeatedly since I came forward is a tendency for people who were at one time close to Graham to "lawyer up" whenever speaking with me. My conversations with such people are not spontaneous. Words are spoken, not freely, but very precisely in a type of hockey legalese. And when I reached out to the local school board in Winnipeg, my only contact was with a lawyer at a firm they hired immediately after I contacted them.

It's an interesting thing, asking questions about the past. People have a natural tendency to run toward success and run away from failure. For a guy who was as successful as Graham was in the hockey world, Graham sure seems to have a lot of people who were once close to him who now say they were never really friends with him—at least, when speaking to me.

I completely understand a desire to avoid any association with a convicted serial child sexual predator. But there should be no shame in admitting to having been conned by Graham. The only shame is in denying it.

In my case, all I had wanted was for people who'd been around Graham to step up and admit that they'd missed it too and that they were sorry it had happened. Maybe, I thought, they might even ask how I was doing and check to see if I was holding it together. All I had wanted was for people to respond as caring humans in a shared community where somebody from their own community had been sexually abused. But I was naive not to understand that when a delicate issue like Graham came up people would understandably focus on potential legal exposure and their personal risk in responding.

Stories of sexual abuse are nothing to run from and they should not be situations where the first thought is to focus on possible legal liability. Instead, they are extreme examples of a failure in the human fabric that leaves behind victims who are in desperate need of the best that humanity has to offer.

A LAW SCHOOL classmate of mine, now a senior professor at the University of McGill Faculty of Law, invited me to Montreal to deliver a lecture. She was interested in my story as it related to whether the law adequately protects the most vulnerable in our society. In speaking to the students and other professors in the lecture hall that day, I conveyed what I thought is perhaps the fundamental problem with our legal system: an increasing absence of humanity. Harkening back to my own thoughts in first year criminal law, I reminded the audience that the law is meaningless if you forget that every case in every set of precedents involves real people who may have suffered actual harm and indignity. I asked that they never again read another legal case without thinking long and hard about the people involved and what had happened to them, rather than focusing only on the legal principles at stake. Only then will the law develop in a humane way.

The lecture went well, but I was dealing with another issue that day that was more than slightly distracting. Graham was reportedly living in the Montreal area. Despite the progress I had made, I was seeing ghosts. The lecture had been publicized. Would he show? I kept glancing around the room. Of course checking for him made no sense. Of course he wasn't there. But I started to panic, to sweat, to fear him once again. He may not have been in the hall, but he was out there, somewhere.

Montreal, glorious Montreal, home of Les Canadiens, my second favorite hockey team next only to the Winnipeg Jets, bonds that had been formed back when I was a young boy, when it was possible to cheer for both the Jets in the WHA and the Habs in the NHL. Was Montreal now a poisoned place for me? Of course not. This fear of seeing Graham in Montreal was so silly, so irrational, of course it would instantly go away. But it didn't, and it was a very long day.

There is nothing in hockey as awe-inspiring as watching the Montreal Canadiens play at home, back in the day in their whites, now in their reds. I grew up playing for the St. James Canadians, with the anglophone "a" instead of an "e," but in identical uniforms, dreaming my hockey dreams. I loved everything about the Habs. Even now, decades later, back home and miles away from Montreal, I watch them. But then, in an instant, I find myself wondering whether Graham is at the Molson Centre for their home games. Without realizing it I find myself changing the channel away from the game to ease the blip in my stress level until I get it back under control.

I am so much better.

I can manage it now.

But I also understand that he will always be there.

ALIVE AND KICKING

It were better for him that a millstone were hanged about his neck, and
he cast into the sea, than that he should offend one of these little ones.
  —Luke 17:2

A M I TO forgive him? Am I to believe that in completing his time behind bars he has fulfilled his debt to society, that he is entitled to forgiveness, that he should be free to start life anew, and that anything less makes him a victim of something far worse? Was his time behind bars, reduced for the very reason that he is so hard done by on account of the public's awareness of who he is and the crimes he committed, all he should have to endure?

I have learned so much about myself through my recovery. I have learned that I am far stronger than I ever imagined I could be, that my very existence is testament to my ability to fight harder than most may ever have to fight.

But I'm not strong enough to forgive.

IN THE END, whatever happens to him now, it doesn't change who I am or what I will be able to do with the rest of my life.

I long ago accepted that no form of justice or validation would ever come from a third party. As much as I craved closure from our legal system or from Graham himself, I came to understand that finding value and meaning from within was really the only thing that had ever mattered.

In coming forward, I reconnected with my mother (now dead), brother, and sister. I have begun reconnecting with friends who ask no questions and who forgive me for having dropped out of their lives.

I will continue to heal so that the past will no longer define me. The past will always be a part of the tapestry of who I am, it will always be there, but it need not dictate my future.

I am not too proud to admit that I still need help.

Although the story of my life isn't finished, I like to think that the story is one of hope, of survival. I have learned to value the knowledge, understanding, and empathy I have developed as a result of my experience, and I believe that the experience has in a strange way made me a better person. Good has come out of the bad, and I wouldn't trade my life for anybody else's.

Some may find that to ring false. After all, several summers ago my Princeton classmate Jeff Bezos, founder of Amazon.com and a *Time Magazine* Person of the Year, successfully launched a rocket on a day when my biggest accomplishment had been to go to the store and buy ketchup. Insult was added to injury when it was pointed out to me that I could have stayed home, ordered the ketchup online through his company, and had the product delivered to my door. Yet, life is about achievements and lessons of all kind, with each and every one of us having our own experiences, each of us looking back on our own pasts as "an arch wherethrough / Gleams that untraveled world, whose margin fades / For ever and for ever when [we] move" (Tennyson). I'm just thankful for my own life, a life that has never been without challenge, learning, and, ultimately, growth.

I refuse to continue to feel victimized and overwhelmed, and I am determined to maintain a sense of well-being. I was told not long ago by a person I love deeply that I have a beautiful soul, and that, to me, is the greatest affirmation I could ever receive, one I believe would not have been possible if I hadn't gone through what I did.

I choose to believe that my past has made me better, and this belief only makes me stronger as I transition from one who has survived to one who can once again thrive. I have a lot of life left to live and to give, and while certain opportunities are gone, others have yet to present themselves. Once a victim of the most horrible form of abuse, I am now moving forward with hope and resolve to live a life full of love and happiness, a life of worth, for I am indeed worthy of living.

It's difficult to say what I gained from coming forward. It would be easy to say nothing but trouble, but coming forward opened my eyes and forced me to rededicate myself to an even more intensive recovery—one at which I am succeeding.

I wrote this book to give myself closure on that part of my life, to force myself to confront the past and explain as honestly as possible how it affected me, to crystallize my belief that although the abuse will always be part of who I am, it need not define me.

Giving voice to what it is like to go through that abuse and to try to come to grips with it has been a difficult process that has taken me to disturbing places. But I'm still here, and as bad as things got, they didn't defeat me but instead gave me a perspective that allows me to see the beauty in a fallen leaf when others might be too occupied to even notice it or too worried about whether or not the wind is messing up their hair.

This book is my statement of survival after a horrific experience. It took so long to get it right. And maybe earlier a part of me wasn't ready to move on yet, maybe I was comfortable in my pain, maybe I was afraid of what life would be like when I finished writing it and it would be time to move on to the next chapter of my life, whatever that may be. Maybe I was afraid that I really was all of the horrible things I thought about myself, that I had it right when I thought I had no worth or value to anybody, that maybe I really don't belong.

To get to the point where I could write this book, I first had to get to the point in my recovery where I could take a hard look at everything in my past, no matter how ugly, and accept that all of that is a part of who I am. To get to that point, I had to understand exactly who I was and what had happened. But to gain the tools to do that, I had to first decide to deal with what happened and tell somebody what happened. I had to decide that I wanted to live, because telling somebody else about what happened feels like death itself. To really understand that I did in fact want to live, I had to confront the alternative of death head on.

And I did.

That seemingly golden life of mine was anything but. I had a terrible secret that I had kept from everyone but that was always there, that had a life of its own inside my head, that was my reality after being groomed and sexually abused. I kept things together as best as I could, but it was always there, speaking to me in a way that only I understood. In my mind, I had an idea of who I was, a reality that went with me wherever I went, whatever I did. But it did not mesh with the reality the outside world saw. The world couldn't see what I "knew" to be my reality.

I have spent almost forty years trying to forget everything about Graham, trying to forget about all of it. Everything I have done ever since I first met him has been an attempt to run away from him, to run away from it, to run away from myself. But those dead shark eyes, his eyes, are still there, haunting me.

I'm getting better now. I'm finally able to look back with greater understanding, I can look forward and see that there is a road ahead, a path to a bright future, a future I was always supposed to have.

I made it through and have come out better than I was going in. I can now both say the words and keep fighting to live them:

I was a victim. It wasn't my fault. I'm not responsible for what Graham did to Todd or Theo or Sheldon. I deserved Princeton. I deserved whatever success I had there. I deserved U of T law school and the Varsity Blues. I deserved Torys, CanWest, Cookie Jar Entertainment, and the rest. I deserved to be married. I deserve my friends. I deserve to be healthy and in great physical shape once again. I deserve a good life with a happy ending.

I was a nobody. Coming out of the abuse I became nobody at all. But now I have come to believe that I am somebody, somebody with a future who can have that happy ending. Now, I am somebody.

I am Greg Gilhooly.

POSTSCRIPT

OH, AND IF there is a God, I can't believe he or she didn't arrange things so that Ken Dryden's skates fit me. I used to think that when they didn't fit it meant that there would be no recovery, no Hollywood ending, that good things were never meant to be, that there was nobody watching over me. Now? Maybe it was a good sign after all. Maybe it just showed that I was meant for something bigger.

ACKNOWLEDGMENTS

THIS BOOK TOOK me years to write as I moved through stages in my recovery. I started and stopped and started again so many times in an effort to try to convey just what it is to go through what I went through, what I continue to deal with. I couldn't have gotten through this without the help and support of so many. The words in this book are mine—there is no ghostwriter. But that doesn't mean that I'm the only one who had a hand in writing this book. Far from it.

So many reached out to me and kept me going, kept me alive, just by being there for me. Some were complete strangers who made contact just to let me know that they supported me. People from my past have crept back into my life. It has all been so humbling.

Michael Levine, my agent, was there from the very start, telling me that I needed to write my story. I thank him and the rest of the team at Westwood Creative Artists who connected me with my publisher, Rob Sanders, and his group at Greystone Books. Rob—a true gentleman in every sense of the word—and everyone else at Greystone, showed me so much patience as I struggled to confront my past and write this book while still working to recover.

Special thanks to my editor, Nancy Flight, who put up with me and my quirky style while always showing a soft, gracious touch when reining me in and refocusing me on what was truly important. I couldn't have done this, something that has proven to be so cathartic and helpful in my recovery, without her.

And of special note, both Nancy and Lesley Cameron (my copy editor who also made so many excellent suggestions) rigidly enforced American English spelling throughout this book. It is to my great shame and <u>dishonour</u> that I was unsuccessful in moving them from their position.

I had the good fortune during my career to work with so many wonderful people in the legal community, first at Torys and later at Heenan Blakie, and then Blakes. Words cannot begin to describe the respect I still have for all of my colleagues from my days at CanWest, and especially for the Asper family—I thank them for bringing me in for the ride of a lifetime, no matter what fireworks may have ensued. I fully expect K.C. Bascombe to write and direct an award-winning film produced by Nick Seferian that is both filmed on location at and set in The Haig in Buenos Aires. And to Michael Hirsh and the rest at Cookie Jar, my eternal thanks for supporting me as long as was possible while I came forward.

I want to thank those at Hockey Canada for the special humanity they showed me. It was truly life-sustaining. To Roy MacGregor, Bruce Cheadle, James Bronskill, Reg Sherren, and Gerry Arnold, your graciousness in dealing with my story made it possible for me to consider telling it in greater depth. And to Winnipeg Police, the Crown prosecution, and especially to Milco de Graaf, you all helped so much with an unbearable legal process.

The Princeton hockey world has given me so much support, and I thank especially Troy Ewanchyna, Tim Driscoll, and Marc Daniel. As for the rest of my Princeton community, there are simply too many to name, though I do want to make special note of Caroline Coleman for her advice on writing and Julia Hicks de

Peyster for her consistent humor as an inspiration. And to my roommates in my senior year—Michael Cragg, Michael Denham, Greg Jenko, Christian Kemp-Griffin, Chris King, Brian MacFarlane, Scott Scharfman, and Ben Webster—words are not enough to thank you all.

An abuser can leave behind many types of victims in his wake. Paul Buchanan, you are a special man who suffered so much by standing up to Graham.

Theo Fleury and Sheldon Kennedy, both former high-profile professional hockey players, have a platform and use it effectively to raise awareness and provide support for those who suffer from child sexual abuse. Todd Holt helps so many by speaking publicly and telling his story, something that makes it possible for other victims to come forward and progress with their recovery. They are all more than capable of telling their own stories, and they have done so. But I would be remiss were I not to point out their leadership in this regard. Their accomplishments are often cited in the media, but the media's bright light can be fickle, and one never knows when it will shift elsewhere. I hope that the institutions that both Sheldon and Theo have created will remain in the public eye as priorities for years to come. Victims understand the dramatic costs associated with sexual abuse. It frustrates us when people looking at the legal system focus on the costs of convicting and incarcerating criminals while missing all of the costs associated with the carnage the abusers leave behind and the rehabilitation that victims require. For too long our focus has been on only one side of the equation.

It has sometimes been difficult to remain my friend while I dealt with the mental health issues arising out of the abuse. Yet I have two friends, Rod Pertson and Brent Littlejohn, two remarkable men, who have always been there for me and who somehow managed to make my living hell not just bearable, but enjoyable, for a moment in time without even knowing they were doing so.

John Macfarlane, Paddy Torsney, Brian Koturbash, David Lomow, Andrew Diamond, Sandra Antidormi, Paula Todd, the Oakville hockey guys, the list goes on. And I have had with me a man I look to as a mentor, David McCarthy, who never asks questions or puts pressure on me, who just understands me.

I am now close with my brother and sister and their families, and this makes me so happy and provides me with so much support, with my parents no longer with us. I thank you so much for all that you do for me.

In the end, I couldn't get around to writing this book until I made peace with myself in my own heart. In finding Stephanie Smith I finally found somebody who didn't see me for what she thought I could become, who didn't make anything conditional on how I might recover, she just saw me for who I was and loved me for it. And because of that she became my muse. Finally, it was enough for me to just be me, and because of that, I wanted to be better. She has made me and my life better, and I can't thank her and her children—Evelyn and Damian—enough for welcoming me into their lives.

And there is somebody else out there, somebody who, because we live in a world filled with lawyers, can't be mentioned, but please know that you are the most important thing in my life. You are practically perfect in every way, and I cherish everything about you. I may not be able to use your name in this book (or even refer to you being a part of my life), but please know that I want to shout it out to everyone to show my pride in you and the joy you bring me.

Without all of you, I am nobody.

ABOUT THE AUTHOR

G REG GILHOOLY IS a graduate of Princeton University and the University of Toronto Faculty of Law. He was a successful corporate lawyer and senior business executive, a man who could seemingly succeed at the highest levels with little effort. Yet there was something about Greg that nobody could see, a secret that he had been keeping for decades.

Greg was also a victim and survivor of sexual abuse at the hands of Graham James, one of the sporting world's most notorious child sexual abusers, perhaps Canada's most notorious sex offender, a man who had also abused Sheldon Kennedy and Theo Fleury, among others.

Greg's story has been featured in national and international media. He makes regular media appearances on the subject of sexual abuse generally, and has testified before the Canadian Parliamentary House Standing Committee on Justice and the Senate Committee on Legal and Constitutional Affairs. He broke and told the story of Graham James's pardon, which led to immediate changes to Canadian pardon and parole laws.

In addition to being a highly qualified business and legal executive, Greg is a powerful and public survivor of child sexual assault with a strong voice and media presence. He has a proven record of community service and a strength of character that has facilitated sustained accomplishment in the face of difficult circumstances.

As a savvy, informed, and passionate media commentator on national news and sports radio and national television and news media outlets, he is in demand as a public speaker for groups concerned with hockey, abuse, mental-health stigma, and the law, including the hockey community across Canada, law students and graduates, law firms, parent groups, police groups, school groups, and NGOs.

Several psychologists have called Greg a "highly functioning victim" who, because of his intellectual abilities and legal training, has the rare ability to provide a detailed and thorough perspective on the emotional and psychological impact of abuse, while also addressing the relevant issues and principles at play within our legal system and our society.